OPERA

AS

DRAMA

OPERA
AS
DRAMA

Joseph Kerman

VINTAGE BOOKS

A DIVISION OF RANDOM HOUSE

New York

To my Mother and Father

Foreword

To THE editors of *The Hudson Review, Opera News, High Fidelity,* and *Partisan Review* I am thankful for permission to reprint material that first appeared in their magazines, sometimes in rather different shape. My gratitude to the editors of *Hudson* goes much deeper, for they have encouraged or at least suffered me to develop my ideas and the form of my ideas for eight years now in their pages. This at a time when musical criticism finds little support, and lapses. And to one of those editors, William Arrowsmith, I owe a debt of good friendship for poring over chapters with relentless, sympathetic critical judgement matched only by that of my wife. Warm thanks also to Mrs. Althea Doyle and Roger Levenson; Herbert Weinstock; Charles C. Cushing, Seymour Shifrin, and Seth P. Ulman. A year ago the members of the Company of the Golden Hind in Berkeley taught me a good deal when I worked with them in an operatic production, and pleasantly delayed the early stages of this book.

J. K.

Berkeley
April 3, 1956

Contents

OPERA

AS

DRAMA

Introduction: Opera as Drama

I MAKE NO APOLOGY for the Wagnerian title. This book is far from Wagnerian, but the point of view it develops is really the basic one celebrated by *Oper und Drama*, that astonishing volume of a hundred years ago, Wagner's chief theoretical statement and the important opera tract of his time. The view is trite, but always freshly suggestive: that opera is properly a musical form of drama, with its own individual dignity and force. Now, what Wagner said over and above this amounts to a very great deal, and gives his writing its particularity, and grows more and more insupportable as the years pass. What remains is his violent championship of the old tautology, opera as drama. Wagner's operas and his writings forced the nineteenth century, and the twentieth, to approach opera with a new high-mindedness, which is waning only today. No one has ever pleaded the cause so efficiently.

The cause had many earlier champions, as well as worthy opponents. Since the days of the half-literary, half-musical academy that willed opera into being, musical drama has fascinated critics almost as steadily as composers; the speculative, satiric, and polemic literature is very extensive. And lively, thanks to the interest of Saint-Evremond, Addison, Diderot, Kierkegaard, Stendhal, Nietzsche, Shaw, and many intemperate lesser men. Today, as we look back over all the arguments and battles, perhaps the strongest impression is of a pervasive continuity. The examples change, but the central issues remain, constantly reinterpreted in the terms of the time. Is musical drama viable, and if so, how? Is Lully, or Gluck, or Wagner, or Verdi really doing with the form what we think it is capable of? The postulates and ideals, the dissatisfactions and controversies are renewed for every generation.

Musical drama *is* viable, and I believe that the present intellectual climate ought to be especially clement to the idea. We have certain new advantages; but the old disadvantage is still with us—the seeming contradiction between ideals and corrupt practice. Singers, audiences, and impresarios are irresponsible, as they always have been; artistic values are thoroughly confused by the jumble of good and bad that forms our current repertory. This makes a serious consideration of opera both difficult and rare. Sometimes ridicule can cut true, but we should do without that familiar indiscriminate satire on the genre as a whole, delightful or deserved as often this may appear. At present the greater need is for a reassertion of presumptive virtues. Addison and W. S. Gilbert, delightful writers, have had their bad effect on the course of opera in England. The instant appeal of their approach makes it all the more necessary to keep reformulating the humorless, idealistic position.

Today Wagner's terms are impossible; none more so, perhaps. A contemporary view of opera does not owe its novelty primarily to the current situation in the United States, though this seems odd enough in the light of history: the abrupt enthusiasm for opera in the years since the Second World War, for opera that is mostly foreign and old, known mostly from records, broadcasts, and earnest half-amateur "workshops." The novelty is due more fundamentally to the modern approach to an artistic tradition. Historical perspective has led on the one hand to a broader, more imaginative concept of the dramatic, and on the other, to a warmer respect for music of the past than was possible in earlier times. We see much more as dramatic; we see much more as musically expressive; we have the opportunity, the terms, for a quite new interpretation of the operatic problem and the operatic repertory.

In particular, the historicism which so much determined the old view of opera is unthinkable today. Wagner, who found Racine "laughable," would never have given a thought to the operas of Monteverdi, even if he had been able to know them. Music, he was sure, was so simple in the seventeenth century that nothing sensible could be expected of opera. But today we are sure that this is not necessarily so. As the tradition is studied more carefully and more sympathetically, it seems less and less to fall in with any dialectical march to a *Gesamtkunstwerk* of a hundred years ago, to "the Art-Work of the Future." Composers of the past left, not a series of immature experiments, but a number of solutions, each distinct, and each with the potentiality of artistic success within its own limitations. This way of looking at history is no less benign to Wagner in the nineteenth century than to Monteverdi in the

seventeenth. Wagner might have cursed it as flabby
relativism, but to us it represents a breadth of vision
as inevitable as it is hard to maintain. And it does allow
us to encompass more.

Flabby relativism is certainly the danger, as anyone
ought to know who buys an opera season ticket. Under
the tacit assumption that everything is all right in its
own terms, extremes of beauty and triviality are regularly placed together. The extremes, I think, are even
more grating than with other contemporary arts: in
our opera houses, art and *Kitsch* alternate night after
night, with the same performers and the same audience, to the same applause, and with the same critical
sanction. Confusion about the worth of opera is bound
to exist when no distinction is drawn publicly between
works like *Orfeo* and *The Magic Flute* on the one
hand, and like *Salome* and *Turandot* on the other. As
for operatic criticism—but unintellectuality is another
odd feature of the current American vogue for opera.
Talk is never about meaning, but about peripheral
topics like opera in English, "modern" production
methods, and television techniques; all without an idea
of what opera can or should be, and what is in the
first place worth translating, producing, and televising.
This may be understandable in our first flush of enthusiasm of discovery, but it is hard to think that all
our operatic activity can proceed much longer without
standards.

A serious search for dramatic values, with the kind
of informed respect for the tradition that is elsewhere
second nature nowadays, can begin to provide a basis
for standards. At the same time, such a search can begin to subvert the general indulgence towards anything
that happens to hold the stage; it need not lack Wagner's steady hostility toward cheapness and philistin-
ism. The postulate is that opera is an art-form with
its own integrity and its own particular limiting and

liberating conventions. The critical procedure involves a sharpening of musical awareness and an expansion of our range of imaginative response to drama.

2

OPERA as drama. What are we to comprehend as drama? There have been many general answers, all necessarily partial. For my purpose, at the moment, it may be enough to mention briefly several things that drama is not, and then to follow up an obvious analogy. Drama is not, exclusively, a matter of the effective deployment of plot. Skilfully contrived situations, clever exits and entrances, and violent *coups de théâtre* do not compose the soul of drama. Neither does strict naturalism in character, locale, or detail; "imitation of an action" does not mean photographic reproduction. Yet when an opera is praised as dramatic, the judgement generally seems to be based on some such limited view. What is meant is little more than "theatrical" or, rather, "effective according to the principles of the late nineteenth-century theater." *Tosca* is "dramatic"; not a very subtle piece, perhaps, or a gracious one musically, but at least "dramatic"—and so it holds the stage.

It should hardly be necessary to observe that other dramatic traditions exist besides our immediate one, the so-called Naturalism of the late nineteenth century, and that they have differed as widely in technique as in range of expression. Dramatic criticism is concerned with Æschylus and Euripides, the medieval stage, Shakespeare and the other Elizabethans, Racine, Goethe and Schiller, Pirandello, Lorca, and Eliot, as well as with Ibsen, Shaw, and their less serious followers. A contemporary account of drama has to rational-

ize some appreciation of the particular powers and procedures of many very different dramatists. (The two
best and most influential of recent dramatic studies, by
Francis Fergusson and Eric Bentley, provide an important place for Wagner too.) Drama in its great
periods has been variously conventionalized and variously artificial; the slice of life and the well-made plot
are by no means essential. Indeed Naturalism, whatever its merits, is less useful to the understanding of
opera than are most other modes of spoken drama.

Most of those others are poetic modes; this fact
alone brings them closer to opera. The comparison
with poetic drama can help us with the problem of
dramma per musica, as opera was called by the early
Italians—drama through music, by means of music.
The analogy should probably not be pressed too far,
but fundamentally it is just: in each form, drama is
articulated on its most serious level by an imaginative
medium, poetry in the one case, music in the other.
In his essay *Poetry and Drama,* T. S. Eliot puts it as
follows:

It is a function of all art to give us some perception of an
order in life, by imposing an order upon it. The painter
works by selection, combination, and emphasis among the
elements of the visible world; the musician, in the world
of sound. It seems to me that beyond the nameable, classifiable emotions and motives of our conscious life when
directed towards action—the part of life which prose
drama is wholly adequate to express—there is a fringe of
indefinite extent, of feeling which we can only detect, so
to speak, out of the corner of the eye and can never completely focus; of feeling of which we are only aware in a
kind of temporary detachment from action. There are
great prose dramatists—such as Ibsen and Chekhov—
who have at times done things of which I would not
otherwise have supposed prose to be capable, but who
seem to me, in spite of their success, to have been ham-
pered in expression by writing in prose. This peculiar
range of sensibility can be expressed by dramatic poetry,

at its moments of greatest intensity. At such moments, we touch the border of those feelings which only music can express.

The function of dramatic poetry is to supply certain kinds of meaning to the drama, meanings that enrich immeasurably, and enrich dramatically, and that cannot be presented in any other way. What is essentially at issue is the response of the persons in the play to the elements of the action. In this area poetry can do more than prose discussion or the placement of actors into physical and psychological relationships. The particular aspect or weight of such relationships, of events and episodes, is determined by the quality of the verse; and in the largest sense the dramatic form is articulated by the poetry in conjunction with the plot structure. The same can be true of music.

As Eliot says, ". . . when Shakespeare, in one of his mature plays, introduces what might seem a purely poetic line or passage, it never interrupts the action, or is out of character, but, on the contrary, in some mysterious way supports both action and character." More profoundly yet, an extended poetic passage can critically determine the whole course of a drama by its quality of feeling. In such a case poetry becomes the vital element of the action. An example comes to mind (for a special purpose) from *Othello*: the entrance of Othello with the candle in the last scene, before he kills Desdemona. To say that he comes no longer as a jealous murderer, but in the role of judge, is merely to give the scenario of what Shakespeare projects by poetry:

It is the cause, it is the cause, my soul.
Let me not name it to you, you chaste stars!
It is the cause. Yet I'll not shed her blood,
Nor scar that whiter skin of hers than snow,
And smooth as monumental alabaster.
Yet she must die, else she'll betray more men.
Put out the light, and then put out the light.

If I quench thee, thou flaming minister,
I can again thy former light restore,
Should I repent me; but once put out thy light,
Thou cunning'st pattern of excelling nature,
I know not where is that Promethean heat
That can thy light relume. When I have pluck'd the rose,
I cannot give it vital growth again;
It needs must wither. I'll smell it on the tree.

He kisses her.

Imagery and poetic music combine to give a grave beauty to Othello's behavior. First, I think, by means of the heavy rhythm of the opening repetition, with the recurring soft assonant "is . . . cause" interrupted by the flow of the second line to its majestic halt at the slow, again assonant, spondee "chaste stars." A moment later the repetitions are resumed and developed, four-fold with echoing t's, and with a particularly beautiful intensification in the rhyming and weighting of "thy light." Second, the metaphors, homely and poignant —the putting out of light, plucking a rose; the quiet syntax, imagery, and rhythm combine to create a gentleness, inevitability, and clear-eyed grandeur that no amount of prose or plotting could have matched. This is all brought out by the fine dramatic contrast with Othello's tone at his previous appearance, all k's and p's and spitting rhythms; Desdemona was not a rose but a sweet-smelling weed, "a cistern for foul toads to knot and gender in" and many other complicated things. In turn, the soliloquy reflects forward to the great final speeches in which Othello seeks to summon up his former self-image. One's response to the play as a whole hinges on the feeling of this soliloquy, and on other elements of this sort.

The musician's ear responds to analogous elements in opera, wherein the imaginative articulation for the drama is provided by music. Consider the parallel scene in Verdi's *Otello*—it is not exactly parallel, of course, for Verdi wanted a different quality, and to get it altered the "scenario" (it was not the libretto that altered the quality). Otello enters making the decision, not already resolved; rather than the sobriety of tragic anticipation, Verdi wished to present love and fury tearing at Otello's soul. The scene begins on a celebrated note of menace, muted double-basses interrupting the ethereal close of Desdemona's *Ave Maria*. What defines it as much as the grotesque color and pitch is the key contrast, E thrust into A♭. The double-bass line becomes more mellow, and limps, punctuated by an urgent motive, at first bleak, then flaring up as Otello makes to scimitar Desdemona at once. A crying figure seems to restrain him; answering it, with an abrupt harmonic shift again, a dull-rooted melody grows out of the first notes of the double-bass line, harping on the minor sixth degree:

This turns radiantly into the major sixth, and a beautiful phrase that we recognize with a flash of understanding: the climax of the love-duet of Act I, ardent, articulate, assured. But as Desdemona awakes to his kiss, this possibility is cut off by means of the most wonderful harmonic change of all, a turn from E to f minor which sounds suddenly the real note of tragedy.

One's response to the drama as a whole hinges crucially on the feeling of this scene in its context. Very obviously so, in this case; for by means of the phrase associated with the kiss, Verdi directly links the scene backward to the early serenity of the first night in Cyprus, and forward to the final moment:

> I kiss'd thee ere I kill'd thee. No way but this—
> Killing myself, to die upon a kiss.

When Otello stabs himself, the motive with the minor sixth is heard again, and there is new pathos now to its transformation into the luminous music of the kiss. Nothing escapes Otello's consciousness; the F returns as a Phrygian cadence to the tonic key of E. Where Shakespeare recalls the past feeling, Verdi, by the force of musical recapitulation, actually recaptures it, and even intensifies it, by means of certain changes in detail. If Verdi's man does not achieve the new integration of nobility attempted by Shakespeare's, he does recover the fullness of his love, no inconsiderable dramatic feat. It is the music that sums up, forms, and refines.

In a verse play, those all-important feelings which make the difference between scenario and work of art are supplied by the poetry; in an opera, by the music. The speed and mental pliability of words give verse drama an intellectual brilliance impossible to opera, and indeed the luxuriance of detail presents a challenge to the poet, who has to organize it firmly to his central dramatic idea. Poetry is much more precise in the treatment of specific matters; narration, discussion, and subtleties of character development come naturally to verse drama, but have to be treated with circumspection in opera. Mr. Eliot's problem about "saying homely things without bathos" is much more severe for the opera composer. But in spite of all the flexibility and clarity of poetry, even the most passionate of speeches exists on a level of emotional reserve that music automatically passes. Music can be immediate and simple in the presentation of emotional states or shades. In an opera, people can give themselves over to sensibility; in a play nobody ever quite stops thinking. Music is also a natural medium for the projecting of various kinds of mood and pageantry, and is so used in the spoken theater. As dramatic elements, these are often misused, but need not be. And in the larger sense of form, music has the clearer, stronger outlines. Recapitulations, cadences, transitions, interrelations, and modulations are devices that music has learned to handle most powerfully.

These and other differences surely exist, and account for the different forms developed for spoken and musical drama. But in spite of differences, I would emphasize again that the imaginative function of music in drama and that of poetry in drama are fundamentally the same. Each art has the final responsibility for the success of the drama, for it is within their capacity to define the response of characters to deeds and situations. Like poetry, music can reveal the quality of action, and thus determine dramatic form in the most serious sense.

In the following chapters, I shall develop this idea in reference to the great musical dramatists. They differ, perhaps, as widely as Shakespeare and Sophocles and Strindberg in their dramaturgies and in their personalities. But for all of them, opera was not a mere concert in costume, or a play with highlights and an overall mood supplied by music, but an art-form with its own consistency and intensity, and its own sphere of expression. Opera is a type of drama whose integral existence is determined from point to point and in the whole by musical articulation. *Dramma per musica.* Not only operatic theory, but also operatic achievement bears this out.

3

IN FORMULATING this view of opera, I certainly have
no thought of claiming it as a novelty. It is the view
that has kept operatic criticism alive for 350 years,
and one that many people today probably hold—but
lazily; nobody seems ready to go out and meet it, think
it through, and assume its consequences. At present,
indeed, there seems to be more vigor in other attitudes,
which go against opera as drama, either directly or in-
sidiously.

The frankest assault comes from certain dramatic
critics of particular literary bent, who tend to question
the dramatic efficacy of any non-verbal artistic medium.
They do not doubt that music in the last few hundred
years has attained enough maturity to meet very strin-
gent demands; they may be keen music-lovers. But
they feel that because of a characteristic lack of detailed reference, music cannot qualify ideas and there-
fore cannot define drama in a meaningful way. Thus
Eric Bentley in *The Playwright as Thinker*:

. . . every dramaturgic practice that subordinates the
words to any other medium has trivialized the drama
without giving full reign to the medium that has become
dominant. . . . Above all, music performs its dramatic
functions very inadequately. Though Wagner and Richard
Strauss have carried dramatic music to extraordinary
lengths, they not only cannot, as the latter wished, give an
exact musical description of a tablespoon, they cannot do
anything at all with the even more baffling world of conceptual thought. They cannot construct the complex parallels and contraries of meaning which drama demands.

Now just what music *can* do is of course a famous
aesthetic problem. According to the classic solution of
the seventeenth century, music depicts "affects." But
the twentieth tends rather to discern certain kinds of

meaning in music, significances impossible to define in words by very nature, but precious and unique, and rooted unshakeably in human experience. Meaning, we are inclined to say, cannot be restricted to words. If even ostensibly abstract instrumental music is thought to have meaning, the case is surely stronger with opera, where the specific conceptual reference is continuously supplied—by the libretto. Supplied as clearly as possible by the presentation of situations and conflicts, and by the use of words in their "denotative" aspect. Around such references music is free to indulge its most subtle connotative, expressive powers. Mr. Bentley leans towards the "drama of ideas," which Wagner took over as enthusiastically as he took every other aesthetic notion known to him. But literary drama has more regularly—and more successfully?—dealt with qualities of experience, not principally with ideas. Feelings, attitudes, and meanings "beyond the nameable, classifiable emotions and motives of our conscious life" (in Eliot's words) do not necessarily find expression in the most elaborate scenario or in the most trenchant dialectic. No artistic medium that exists in time and on the stage can be denied at the very least a theoretical opportunity to articulate drama. Music has done it very well.

Music critics, however, have not seriously challenged or disproved the intransigently literary point of view. Most of them, I think, do not even recognize the problem. Perhaps they are to be excused for having an elementary notion of drama; but with *Tosca* as a dramatic ideal, "opera as drama" really has no import at all. While we have developed considerable insight into the means whereby music can and does contribute to drama, this insight has rarely been integrated into a full account of the complete work of art. Musicians, doubtless, are no duller in the theater than literary men are in the concert hall. But however this may be, dramatic unawareness underlies almost all current writing about opera, from the most philistine to the most professional.

A striking recent example of the latter is *Mozart's Le Nozze di Figaro,* an exhaustive, not to say scholastic, monograph by Siegmund Levarie. It may seem solemn to tilt at anything as manifestly windy as this; still, the book has an imposing technical apparatus and a certain distinction as the first exposition in English of the influential theories of Alfred Lorenz, the German Wagner analyst of the 1920's. The assumptions and procedures of Lorenz's analytical method are questionable enough, but the main point is this: the system is in fact a pre-existing purely musical one, for which dramatic details are regularly invoked to "explain" musical details that do not fit. The "explanation" is made with a logical naïveté that matches the dramatic insensitivity. Thus the "unity" of the work as a whole is ultimately proved by reducing it to a cadence formula, I–IV–V–I; and regarding the peripety, it is said:

The reconciliation of the married couple takes place in G major, the Countess' realm; but the final scene is in D major, in which a straightened-out Count may be expected to prove his dominance over a supporting wife.

No amount of harmonic explication can explain this mistaking of the Almavivas' domestic situation. As in the worst peripheral excesses of the New Criticism (which has been innocently invoked to support Mr. Levarie's method), the work of art has been lost in ticker-tape. For the work in this case is a drama, not a harmony exercise. Lorenz and his followers show the absurdity of an intransigently musical view of opera.

More popular writers on music eschew, indeed scorn, any close analytic approach to opera. Having no dogma and no intractable mass of detail, they lose the work of art in other ways. Some can never really

accept the basic operatic convention, try as they may;
so it is ridiculous for starving Florestan to start singing on a loud high G. Some lack the courage of their
own presumptive love of music; in the concert hall
Beethoven can sustain the *Ode to Joy,* but in the
theater he cannot sustain the ending ecstasy of
Fidelio. Some have inherited Victorian qualms about
operatic music; *Otello* is somehow vulgar compared
with a good fugue by César Franck. Contradictory
timidities mix to produce a characteristic vagueness
of position, at best alleviated by an occasional insight.
Here bad music is excused as suitable to some crude
theatrical effect, there drama is dismissed, or bad
drama is excused, as a pretext for pretty music. Even
Ernest Newman, the most venerable, the most widely
read, and far and away the best of operatic critics, can
write as follows of *The Magic Flute* in his latest book:

. . . undue stress has been laid on its "ethical" virtues—
its laudation of Virtue, Justice, Humanity, Universal
Brotherhood, and all the rest of it. These academic expressions seem a little fly-blown today, and we have got
past the stage when we can take a work of art to our bos-
oms merely because it spouts lofty sentiments: in a work
of art it is only the art that finally matters. Still, these
sentiments played a large part in making the music of such
works as *The Magic Flute* and the choral finale of the
Ninth Symphony what it is, and so we must be content,
for the time being, and for purely artistic reasons, to accept them at the valuation Mozart and Beethoven placed
on them, just as when watching *Hamlet* we do not admit
that ghosts exist, but merely suspend temporarily, for the
sole purpose of playing the game along the lines laid down
by the poet, our disbelief in them.

The worst of these critics have made Puccini's *Tosca*
into a sort of *locus classicus* for musical drama.

I think it may be worth while to consider *Tosca* a
little. Let us look at the last act, at least. The fact that
it shows some similarities to the final act of *Otello*—

and does not Scarpia invoke Iago in Act I?—should facilitate analysis.

Like Verdi, Puccini found himself beginning his last act with memories of great tension and violence, and with a situation conducive to an impressive hush before the catastrophe. With the "Willow Song," Verdi made this into an ominous hush which seems directed; as Puccini did not capture this quality, his scene seems rather to wait. He too employs a folksong, sung off-stage by a Shepherd Boy as a misty, pink dawn is about to break. Presently a lengthy orchestral passage overloaded with Matin bells introduces the hero Cavaradossi, who converses briefly with the Gaoler; unlike the orchestral entrance of Otello, this is static, a single mood. Left alone, Cavaradossi recalls a rather warm dream of love in his famous aria "*E lucevan le stelle.*" Tosca enters with news of the "reprieve," and the score is heavy with leitmotives. As soldiers come, the action progresses swiftly to the final *coups de théâtre.* Tosca leaps off the parapet, and the orchestra concludes *tutta forza con grande slancio* with a repetition of the melody of "*E lucevan le stelle.*" The scheme is, again, superficially like that of *Otello.*

Now the first part of this act, up to the entrance of Tosca, is one of the most undramatic things in opera; *not* because nothing much happens on the stage, but because nothing happens in the music. It is indeed the penultimate demonstration of Puccini's insufficiency before the demands of Sardou's obvious melodrama. (The ultimate demonstration is the curiously passionless dialogue with Tosca that follows.) Possibly the Shepherd's song might have been integrated dramatically, but Puccini wished only to strike a mood of melancholy, which is inappropriate to Cavaradossi's position on its own, and doubly so when it leads into the attenuated bell-passage at his entrance, then into his mawkish aria. If Puccini had no more insight into

or sympathy with the condemned hero's feelings at
this crisis, he would have done better to leave them
alone, as Verdi did with Manrico's at the end of *Il
Trovatore*. But patently Cavaradossi was not the primary concern. What mattered was not his plight, but
the effect it could make on the audience. Puccini's
faint emotionality is directed out over the footlights;
he will let us have a good cry at Cavaradossi's expense.
This at once makes for a complete extinction of the
poor painter as a dramatic protagonist, and forms a
shield against any serious feelings which Sardou, even,
might have hoped to arouse in us.

As for the Shepherd's folk-song, it appears then to
be as extraneous as the choirboys and the cardinal of
Act I, an insertion not for any dramatic end, but for
display of floating lyricism. This kind of thing is a
weakness even with a composer of truer lyric talent.
It is hardly necessary to contrast the parallel element
in *Otello*, the "Willow Song," which not only makes
Verdi's hush, but also wonderfully fills Desdemona's
character and clarifies her fate. In the last act of *Otello*,
the music for the hero's entrance, too, is crucially involved with the drama. Never once in four acts does
Verdi interpolate pageantry or lyricism without a telling influence on the drama.

Tosca leaps, and the orchestra screams the first
thing that comes into its head, *"E lucevan le stelle."*
How pointless this is, compared with the return of
the music for the kiss at the analogous place in
Otello, which makes Verdi's dramatic point with a
consummate sense of dramatic form. How pointless,
even compared with the parallel place in *La Bohème*,
where Rudolfo's surge of pain does at least encompass
the memory of Mimi's avowal. But *Tosca* is not about
love; *"E lucevan le stelle"* is all about self-pity; Tosca
herself never heard it; and the musical continuity is
coarse and arbitrary. Once again, this loud little epi-

logue is for the audience, not for the play. What a shame (we are to feel), what a shame that butterflies are broken on this excellently oiled wheel. For they are, after all, still the fragile butterflies of the new Arcadia that is Puccini's Bohemia, flirting, fluttering, carefully fixing their crinolines in garrets. Cavaradossi is Marcello, with a commission, but with no more sense of reality; Mimi is caricatured as La Tosca, with her simpering "*Non la sospiri la nostra casetta*" and her barcarole love-theme. But what had a certain adolescent charm in the earlier opera is preposterous here, with Spoletta, Sciarrone, Baron Scarpia, and the headscrew. I do not propose to analyze the musical texture of *Tosca*; it is consistently, throughout, of café-music banality. If Joyce Kilmer or Alfred Noyes had taken it into his head to do a grand poetic drama on Tosca, that would have been something analogous in the medium of language.

But it is scarcely believable that such a play would have held the stage, or that it would be bracketed with Shakespeare, or that it would have become a favorite criterion for poetic drama. It would have its adherents, no doubt; and before those who would be impressed by the quality of the verse, one could only maintain discreet silence, as before those who are awed by Scarpia's chords or touched by the "*Vissi d'arte.*" The really insidious errors are three: first, the idea that Puccini's banality and Sardou's can somehow excuse one another and elevate each other into drama; second, that this is worth staging and buying season tickets to watch; and third, that this represents the true achievement of the art of opera.

The more fully one knows the real peaks of this achievement, the more clearly one sees the extent of Puccini's failure, or more correctly, the triviality of his attempt. A later chapter will examine his operas again, together with others that clog our standard repertory, in a clearer context than is possible at the present point. This book, however, aims much more at an appreciation of important works of art than at the divestment of unimportant ones. The positive accomplishment of *dramma per musica* will occupy our attention, happily—from the first attempts of Monteverdi to the arrogant structures of Wagner, from a huge tradition that culminates in Mozart to another that culminates in Verdi, from Purcell to Stravinsky, from Metastasio to Alban Berg. In 350 years opera has established an impressive canon of fine works. Among them are some masterpieces. Among them, also, are some excellent operas in which the dramatist's vision is not entirely sustained; and in dealing with these, I shall make no effort to gloss over limitations. Both the *Orfeo* of Monteverdi and the *Orfeo* of Gluck, for instance, fail to encompass the final catastrophe implicit in the Orpheus legend within their different, and in some ways opposite, dramatic conceptions. But these operas fail in quite a different sense than *Tosca*. With all their imperfections, they are still seriously dramatic, still works of spirit and sensitivity.

Of the many current partial attitudes towards opera, two are most stultifying: the one held by musicians, that opera is a low form of music, and the one apparently held by everybody else, that opera is a low form of drama. These attitudes stem from the exclusively musical and the exclusively literary approaches to opera, to which I have already indicated my objections. Opera is excellently its own form. The role of music in this form has been defined simply but exactly by Edward T. Cone, in the course of an essay that one might wish were more typical of recent operatic criticism:

In any opera, we may find that the musical and the verbal messages seem to reinforce or to contradict each other; but whether the one or the other, we must always rely on the music as our guide toward an understanding of the composer's conception of the text. It is this conception, not the bare text itself, that is authoritative in defining the ultimate meaning of the work.*

The final judgement, then, is squarely musical, but not purely musical, any more than it is purely literary. Music articulates the drama, and we can no more suppose that a small composer can write a great opera than that a poetaster can make a great play. To estimate the meaning of a work of art of the past, to reconstrue the composer's conception in terms that are meaningful now—this takes an imaginative effort, as always. Strangely or not, something of the same effort is required to comprehend the contemporary masterpieces, which complement and continue the great operatic tradition.

* "The Old Man's Toys: Verdi's Last Operas," *Perspectives USA*, Number Six, Winter 1954.

THE TRADITION

*

1

Orpheus: the Neoclassic Vision

*Io la Musica son, ch'ai dolci accenti
so far tranquillo ogni turbato core,
ed or di nobil' ira ed or d'amore
poss' infiammar le più gelate menti.*
—THE PROLOGUE, MUSIC,
IN MONTEVERDI'S *Orfeo*

FIRST there was the neoclassic vision of a drama reanimated by the co-operation of music. Doubts grew up only later.

The vision itself came as a climax to the whole tendency of Renaissance musical speculation and practice. In the sixteenth century, for the first time, the problems of musical expressivity became central for many theorists and composers; here as elsewhere, the Renaissance contributes the essential modern point of view. Long before the first classicizing librettos of Count Bardi's academy, the *camerata*, humanists had insisted that if music in ancient times had imitated and stirred the emotions with matchless power, it could and should again. Musicians, accordingly, had devoted their attention to the means of emotional expression, experimenting sometimes with great psychological understanding, and over the years with developing ingenuity and effectiveness. The dominant musical form was the madrigal, a short vocal piece bound intimately to its poem—at best, and most characteristically, to a Petrarchan sonnet, an isolated stanza from Ariosto, or a lyric by Tasso. Images, moods, and "affects" were translated into musical terms. The rich tradition of the Italian madrigal, from Cipriano de Rore to Luca Marenzio and Claudio Monteverdi, determined the expressive course of music during the last half of the *cinquecento*.

The ultimate step, perhaps an inevitable one, was from the lyric to the dramatic: music was to step on to the stage, as Monteverdi's Prologue does, in order to inflame variously even *le più gelate menti*, the most frigid of minds. To attain its most far-reaching influence, music had to aspire to the high form of drama. This remained an aspiration, no doubt, except for a few works; in any case it was less a deliberate goal than the natural outcome of *fin de siècle* essays in exaggerated expressivity. Many currents led in to the famous musical "revolution" of 1600, from which we date a little too crudely the beginning of modern music, the invention of the *basso continuo* or thorough-bass, the triumph of melody over counterpoint, and the first opera. This revolution is best seen as a violent, baroque extension of tendencies of the prior century. In many ways Monteverdi cuts off sharply from Cipriano de Rore and Palestrina, but the continuity is also clear; the first great opera composer was also the last great madrigalist. Musical drama was the last and most extreme product of the sixteenth century's faith in the moving power of music.

To the humanists and those who shared their enthusiasms at second hand, evidence for the great power of music was everywhere convincing. They knew that the Greek lyrics had been sung, and likewise the tragedies themselves—certainly in part, if not entirely. In 1585 a version of *Œdipus Tyrannus* was performed

with the choruses confidently set to music by one of
the most important madrigalists, Andrea Gabrieli. But
an even deeper inspiration was to be found in the
musical stories revered by classic authors—by Plato
himself, who would have banished certain modes of
music as too powerful, too dangerous for the well-
being of the state. Great musical exploits are told of
Amphion and Eunomus, Terpander and Timotheus,
Pan and Apollo. The legend of the Thracian singer
Orpheus is especially well developed, problematic, and
rich, and is remarkable for the simple beauty of its
action. Already in its classic sources the myth is half-
way to the dramatic form in which Politian and
Ottavio Rinuccini, Lope de Vega, Monteverdi and
Gluck, Cocteau, Milhaud, and Stravinsky were sub-
sequently tempted to shape it.

The lasting myths contain in them the lasting problems of man. The myth of Orpheus, furthermore,
deals with man specifically as artist, and one is drawn
inevitably to see in it, mirrored with a kind of proleptic vision, the peculiar problems of the opera composer. Initially Orpheus is the supreme lyric artist. In
the classic view he is the ideal of the prize-winning
kitharista—or, in Christian allegory, the evangelical
psalmist who charmed the melancholy Saul. To the
fourteenth century, he is the minstrel who exacts his
boon from the Fairy King; to the sixteenth, perhaps,
the madrigalist; to the nineteenth, proud Walther who
persuades the German pedants. The eighteenth century painted him, tremulously, as the amiable singer
of Metastasio's faint verses who entranced the King of
Spain. But for Orpheus the lyric singer, the crisis of
life becomes the crisis of his lyric art: art must now
move into action, on to the tragic stage of life. It is a
sublime attempt. Can its symbolic boldness have es-
caped the musicians of 1600, seeking new power in the
stronger forms of drama? Orpheus' new triumph is

to fashion the lament that harrows hell out of his own great sorrowing emotion—this too they must have specially marked, wrestling as they were with new emotional means, harrowing, dangerous to manage. But the fundamental conflict of the myth transcends that time and this medium, and extends to every artist. It is the problem of emotion and its control, the summoning of feeling to an intensity and communicability and form which the action of life heeds and death provisionally respects. All this Orpheus as artist achieves. But as man he cannot shape his emotions to Pluto's shrewd decree; face to face with the situation, he looks back, and fails. Life and art are not necessarily one.

The quality of Orpheus' failure here is obscure in the myth, but for the dramatist it is the crux of the matter. Around it, Monteverdi and Gluck attempted to crystallize the very different dramatic ideas that guide their versions of the legend. We shall try to understand and gauge the quality of their success, or failure. To be sure, this "problem of control" is an abstraction; few artists, and certainly not Monteverdi or Gluck, have drawn so clean and scientific an issue. Nor did Orpheus, in the simple, unelaborated myth. It is the dramatist's task to clarify the issue for Orpheus. The critic's is to clarify the parallel issue, the artist's problem of control; not for the dramatist, but for an audience which needs to grasp the dramatist's methods in order to share his vision.

2

THE FIRST two operas that have been preserved are settings by Peri and Caccini of *L'Euridice*, a pastoral play by Ottavio Rinuccini, the Florentine humanist

poet of Count Bardi's *camerata*. The first great opera
is Monteverdi's *La Favola d'Orfeo*, written at Mantua
in 1607; and *Orfeo* is the first opera to reveal the
characteristic composer's struggle with the libretto.
The composer is the dramatist, and his particular
powers will determine the integrity of the drama. From
his point of view, then, those elements in the libretto
which suit his powers can be realized; other elements
are either triumphantly distorted, or do not matter,
or defeat him. In the end, the libretto is the limitation. But from another point of view, it is usually
true that the composer's powers have hardly been
shown beforehand, and come out only in the musical
setting of the libretto. In the beginning, the libretto
is the inspiration.

So it was with Monteverdi. He was not a master of
recitative who went to Alessandro Striggio for a libretto
to incorporate this special strength. Striggio, let us say,
brought him the book; and, in setting it, Monteverdi
discovered recitative—he did not invent it, but in the
deepest sense he certainly discovered it. From then
on recitative was his greatest achievement. It forms
the basis for *Orfeo*, and completely dominates and
determines his masterpiece of thirty-five years later,
L'Incoronazione di Poppea.

Recitative is one of the fundamental, constant elements of operatic dramaturgy. But actually it already
began to decay into convention with Monteverdi's
pupils, and in spite of impressive renewals in later
centuries, it has never been used again with Monteverdi's confidence, imagination, and conviction. As a
result, it is hard for us today to think of recitative
as anything but second best, a necessary link between
arias. In 1600, however, there was as yet no concept
of the considered emotional experience that later composers were to elaborate in purely musical forms—Bach
in the fugue, Beethoven in the symphony, Handel and

Verdi in the aria. It remained for Gluck to bring this modern concept of musical coherence to the Orpheus legend; Monteverdi understood nothing of it; in the tradition that he knew, musical expressivity was directed only to the painting of moods and images in madrigals. Now there was a more specifically neoclassic ideal: music instead should imitate the accents of passionate speech as best represented by the grand, exaggerated rhetoric of a great actor. Music should follow the cadence and thus the moving implication of the individual word, with little heed to the phrase, the sentence, or even the total feeling. The result was recitative, tumbling emotion, a continuing heart-cry, undistanced, "the naked human voice" behind the measured voice of the poet. Its magnificence and immediacy stem exactly from its impulsive nature, from its lack of forming control.

Monteverdi met this ideal with a perfect genius for declamation; words formed themselves musically for him. And to whip the recitative line into passion, he harrowed every available musical means for tension. Declamation guided him to sudden halts and spurting cascades in rhythm, and to precipitous, intense rises and falls in melodic line. Though he sometimes juxtaposes chords in radical ways, his basic harmonies are generally simple; harmonic tension is implemented by dissonance between the voice and the chords below. Occasionally he even emphasizes violent dissonance above a harmony without any suggestion of relief (in technical terms resolution, passage into calmer consonance). Or when, more usually, he does resolve dissonance, the effect may be partial and bitter, or else compromised with new subsidiary tensions introduced in passing by searing extra-harmonic notes. The great advantage of the modern monodic style of the 1600's, the "new music," was that the voice could range unencumbered above the *basso continuo*, which all alone provided a simple harmonic support. Rhythm, line, and dissonance were actually freed for the most expressive contortions. In the essential simplicity of the total texture, they could not destroy the clear, quiet authority of the bass.

Monteverdi's use of syncopation is particularly striking. Syncopation is rhythmic tension, just as dissonance is harmonic tension; traditionally the two had been carefully used together, mainly for the purpose of strengthening a coming cadence. But Monteverdi made syncopation of the recitative line into a positive mannerism, producing a curious sense of ready displacement, a latitude that allows the singer to drag or rush irrespective of the sober metrical beat. In the musical example below, the lower lines show Monteverdi's syncopated recitative line and its bass; above I have tried to reconstruct the conventional, non-syncopated version of that line which the bass would normally imply. Six times the voice seems to come in too late for its accompaniment—and usually its lateness has caused a sharp, scarcely resolved dissonance. At the end the voice twice stumbles in ahead of time, with an even more excruciating effect. This has just the expressive force of *rubato*:

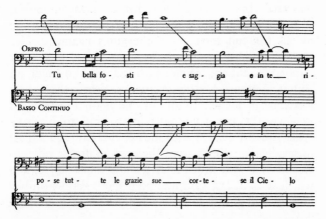

No doubt Monteverdi wanted the dissonances for their own sake, but he was also interested in an impression of unbridled ebb and flow, and in the immediacy of response which this creates. It is as though the singer were in such transports that he can no longer restrain himself to the artifice of the steadily marching bass. The example, moreover, is simple in that Monteverdi here has regular movement in the bass, for a special reason; usually the bass is also erratic, giving a remarkable sense of flexibility, torsion, and expressivity to the whole complex. The musician tries to capture the metrical fluidity of poetry, poetry as spoken on the stage. The result is a declamatory style of unexampled raw emotionality.

This art of recitative is what Monteverdi brought to the story of Orpheus, an artist who could move hell by his grief, a lover who could not dominate his passions. Striggio's libretto does everything to refine a view of Orpheus as an unreflective creature of impulse, acting strongly and with the greatest instinctive bravery. In the first act we hear him only briefly, breaking into the Arcadian atmosphere with an enthusiastic hymn to the Sun, rejoicing in his success at finally winning Eurydice. But in Act II the pastoral tone is shattered by a most explosive Messenger, Silvia, *"ninfa gentile,"* who suddenly and for the first time reveals the full force of Monteverdi's recitative. Her superb, rapid lament acts as a kind of trigger for Orpheus' emotion; his part in this act is also small, an abrupt, intense, half-unconscious decision to seek Eurydice in Hades. In Act III he is on the bank of Styx with Hope, who must leave him, to his very articulate distress. Hopeless, he nonetheless sings a huge formal lament to Charon; the lament breaks off into an informal plea which is even more impassioned, and which does at last gain him admission. Rather ambiguously, though: Charon, evidently a half-comic character, is still adamant, but falls asleep (like Cerberus in mythology). In Act IV, when Eurydice is released, the drama quickens as it reveals Orpheus' rather terrible insufficiency. His reaction is neither gratitude nor real affection, but a hymn of praise to himself and to his lyre. Fearing that Eurydice may be snatched back, he turns fitfully to see her, as much out of overconfidence as for love. When she fades away from him, he utters another piercing cry, such as Monteverdi alone could handle in recitative. How inadequate Gluck is at this place, in the heat of the moment! Monteverdi's Orpheus is agonized, and the Infernal Chorus mercifully cuts him off.

This chorus observes that success comes only to those who can moderate their feelings, a moral which indeed is spoken by everybody: by a Spirit who warns of *giovenil desio* as he fetches Eurydice, by Eurydice herself in her dying words "*Così per troppo amor . . . ,*" and in the next act by Apollo *ex machina,* who echoes her speech and further rebukes his son: "*Non è consiglio / di generoso petto / servir al proprio affetto.*" But Orpheus learns nothing. In Act V, before Apollo comes to him, he is lamenting again in Thrace, with more intensity than ever, but with scarcely any higher awareness. And his subsequent ascent to heaven is more or less meaningless, the most disappointing thing in the opera.

To distinguish between the attitudes of the librettist and those of the composer is often hard. Striggio was experimenting, just as Monteverdi was. While the first act of the libretto is purely lyric in quality, like the *Euridice* of Rinuccini, the later acts show striking dramatic tendencies, especially by contrast with Rinuccini. But Striggio did nothing to bridge the gap between Orpheus' heroic achievements in song or action and the callow impulse (to consider it coldly) which is his only response to them. In a libretto, poetry can do nothing for Orpheus; even if Striggio had the poetic art, he lacked the time and the form. But through Monteverdi's recitative, impulse becomes passion; it is impossible to consider Orpheus coldly. What seems in the book to be instinct or caprice becomes under the pressure of the music an absolutely compelling emotion, so that we are no more in doubt of Orpheus' integrity than are the wild beasts of Thrace and the creatures of Hades, whom he likewise sways. A libretto provides a framework, but the essential dramatic articulation is provided by the music. By means of Monteverdi's recitative, Striggio's blank or contradictory character attains tragic reality.

Monteverdi also grasped the need for elements to bind and weight the primary texture of recitative, to control it from the outside, since it knew no inner restraint. He used short songs, brief orchestral sections called *ritornelli* or *sinfonie*, and choruses ranging in style from serious madrigals to light fa-la's. None is very expressive in itself, indeed many can be said to be awkward, neutral, and antiquated; but they make a perfect ballast for the form. In the task of dramatic construction, Monteverdi was helped by having a poem shaped along bold, simple lines. Striggio appears to have worked from a sort of ideal scheme for an act, a scheme which forms itself during Acts I and II, reaches full articulation in Acts III and IV, and decays in Act V. His tendency was to start each act with a static situation, follow it by a single important action, show Orpheus' reaction to it, and then sum up in a choral conclusion. Especially the great Infernal Chorus, flanked by the trombones and *cornetti* which alone survive in Monteverdi's hell, beautifully reflects the success of Orpheus in Act III, and then his failure in Act IV. The solemn Venetian madrigal polyphony, stiffly controlled as though sculptured, answers and deepens the impassioned voice. *Orfeo* shows a wonderful sense of clear dramatic movement; Striggio had not studied and translated Greek plays for nothing. And Monteverdi, past master of the highly developed choral art of the sixteenth century, was able to give the chorus, in particular, a dramatic importance second only to that of the recitative.

As I have said, one virtue of the libretto is that it gives Orpheus many occasions to react violently in moments of crisis: the news of Eurydice's death, the departure of Hope, the rejection by Charon, the return of Eurydice, and her second death. These moments are precisely suited to Monteverdi's power, and mark indelibly the character of the drama. But at two crucial points in the play, Orpheus is confronted with the necessity of dealing with considered feeling after the moment of pain has passed; he is to summon up all his art, his control, to comprehend pain in a purer consciousness. For a later composer, these would have been natural "aria situations."

The first of them is the formal lament to Charon; and Monteverdi, who could not write a true aria, triumphantly distorted the libretto. Striggio wrote six tercets of *terza rima*—knowing that Monteverdi was usually very respectful of poetic form. Monteverdi set the first four tercets as an increasingly brilliant musical display, with fabulous coloratura for the singer, broken by ornate instrumental interludes. But as this does not impress Charon, Orpheus forgets himself abruptly and delivers the fifth tercet as a free and (in context) doubly piercing recitative. Then, by a wonderful inspiration, the final tercet is completely calm, without coloratura or passion; Orpheus and the instruments come together for the only time in the opera, in a style vaguely ecclesiastical, part-music to which Orpheus kneels with the viols, exposing most purely the quiet bass pattern which had united the earlier stanzas. Charon is indeed stony-hearted. With intolerable passion, the recitative plea is resumed, culminating in the famous refrain *"Rendetemi il mio ben, Tartarei Numi!"* As Orpheus enters Charon's boat, the Infernal Chorus speaks its sober sentence:

> *Nulla impresa per uom si tenta invano*
> *Nè contr' a lui più sa Natura armarse . . .*

> No undertaking of man is tried in vain,
> Nor can Nature arm against him further . . .

The other "aria situation" is of course the scene in Act V, which begins with a fifty-line lament for the despairing Orpheus. Striggio built the passage metrically to a pulsing climax; apparently the idea was to carry Orpheus forward from mere depression and bantering with his echo to a state of ecstasy in which he could sing a hymn (at last) to Eurydice. It is worth emphasizing that previously Orpheus has sung only in praise of his success in winning her, and then again in praise of his lyre. But Striggio's long lament turned out to be one of those elements in a libretto which defeat a composer. Monteverdi's recitative is perhaps never so impassioned and powerful as here, but he had no way to present the more serene vision that Orpheus may be expected to attain as he looks back on events from the Thracian fields. Monteverdi must have been dimly conscious of a "problem of control" in recitative. He attempted to organize it by means of refrains, sequences, rhythmic and melodic goals, even sometimes by a sort of tonal plan, and most strikingly by loose repetitive structure in the bass. That is, the free flow of the declamation is unified by the repetition in the bass of a fairly extensive pattern. Even this device, however, does not produce the cohesion of musical substance that gives consistency to emotional effect. Recitative is still too bound to the words; the technique of the aria was not yet developed. Having learned nothing, Orpheus is still reacting on impulse.

And when the force of instant passion fails for Orpheus, Monteverdi was at a loss for a further action or a final comment. I see no reason to doubt that Monteverdi saw into the delicate balance between character and action implicit in a drama. He was able to develop Orpheus' character in music so that his actions have dignity and sense; Orpheus' failure in Act IV begins to touch us tragically. But in the implied tragic end of an Orpheus play, there is another necessary balance: between the consciousness that grows in the hero and the tragic fate for which this prepares him, and which it lets him then transcend. Orpheus must somehow rise to meet, or deserve, or require the tragic fate. This progress Monteverdi could not show. So the conclusion of the drama presented a serious problem.

Monteverdi solved the problem by conducting Orpheus to heaven, with the prospect of meditating upon Eurydice fixed among the stars. It must be said that this Platonic apotheosis is musically and intellectually blank. But at least it is an act, and ends the piece efficiently; that is more than Striggio would have done; he meant originally to bring in the Bacchantes, but unlike Politian did not venture to offend the court by having them tear Orpheus. Monteverdi, we may well imagine, would have nothing to do with this undramatic prevarication. Even if Orpheus could not be shown to progress in Act V, dramatic form demanded some full action, some solid realization in terms of plot. Custom would not have deterred Monteverdi from carrying through Striggio's hint of tragedy if he had wished. Perhaps he refused to do so on account of an instinct of his own limitation.

Apotheosizing Apollo has no personality at all. But earlier, there have been beautifully pure little pictures of minor characters. The first is the passionate Messenger of Act II, who, after Orpheus has sung and left, continues her tremendous lament, self-centered as the hero himself, even infecting the Nymphs and Shepherds with her recitative refrain. In the next act, an even smaller role, parallel in function to that of the Messenger, is Charon; grotesque, scabrous, bitter with memories of violation and deceit. After Orpheus' song, Charon grumbles over the same bass pattern that had accompanied his original outburst; he is touched but determined not to budge. The vivid consistency of characterization and the opportunity provided for Orpheus to intensify his plea more than make up for Charon's unlikely drowsiness. He is a genuine test both of Orpheus' bravery and of the power of song.

Finally, there is the earnest figure of Music, who sings a simple strophic song as Prologue. She carries on her shoulders the artistic anxiety of the time. As, at the end, her song changes from gay to sad and she charges the birds and waves and winds to silence themselves, we wonder—will they yield in Mantua, as once they did in Thrace? Twice during the course of the drama Music is heard to return, as though to enquire and encourage, dumbly through the viols of her original *ritornello*. Can passion move into action? In Vienna in 1762 the issue was again to be in doubt, in a new atmosphere of experimentation with the means of musical expression. The matter was still not to be settled unequivocally.

3

WHAT Music had learned in a hundred and fifty years is shown swiftly by the opening scene of Gluck's *Orfeo ed Euridice*. Gluck plunges at once into the heart of the story with a funeral chorus for Eurydice, a somber musical block of the sort that Monteverdi knew well how to manipulate, though the tone here recalls rather Rameau. But neither Monteverdi nor Rameau could have conceived the part of Orpheus during this chorus. Sporadically, he utters three slow cries of the one word *"Euridice"*; he seems unaware of the mourners' presence, but it is the heavy, formed, ritual pattern of their dirge that sets off his uncontrolled and lacerating emotion. This is the first of many magnificent inspirations in this opera; Gluck must have congratulated himself on the classical economy whereby twelve notes sufficed to set Orpheus' broken grief. The point, however, is in what follows. After Orpheus asks to be left alone, the chorus departs, repeating most of its music, but he is now silent, contemplating. Then at once he begins his first aria, *"Chiamo il mio ben così"*—the elegy is sung by Orpheus in this opera, not by the chorus, as in Monteverdi's. Orpheus is equal to it; his previous inarticulate wailing is transformed to a tranquillity beyond anything that Monteverdi could achieve. Through his two utterances, Orpheus is shown to pull himself together, to a point where grief is viewed and understood, no longer lived, but not shunned either. He transcends his sorrow by controlling it into song.

This art of control was what had been learned: the art of the aria, after recitative the second of the two fundamental elements of operatic dramaturgy. Composers now could take a momentary sentiment and project it as a realized emotion rather than as an impulsive flash of passion in the manner of Monteverdi. Ideally the lyric aria comprehends a full, considered experience, and fixes it by means of musical form. Of course the modulation of lyricism into drama has been much misused, in *Turandot* and *Lucia di Lammermoor* and even *Don Giovanni*, as well as in the countless Metastasian *Didones* and *Egistos* of the eighteenth century. Nevertheless, the aria or some lyric substitute for the aria has become the prime power of musical drama, and no one has ever understood its function better than Gluck.

He was himself a product of the huge Italian school of *opera seria* that flourished in Naples, Venice, Vienna, and London; some of its best composers were *tedeschi*—Handel and Hasse and Johann Christian Bach, as well as Gluck. This school developed and abused the aria fantastically. The incentive for development came in the formal arrangement of the librettos of Metastasio, the poet who determined the aspect of that opera more strongly than any single composer. But the main abuse was due to musicians: over-elaboration, both in coloratura, thanks to the singers, and more basically in musical form, thanks to composers. In a sense, of course, every work of art, every aria, is its own form; but when standard patterns grow up, one can trace roughly the characteristic kinds of feeling to which they correspond. In Gluck's time aria form was extremely elaborate—I do not say complicated, for that would imply a psychological depth which musicians did not yet know how to sound, but elaborate, highly decorative, ruminative and elegant, exhaustive and exhausting. Feeling was attenuated to the destruction of drama. When Gluck wrote arias of stark formal simplicity, new truth and intensity of emotional expression came with the force of a revelation. This imaginative realization of the aria remains the greatest of Gluck's much-discussed "reforms."

Form can always be analyzed profitably up to a point, if never up to the ultimate point. "*Chiamo il mio ben così,*" Orpheus' first aria, is merely three identical strophes in a perfectly plain binary arrangement: 9 + 4 bars to the dominant key and 11 + 6 bars back to the tonic, with a positive minimum of other harmonies, no *ritornello,* and as adornment only a one-bar upbeat and exquisitely balancing echoes. These strophes correspond to the stiffly parallel three stanzas of the elegy. Between them are two epistrophes, in which the poet Calzabigi's conceit was to have the name Eurydice echoed by woods and glades, according to the best pastoral cliché. But there is a deeper echo: of Orpheus' initial lament with the mourning chorus. Gluck set the epistrophes as meditative, highly organized recitatives with echoes; and the very fact that the orchestra now always answers Orpheus' invocations of *"Euridice"* distances and forms his grief and illuminates the extent of his progress. The recitatives do introduce some richer harmonies, shifting tonally—the first to minor tonic and dominant, the second back through both mediants. One can grasp the economy and consistency of this scheme, and also the sophisticated irregularity of phrasing which alone could save it from banality. But in the last analysis Gluck's celebrated purity of line and nobility of musical conception are among the hardest things to "explain" in all music. Handel, the greatest of traditional opera composers, said that his cook had a greater command of counterpoint than the Chevalier Gluck. Perhaps so. Gluck was no more interested in the organ loft than in the kitchen; his iron control was over the means to far different spiritual pleasures.

The aria, for all its abuses, was the great strength of early eighteenth-century opera—its only strength, one is inclined to say. The aria is also the cornerstone of Gluck's operatic edifice. In recitative he pales beside Monteverdi; the genre had become conventionalized, decorous, and stilted. To be sure, Gluck worked hard to strike flame out of recitative, and, especially in the operas from *Alceste* on, achieved a certain force with it. But he did so, characteristically, by building recitative towards the aria: first by orchestrating it up to the level of the arias, and then by binding it as firmly as possible by means of accompaniment texture, tonal scheme, bass pattern, or general rhythmic pulse. Exactly these devices make it impossible for recitative to render the instant passion that its original master had so dearly loved. Most successful, in Gluck's *Orfeo*, are the tightly echo-bound recitatives within the first aria, "*Chiamo il mio ben così*," and the sublime climactic arioso (almost an aria) for Orpheus in the Elysian Fields, "*Che puro ciel.*" Something can be said too for the passages of angry declamation tied up with *tremoli* and decisive motives (in Act III, with Eurydice; in Act I right after the aria, as Orpheus rages at the gods and thinks of going to Hades; again at the end as he resolves). But these passages cannot be compared in emotional force to the lyric expression of the arias and choruses; the most impressive recitative is always at an unfair disadvantage in such company. Gluck's recitatives cannot convince us of Orpheus' fury and pain in the way that Monteverdi's do.

Understanding this, perhaps, Calzabigi presented Gluck with a libretto containing a minimum of situations in which Orpheus is shown to act on impulse. The arrangement is exactly opposite to that of Alessandro Striggio working for Monteverdi; here everything is maturely reasoned. In Act I, Orpheus is mourning at leisure, and is disturbed by no disruptive Messenger. He does think of going to Hades, but not as a momentary impulse, and the initial thought is not the decision; even after Cupid comes to support him, Orpheus debates the matter before making up his mind. It will be a difficult task, for will Eurydice accept the condition that he shall not look at her? He fears the worst, but nonetheless resolves to go. The contrast with Striggio is striking in Act III, at the crux where Orpheus regains Eurydice. Far from stemming from over-confidence and lack of restraint, the catastrophe is promoted by a very vibrant Eurydice, who goads her husband at great length to turn. Orpheus, who has been steeling himself for this ever since Act I, resists heroically as the scene drags on. They sing a duet at cross purposes; Eurydice sings a proud, passionate aria refusing to follow him under what she takes to be his condition of abstinence. They dispute repeatedly in recitative, the quality of which seems to emphasize the nagging hopelessness of the conflict. At last Orpheus turns to her, with full consciousness of self-sacrifice, and she dies. For a moment he rages (unconvincingly); then, once again, with a superhuman effort, distils his grief into song. "*Che farò senza Euridice?*," the second and last aria for Orpheus, brings him again on top of his feelings, comprehending them, refining them, projecting them in artistic form. Hanslick's famous objection that the piece does not sound instantly gloomy misses the essential point: the aria is beyond grief, and represents a considered solution, a response to the catastrophe.

Can we believe this accomplishment, this fantastic self-control in the face of disaster? The aria is constructed as a sort of undeveloped rondo, with the grand melody and the words "*Che farò senza Euridice?/ dove andrò senza il mio ben?*" sung three times almost identically, but with increasingly beautiful effect. Between these appearances are brief, tuneless episodes hingeing (once again) on a bare cry to the name of Eurydice; and these recall again the inarticulate grief of Orpheus at the very beginning of the opera. Thus within this aria, Calzabigi and Gluck write the same progress as between the opening mourning chorus and the succeeding elegy. Even in form, "*Che farò senza Euridice?*" is something like an intense compression of "*Chiamo il mio ben così.*" The process of sublimation is repeated now on a higher plane of action, if not perhaps of awareness.

The clearest clue to Gluck's conception, however, is in the *Gestalt* of Act II. This is perhaps the most moving and perfect act in all opera, and perhaps the

simplest. The first half shows the gradual success of
Orpheus' plea to the Furies; the second shows him
transported to the Elysian Fields, where, as though in
a dream, Eurydice is returned to him just before the
curtain.* For the taming of the Furies, Gluck did not
write an aria for Orpheus, as even Monteverdi had
done. In Gluck's sternly consistent scheme, Orpheus'
arias are occasions for spiritual exposition, and this
was not quite the place for one. Orpheus is already composed, master of the situation; he sings a long tranquil
arioso, modest, manly, and clear-eyed; he will prevail
by the frank force of his personality or not at all.
Even the terrifying repeated "No!" of the Furies cannot
urge him into special pleading, coloratura, or rhetoric.
Gently his harp accompaniment and his vocal line expand and intensify, but essentially his success is articulated by the decreasing force of the Furies' replies;
Orpheus has only to hold his own. Needless to say, he
does not (like Monteverdi's hero) forget himself magnificently for impromptu recitatives. Nor is there jubilation as the Furies cede and convey him to the Elysian
Fields. His reaction is of serene wonder, approaching
worship, and his longing for Eurydice seems even further chastened.

It was remarkable of Calzabigi to have put in the
Elysian Fields, Vergil or no Vergil; but obviously
Gluck wanted them, and made this scene into the
opera's unforgettable climax. Its dramatic meaning,
then, is of literally first importance. Certainly the scene
is not intended to place Eurydice; the lady we see in

* Later, in Paris, Gluck expanded both halves by adding three
wonderful numbers, among others: the Dance of the Furies, the
Dance of the Spirits for flute, in d minor, and the Chorus of
Spirits led by a soprano soloist, *"Cet asile aimable."* So far as I
can judge, these numbers slow the action without altering it significantly. In this discussion I follow the original Italian version
because it is purer in dramatic construction. I should not, however, wish to sacrifice the many improvements of detail in the
French version.

the next act does not fit in Elysium, and we can only imagine her maintained there by means of the Stygian draught. But Orpheus manifestly does belong there. The whole aspiration of his spirit is realized in the glittering gray light of Gluck's perfect heaven, where passion has been finally purified away. Orpheus responds to the vision of Elysium with a calm rapture comparable to that of Winckelmann before a Tuscan ruin:

> *Che puro ciel, che chiaro sol,*
> *che nuova serena luce è questa mai!* . . .

The orchestra unfolds a great arioso held together by a sublime oboe melody and by rustling flutes and violins around it. Some such harmony, seven-stringed, Æneas in search of Anchises was to hear Orpheus strike from his lyre. Orpheus lingers; he is loath to leave; he thinks of Eurydice, to be sure, but the scene is organized by the sounds of heaven, not by those of earth and love. Eurydice herself has nothing to say (and it is a bad mistake in the French version to give her the part of the Happy Spirit in "*Cet asile aimable*"). Obviously, the scene-change to the Elysian Fields comes as a great relief after the tension of the Furies in the earlier part of the act. Thus in the deepest sense, Orpheus' reward for the beauty of his song and his heroism is Elysium, not Eurydice. We trust first what is most emphatic in the music.

For Gluck's thoroughly Vergilian paragon, this otherworldliness comes as easily as self-control and aesthetic sensibility. His virtue has been exposed gradually under the stress of a stately series of events. But towards the end we begin to remark that obstacles are transcended rather than overcome, that the power of Orpheus' art is directed within himself rather than out into the action which it is said to regulate. There is something extraordinary about his passive response to Eurydice's reproaches, though he is as always correct, guided by reason, and not a little saintly. He makes no more effort to meet her on her terrestrial plane than she to meet him on his. Though things are more dramatic —supremely so—as Orpheus summons everything together for "*Che farò senza Euridice?*," yet there is almost a sense of relief to the song; his heart is not in the conflict, but in his own lyric introspection. To be sure, in this he is only being true to the ideal of the lyric singer and to that of the eighteenth-century operatic hero. But in the end Orpheus is in danger of ennobling himself out of the realm of dramatic action. In the state of beatitude to which he tends, mundane conflict seems trivial, and the dramatist's energy seems wasted.

How then could the action relevantly conclude? A tragic ending would be as inappropriate as in Monteverdi's opera, though for a different reason: to have torn apart this perfect hero would have been an act of unnecessary, meaningless brutality. Oddly enough, Monteverdi's apotheosis would have made good sense here. But Gluck was probably confused enough by his hero's tentative leanings towards the religious. The simplest thing was to set the fatuous "effective" conclusion that lay before him in Calzabigi's book.

So Gluck's forming idea of sublimation could no more consummate the drama than Monteverdi's forming sense of passion. After "*Che farò senza Euridice?*," Calzabigi has Orpheus decide to kill himself—as ambiguous an act as could have been conceived. (There is nothing ambiguous, however, about the glorious line of melody which Gluck inserted at the end of his recitative, "*Sì, aspetta, o cara ombra dell' Idol mio*"; even in this rash deed, Gluck seems anxious to assure us, Orpheus is fully conscious of his condition.) The suicide is interrupted by the return of Cupid, who explains that everything has been a trial. Orpheus picks

Eurydice off the floor for a moment of general embarrassment, and then a chorus gaudily cheers the reuniting of the incompatible pair. Their hymn to love has nothing to do with the true merits of the case; but the conclusion is worse than irrelevant, for it tries to deny that there ever had been any drama. Fortunately, I think nobody in the theater will credit that or any other pretension of this conventional excuse for a dramatic solution. Gluck also gives up the ghost at the crux of *Alceste*; the *Iphigenias* and *Armide* end better.

4

HEROIC opera, the quintessential art-form of the baroque, had its beginning when Monteverdi showed suddenly what the form was worth. The great tradition came to an end when Gluck transformed it, and transformed it in its own terms. Orpheus begins and ends an era. The era embraces many neoclassicisms: the late humanism of Count Bardi's *camerata* and the Mantuan court; the *grand siècle* order of Lully and Quinault; the delightful, preposterous fantasy of the Arcadian Academy, with Crescimbeni, Farinelli, and Metastasio; the serene Roman ideal of Goethe, Winckelmann, and Gluck. At every point someone had a vague vision of a modern analogy to the Greek drama; and musical drama somehow came into being. Between the time of Monteverdi and that of Gluck, recitative erupted and decayed, while the aria developed, over-developed, and finally realized itself. It was the time of the true classical tradition of opera.

The lyre of Orpheus extends its charm even farther back, to Peri and Caccini in 1600, and even farther forward, almost to 1800: an *Orpheus* written for London by Joseph Haydn (but never performed) was among the very last of the *opere serie,* decrepit and long past its time. Orpheus' dramatic conflict falls easily into the favorite baroque formulation of instinct and duty, emotion and reason, "love and honor." But a special fascination for the opera composer lay in the almost explicit parallel between Orpheus' action and Orpheus' art. The task for the artist is to assert a purifying control over the emotional source of art, to form and focus it until he can move hell—and also move the audience in the theater. For the man, the trial demands heroism beyond that of daring hell: it is to control his own flood of passion when finally Eurydice returns—and also to convince the audience of the integrity of his actions. With Monteverdi, for whom raw passion was the main reality, the conflict was never solved. With Gluck, whose reality was the sublimation of feeling, the conflict was less solved than passed over; sublimation brought him practically to the sublime, to Elysium. Gluck had reached a point of artistic sophistication at which the problem of emotional discipline was only too simply met. The danger was in losing the very roots of passion. Both dramatists failed in the ultimate task of articulation, lowering their expressive sights and frankly deflecting the conclusion.

Perhaps it was just as well; at least they assumed no more than they knew. This negative virtue stands out in contrast with the next curious operatic metamorphosis of the Orpheus idea, another hundred years later, at another period of expressive experimentation and "reform." In *Die Meistersinger,* Richard Wagner attacked the problem of control head on, specifically, and with his usual relentless enthusiasm. The singer who will not brook laws of art or of orderly bourgeois society is gently taught self-control and musical form, both together, by a higher being who rescues him as arbitrarily as Cupid or Apollo, but who insists on rationalizing the rescue. The complacent tale ends with an unearned hymn to German Art, as the fantastic dramatic machinery purrs to its calculated close. All questions are answered, but no serious ones have been asked; it is not hell that has to be appeased, but the pedants of Nuremberg and the journalists of Vienna. And blind, proud, instinctive Walther has none of Monteverdi's burning passion or of Gluck's heroic self-awareness. The dramatic life in *Die Meistersinger* lies in something that began as a counterpoint to the central idea and then gradually displaced it: the drama of Sachs. It is there, and in other operas, that Wagner asked his important questions.

"Die heil'ge deutsche Kunst"—"Frau Musica" makes a substantial substitute for Monteverdi's shadowy Prologue. But the latter nonetheless remains to haunt our imagination. We imagine her, perhaps, restless on the bank of Styx with Orpheus as he pleads, vainly now, for another opportunity. Like Orpheus, she has her partial success, which is more meaningful than the full victory of others. Like Orpheus, she will continue to confront the dramatist with her elusive, animating challenge:

> I am Music, who with dulcet accents
> Know to soothe each troubled heart,
> And now with passion, now with noble rage,
> My power can inflame the coldest mind.

2

The Dark Ages

THE period between Monteverdi and Gluck was the great age of opera. Singing, scene design, and the composition of music and verse for the stage all saw unbelievable development and unbelievable activity. The output of libretti and scores was enormous; everything was instantly staged, cheered, plundered for the coming seasons, and then thrown away. In Italy, drama meant the opera, and its librettist Metastasio was the universal laureate, the new Sophocles. Outside of Italy, there was the extraordinary phenomenon of Italian theaters—operatic theaters—flourishing from London to St. Petersburg, in the hands of transient or immigrant Italians. And almost everywhere, music at that time meant the opera. Opera guided the evolution of the art, setting its tone as symphony would later, and as Mass and madrigal had before.

Composers were attracted to the limelight like

moths. It was a rare Italian, a disgruntled aristocrat of music like Benedetto Marcello, who could stay away and write a delightfully vicious satire like *Il teatro alla moda*. Opera as Marcello caricatured it was a societal disease: the axis on which every carnival turned, the means to magnify every local Cæsar, the shrine of philistine hero-worship, the grave of masculinity, the trembling issue of Arcadian polemics. Opera, as Vernon Lee showed in her admirable *Studies of the Eighteenth Century in Italy*, caught the spirit of that strangely cohesive age more fully than any other manifestation. The bold blend of music, poetry, and scene; the ornate dramatic convention; the pomp and the splendid, abandoned theatricality; the fierce singleness of operatic passions; the moving architecture, in and out of the ballet—all this sums up with characteristic extravagance the very aspirations of the baroque.

The period between Monteverdi and Gluck can also be called the dark age of opera. In spite of all its extent and fame, baroque opera is thoroughly unknown and discredited today. It is never produced; in fact many of the most important scores remain unpublished. On the whole, scholars have left the field alone, and historians skim over it. Look at Professor Donald Grout's otherwise highly serviceable history. In ominous conjunction with our essential ignorance is our general critical view of baroque opera: that it was all of unparalleled dramatic fatuity. The judgement is equally harsh on French court opera, whose lasting model was formed in the 1670's by Lully, and on the huge tradition of Venice and Naples, which settled in the middle quarters of the next century around the librettos of Metastasio. French opera was a stilted entertainment combining baroque excesses with the driest neoclassicism. Italian opera was a shameless virtuoso display, emasculating classic history into a faint and tedious concert in costume. What remains in the musical im-

agination from French opera is no more than its grave
ballet suite; what remains from the Italian are the witty
attacks of *The Spectator*, *The Beggar's Opera*, and *Il
teatro alla moda*. And some lyric "gems," to be sure,
picked out for students in *Gloires d'Italie* or *Masters
of the Bel Canto*, and even sung sometimes, in oddly
anachronistic versions. But the dramatic futility of the
hundred-and-fifty-year tradition is everywhere taken as
received fact.

I am, obviously, skeptical of this uninformed tenet
of musical criticism, as of many others which would
collapse under even the moderate brilliance of a contemporary point of view. A drastic reassessment of the
whole aesthetic of baroque opera is overdue; it will
have to wait, however, for a lot of tedious work as well
as a really imaginative exercise of historical criticism.
Meanwhile some of the dramatic possibilities of the
baroque are clear enough from their realization in
certain familiar works—whether the central tradition
was corrupt or not. The present study is not particularly concerned with central traditions, but rather with
isolated masterpieces derived from them, however tan-
gentially, and with certain principles embodied in
them, however imperfectly. The important thing is to
insist on the dramatic truth of the peripheral masterpieces, and on the dramatic vitality of the conventions.
These are the primary facts. Certainly the genuine
achievement must not, on account of a reputed general
corruption, be allowed to come into question on *a
priori* grounds.

In any broad consideration of opera, the principles
of the baroque musical theater have a unique importance as the classic principles of the art. Baroque
dramaturgy deals in great, simple, intense blocks; lucid
and naïvely rigorous, it can be employed with magnificent power. The scheme remains central to later
dramaturgies, which are more complex, but less sure

and strong. We cannot grasp the classic normality of baroque opera altogether from Monteverdi, who occupies a primitive position, or from Gluck, who already occupies a destructive one. We need to see composers at the center. Both the French and the Italian conventions, it will appear, had their virtues, and some musicians were impelled to turn them to dramatic account.

2

IN SEVENTEENTH-CENTURY Italy, opera, once planted, developed with tropical luxuriance. By 1680 Monteverdi's *Orfeo* would have seemed hopelessly antiquated to the audience of one of the eight Venetian opera houses. In Versailles, however, it might have been understood, for in certain ways Lully preserved the ideal and technique of *Orfeo* long after Monteverdi himself abandoned them. French opera was reactionary and provincial, and it was soon to become stagnant. But it was also enormously tenacious, and it is pleasant to think that some of its strength came from the solidity of its unacknowledged model. In mood, Lully preserved the high-minded classicizing spirit of the Florentine humanists and Alessandro Striggio. His subjects, still drawn from Greek mythology, were handled with something of the stately simplicity of Greek dramatic action. Venetian opera, meanwhile, had thrown dignity into the canals, and was busy encrusting Latin history with a scandalous picaresque confusion of plot. In technique, Lully's operas also recall *Orfeo*—specifically this unique work, rather than the earlier Florentine operas, or any later ones by Monteverdi or Cavalli. Though Lully wrote seventy years later, the basic elements of his dramatic convention are curiously similar: recitative is still the climactic center of attention, and the vital subsidiary role is taken by the chorus, while little songs or *"airs"* are of mainly decorative interest. Venetian opera, meanwhile, had completely debased recitative in favor of still rather primitive arias, and had completely eliminated the chorus. It was the worst period of Italian opera, between the time of Cavalli and the reform of Zeno and Metastasio. No wonder Lully gained the palm in the invidious international comparisons which delighted critics of that age, as of every successive one.

But of course the old virtues could not be exactly preserved. The difficulty of maintaining this kind of opera was the difficulty of writing Monteverdi's red-hot recitative in the cool atmosphere of Racine and Boileau. Even in Italy the violent passion of the early baroque had yielded to a more formal and disciplined art; the spirit of Monteverdi yielded to that of Corelli. In France order and restraint were even more necessary, and Monteverdi's unbridled style would have been nothing short of subversive. By contrast Lully's recitative is bloodless, its vigor carefully paced, its passion channeled, its nobility stereotyped and labored. Its greatest pride was justness of declamation, a characteristically French virtue which does not mask its dryness of expression.

Yet recitative was still made to carry the central dramatic role, for word and "reason" might not be abandoned for sheer lyric expression. The artificiality of the aria was shunned. To be sure, Racine's formality and pomp are vaguely comparable to Lully's, and we can dream of a neoclassic musical drama compounded of the two. But Lully's circumspect librettist Quinault produced something quite different, both on account of his own insufficiencies and on account of the complicated and depressing critical vise in which he found himself caught. The critics could scarcely forgive him for supplanting Racine, or for clouding the precision of French verse with irrational musical associations, however dry. So with characteristic ingenuity, a new classification was decided upon: *tragédie lyrique*. It was logically unassailable. The diction was to be smooth and resolutely "literary," but the dramatic persons were never allowed to trifle with intelligence.

So while Lully's recitative was much praised, the weight of his opera shifted towards the chorus, together with the ballet and the large scenic effects— what the French aptly consider together as *"le merveilleux."* This was the undisputed field for music, as even *Andromède* and later *Esther* and *Athalie* attest. The danger was that *le merveilleux* might become the *raison d'être* instead of an integrated dramatic element; and the later operas of Rameau, a much better composer than Lully, suffer fatally from this. Lully kept a more careful balance, but his opera is spectacle-ridden too. It is easy to understand his affection for the old mythological apparatus, with its monsters and apotheoses, its choruses of nymphs and tritons, its threnodies, *tombeaux*, and transformations. We are too familiar with the dramatically disruptive effects of *le merveilleux* in French operas of a much closer date (and in *Tannhäuser*) to be sanguine about Lully's compromise. Moreover, while we can read Racine and sing Lully, we can presumably never experience again the fantastic spectacle of the baroque operatic stage.

This is to put the worst aspect on Lully as a dramatist; and the friendliest critic will admit that he labored against great obstacles. But the examination of any one of his scores reveals certain scenes in which the drama is all of a sudden deeply felt and powerfully projected. Next to Euripides or Gluck, Lully's *Alceste* is a joke, but Gluck would not have been ashamed of the great choral scene of mourning for the Queen, with its moving scenery, ballet, and mime. Even Admetus seems miraculously capable of participating in the communal shock and sorrow. Nor were the limitations of Lully's scheme insurmountable for an entire play; *Dido and Æneas*, the crystalline little opera by Henry Purcell and Nahum Tate, is essentially within that scheme. *Dido* is a unique work, innocent of any indigenous operatic tradition, written not for the *roi soleil* but for a young ladies' academy, and dashed off with a cheerful incorrectness which would have horrified Lully. *Dido* is a miniature; like Gluck's *Orfeo*, it dodges the cruel problem of making a full evening's entertainment for a court that demands a decent cut of splendor. Its dramatic perfection is nonetheless in Lully's cast. In spite of the critical anomaly caused by the inclusion of real arias, its dramaturgy is basically determined by chorus, dance, and formalized recitative.

Little enough of Vergil remains, perhaps. Dido is drastically simplified, and Æneas is made into a complete booby; the sense of cosmic forces at play is replaced by the machination of an outrageous set of Restoration witches. The simplification of Dido's character, however, is not without a resulting gain in concentration, and the chorus of her courtiers is admirably Sophoclean in spirit. They give, first of all, an intimate impression of the stake of Carthage in Dido's suicide. Furthermore the carefully worked-out progress of the chorus, in relation to Dido, illuminates and actually defines the personal tragedy.

The first scene contains five short choruses led by Belinda (Vergil's Anna), who doubles as chorus-leader and *confidante*. Repeatedly they encourage the proposed match between Dido and Æneas, finally calling for the Triumphs of Love and the Revels of Cupids as they go off to the hunt. Their trivial, hearty enthusiasm is at odds with the sentiment of Dido's single apprehensive aria—though this too, perhaps, speaks as yet in the accents of courtly convention.

Scene ii shows the plotting of the witches, who substitute for Jupiter and Venus in hastening Æneas' desertion. Dido and her train, of course, know nothing of this, but when we see them in the country in the next act, their song has a strange melancholy, which the "Triumphing Dance" had not led us to expect. The scene opens with what might be described as a masque fragment, a graceful, solemn little suite of song and dance to entertain the Queen while Æneas hunts. But it is the story of Actæon and Diana that comes to mind, in these "lonesome vales" which Venus had been said to favor. The storm dispels the chorus, and —more decorously than in Vergil—Dido too. Æneas is left to hear the witches' "trusty elf,/ In form of Mercury himself," to wrestle with himself cursorily, and to accede to the demands of fate.

In Act III the witches appear again, with a rude chorus of the departing sailors, whose traditional sanguine song of abandoning their girls practically puts the words into Æneas' mouth. After a violent scene with Dido, he leaves, and she prepares to mount her funeral pyre. Two choruses exquisitely frame Dido's famous aria, "When I am laid in earth." As Æneas goes, she sings two lines in recitative: "But death, alas, I cannot shun;/ Death must come when he is gone"; then the chorus, gravely silent during the quarrel, comments: "Great minds against themselves conspire / And shun the cure they most desire." This platitudinous couplet is like those with which the Greek chorus often breaks into a highly charged dialogue. It is all of thirteen bars long, but set in place with a brilliant sense of the drama. It provides a release of tension; a sudden new vantage point, an outside point of balance from which to gauge Dido's grief; a delicate transition from the stabbing dialogue of the quarrel to the lyric pace demanded by the conclusion; a tonal preparation for the ending g minor; and a great passage of time, a lifetime of decision for Dido. The luminous B♭ chords at the start turn to g minor and to quiet repetitions of a poignant figure in the ending phrase. From the flippancy of Act I and the vaguely motivated melancholy of Act II, the chorus comes finally to gravity and awareness.

This puts foolish Æneas and the pantomime witches out of mind; Dido's supreme aria can follow. By the clock, it occupies approximately one-twelfth of the time of the whole opera, and comes with particular spaciousness after the economy of the earlier action. No operatic climax has ever been approached with more direct strength, in a more genuinely classic dramatic rhythm. By relying heavily on a lyric aria, of course, Purcell stepped out of Lully's convention. Lully has his *"airs,"* but they are the simplest and most reticent things, comparable to Belinda's little songs in *Dido and Æneas*. Though French recitative always tends to arioso, the *airs* sound like slightly melodious recitative. The French would not accept the frank Italian convention whereby words and reason yield, at a dramatic crux, to the emotional expression of music handled in its own terms.

As we have seen with Gluck, it is musical form that fixes the emotion. Purcell was no great master of musical form—nor was anyone else in 1690—but he was a specialist at the "ground bass," a naïve and sometimes tedious formal device which is, however, magnificently apposite to Dido's dying lament. Its feeling stems from obsessive repetition: the bass of this aria consists exclusively of nine statements of a single figure, without transposition or variation of any kind. As a matter of fact, this particular descending, depressive bass figure was common musical property. Cavalli employed it regularly for laments; there is one for Hecuba in his *Didone*. Lully worked it into the scene of mourning for Alceste. Bach used it at the *Crucifixus* of the B-minor Mass,

and elsewhere. Purcell achieved an especially leaden effect by stretching it into a five-bar unit rather than the more usual four or six, dragging on the dominant D. For variety, he made the vocal line overlap ingeniously the cadences in the bass, as is shown in the musical example. The harmonies change only slightly with successive repetitions of the bass—until the climax, where on Dido's ultimate cry of "ah" the dominant major harmony is replaced by the modal-sounding, bleak minor chord (compare the first and sixth bars in the example; notice also the slow clashing of dissonant seconds below). In context this simple harmonic effect is tragic, and I use the term in as pure a sense as I know. Then, as Dido ends her song and mounts the pyre, the orchestra runs down a great slow chromatic scale derived from the bass pattern, closing the aria with a sense of quiet excrucation—or rather, breaking through to the concluding choral elegy. The very simplicity of the form, with its unyielding, uncomprehending bass, seems to stress, magnify, and force the insistant grief of Dido's situation.

What is so exactly in the Italian aesthetic, and out of the French, is that the whole piece is strung out to two trivial lines of verse; and that the great climax on the d-minor chord comes on a single syllable "ah"—a pre-verbal cry. Purcell understood that this could be infinitely more expressive than Lully's most elegantly declaimed Alexandrine. But he also understood something better still: how to organize arias into a total, coherent dramatic form. The lament does not end, but flows into the wonderful final chorus, the most elaborately extended in the opera. To a solemn choral dance, "Cupids appear in the clouds o'er her tomb"; Cupids, though, "with drooping wings"; Dido's agony softens and deepens out towards the audience through the mourning community on the stage. All through the opera Dido and the courtiers advance and converge, and at the end the courtiers, grown worthy of Dido's government, can take the stage after her death with full consciousness of the tragedy.

Few operas use a chorus so beautifully, or so integrally. But it is worth emphasizing that the convention employed was well within Lully's ken, and one that might easily be pooh-poohed as undramatic. The plan was simply to end each scene, and to begin as many as possible, with a community song and dance. (Nahum Tate even provided a chorus at the end of Act II, though Purcell does not appear to have composed it.) *Le merveilleux* was as imperative in a school play as at the court of Louis XIV. It presents its challenge to the dramatist; Purcell was able to meet it.

With recitative he was able to do less, though like Lully he devoted a great deal of attention to it. It is very carefully written, and vigorously declaimed, but impersonal, courtly, and bombastic; all that is presented is the shell, the form of passion. From Dido's recitatives we can tell that she is every inch a queen, but only from her arias can we become interested in her as a person. (There are moments, though: "Thy hand, Belinda," prior to the great aria.) Where Purcell trusted his recitative most, it let him down most seriously: in the long recitative for Æneas after he is warned by the Elf, at the end of Act II. This was supposed to make a rousing curtain and to give Æneas dramatic dimension comparable to that of the Queen; the method is Monteverdi's and Lully's. But Æneas remains a nonentity—without destroying the drama, fortunately. Only in the highly organized accompanied recitative for the Sorceress, "Wayward sisters," whose very *ritornello* foreshadows the coming line in the voice, is Purcell really at the height of his power.

3

IT IS hard to say how well Purcell's Italian contemporaries were able to meet their challenges. In 1690, the prospect of writing seventy arias per opera must have daunted even the most enthusiastic dramatist among them; and a sampling of their work does not reveal a genius like that of Purcell. Yet the dramaturgy of Italian baroque opera rests wholly and solidly on the expressive force of the aria. Imperfectly as this ideal may have been realized in the Italy of the seventeenth century, or even of the eighteenth, its legacy is clear in Purcell and Gluck, to say nothing of Bach and Mozart. No doubt the aria is even easier to misuse than the chorus, but its basic dramatic power is even firmer.

As Italian opera worked in practice, the action was halted very regularly for lyric introspection in arias. It was a drama of systematic soliloquy. What had become bizarre beyond the wildest nightmares was reformed by the poet Apostolo Zeno around 1700 into a classical Racinian scheme, which Metastasio a little later executed with an elegance worthy of Racine himself. In *secco* recitative, each little scene presented at least one character with new information or a new situation; his emotional reaction to it occupied the aria to which the scene built. Such scenes and such feelings were relentlessly multiplied and balanced. Like Racine, Metastasio could maintain this precarious artifice only in a world of ideal nobility. The composers simply concentrated their attention on a series of "aria situations"; they were not concerned with the necessary intricacy of plot, for all the details were handled by means of discussions, destined to be set in neutral, devitalized *secco* recitative. No longer the emotional carrier, recitative became simply a conventional manner of speech. When Mozart was rushed during the composition of his half-Metastasian *La Clemenza di Tito*, he had a student compose the recitatives.

This treatment of recitative was at once more workable and franker than that of Lully and Quinault. It eliminated recitative as a dramatic element; such drama as Italian *opera seria* can show depends on the arias, rounded lyric sections arranged in a simple sequence. By comparison with Quinault, Metastasio was more artificial and imaginative, and more justly musical. He gave music a chance, and of course risked bathos as the French never dared to do. At the same time, Metastasio's total form is even more rationalistic: lyric elements are rigorously separated from active ones. The drama is split on two planes, with nothing so problematic as a chorus or an ensemble number.

In theory, the first trouble with Metastasio's scheme was that contemporary music did not command the Racinian subtlety necessary to enliven it. As Purcell's aria shows, the baroque composer could strike a single feeling with wonderful intensity; but he did not have the means to handle psychological complexity. Even during a subsequent period, however, with a composer who did have the means—with Mozart writing *Idomeneo* or *La Clemenza di Tito*—there were other difficulties. The overall Metastasian rhythm, apart from the constant shock of arias jarring in and out of recitative, is impassive and highly predictable. Each scene runs its appointed course to the exit aria, each act balances its scenes, each opera shuffles the standard contrasts. Metastasio's awful symmetry is not naturally dramatic at all; opera was always in danger of collapsing into a catalogue of "affects" spaced off and displayed by means of recitative. The stern compartmentalization of plot action and lyric reaction put into crucial question the relationship of the two. Motivation itself was slighted every time that the expressive level was shut off for recitative, and the gallants in the boxes returned to their snuff and chess.

In practice, even such drama as was possible to Metastasian opera tended to be crushed by the weight of commercial conditions attendant on a genuinely popular art. If French opera suffered under the dictatorship of aristocratic critical doctrine, Italian opera suffered from the lack of any effective control beyond that of vulgar taste for vocal virtuosity. Metastasio's excellently ordered librettos, furthermore, were as stultifying as they were convenient; the composer, instead of blundering around with dramatic problems and perhaps solving some of them, merely provided his two dozen arias according to the specified sentiments of love, vigor, apprehension, and *sdegno*. To quote Sir Donald Tovey on this subject, "The scheme was fatally easy for small musicians and did not stimulate the higher faculties of great ones; while great and small were equally at the mercy of singers." This, of course, was the final limitation: the strong control exerted by the singers' interests. Great *virtuosi* knew only too well that the public paid only to hear their voices, and they were permitted to translate this confidence into an elaborate system of abuses. The resulting state of Italian opera ought to provide the classic lesson on the danger of giving in to the demands of the performing arts.

The grim picture of Metastasian opera is familiar enough. Certainly its obstacles were even greater than those encountered by the opera of Lully and Rameau. But at the same time its potentialities were inherently more exciting to a musician. Take down from the library shelf Apostolo Zeno's *La Merope* as set by Domenico Terradellas, or Metastasio's *Olimpiade* composed by Pergolesi, or his *Alessandro nell' Indie* by Handel (*Poro*), or Mozart's *Idomeneo*. None of them, perhaps, will do as a whole, but within them scene after scene trembles with emotion and dramatic life. Though the dramatic construction of these scenes is stereotyped and artless, even unworkably bare, the aria at the end does everything that is wanted in the little situation. It is the same with Italian opera a hundred years later; nobody calls Donizetti a dramatist, but nobody should begrudge him the simple dramatic success of the last scene of *Lucia di Lammermoor*. Metastasian opera gambled all on the emotional power of the human voice. Much was won. At the same time opera permitted itself to become indebted to *virtuosi* who were more tyrannical by far than the Parisian ballet-masters. It took the genius and tact of a Mozart to cajole the singers, please them, and turn their vanities sometimes to a dramatic end.

Johann Sebastian Bach at least did not have this worry; all the proud singers were at the Opera in Dresden, which he despised. Leipzig had no opera. It may seem capricious to turn to Bach's church music for illustration of baroque musical drama. But we can do so legitimately and profitably because of the nature of the sacred cantata in his time: both Catholic and Lutheran varieties were modeled on the opera. The German cantata was developed while Bach was young. Its guiding spirit, Erdmann Neumeister, a conservative divine, originally planned to restrict the form to a short chain of arias separated by recitatives. "To express myself shortly, a *Cantata* looks like nothing else than a portion of an *Opera* composed of *Stylo Recitativo* and arias together." Some of Bach's cantatas show this minimal form, though generally he (and later Neumeister too) preferred to include some liturgical elements, such as quotations from the Bible, and hymns. Even so, it is hardly surprising that many cantata librettos turned out to have dramatic potential to spare.

"*Jesu, der du meine Seele*," Cantata No. 78, is one of Bach's dramatic cantatas, one of the greatest and best known (or perhaps I should say, one of the less ignored). If I speak of it in terms of a religious drama of conversion, I am of course using the phrase in a special sense. Bach has no stage, no characters, no events; everything takes place in the mind of the Christian, or in Bach's mind, or in the mind of the communal singer. But from meditation to meditation there is a progress, a rhythm that is dramatic, certainly not liturgical. The piece dramatizes the victory over doubt, and the form, in small, is Metastasian. To be sure, Italian opera provides no precedent for the two choruses that weld the cantata together: the first verse of an old hymn is presented in a densely elaborated choral version at the beginning, to portray the soul in despair, and the last verse of the hymn, handled simply, concludes the cantata in a spirit of peace and illumination. But in between, arias and recitatives carry the essence of the drama.

For "exposition" Bach has his opening chorus. No formal drama has ever matched the force of this tremendously vivid opening tableau; it beggars the beginning of *Iphigenia in Tauris* or *Walküre* or *Otello*. It can stand with the first chorus of the *Passion according to St. Matthew*, the famous "scene on the road to Golgotha." The sixteen bars of the hymn "*Jesu, der du meine Seele*" are augmented to thirty-two and then expanded to 144 by means of interludes, an introduction, and a postlude. From the neutral clay of this hymn tune, heavy with association for the pious, Bach molds a despairing prayer in the face of Hell's attack, which he read (dramatically) in the first stanza: seven lines of invocation exploding into the entreaty "*Sei doch jetzt, o Gott, mein Hort!*" The unifying formal device used by Bach is the very same descending chromatic bass that we have just seen in Dido's lament. But both the extent of the form and the required technical feat of fitting the bass to the pre-existing hymn tune determined a brilliant variety in Bach's treatment. He repeats the bass pattern about thirty times. What had been sternly invariable with Purcell is here moved from the bass to other voices, transposed to contrasting keys, variously clothed in strongly motivic counterpoints, sometimes anchored over a pedal, even inverted at the reference to Christ's "*bittern Tod*" —a rising chromatic line has an especially excruciating effect, as already Monteverdi had shown in *Orfeo*. While the soprano slowly intones the hymn tune, the other voices echo the words more excitedly and subjectively, the orchestra has its own expressive web, and the inexorable bass repeats its ever-changing, ever-identical pattern. The piece is a triumph of baroque complexity, and, as always with Bach, complexity is employed to exalt a single simple "affect," in this case the agony of doubt.

Compare this chorus with Dido's aria, which is so similar in the one respect. Bach's rich awareness is striking, particularly as against the narrow thought of Purcell. But the point is in the dramatic position: with Bach a transfixing initial assertion of conflict, with Purcell a stripping away to the essence of tragedy. Bach's complexity would only have clouded the pathos of Dido's death. It is also true that for all its wealth of ornament and energy, Bach's chorus moves or develops even less than Dido's song. It is not dramatic in itself; baroque musical drama comes in the juxtaposition of such blocks.

To enter into the brilliance of a baroque church from the narrow gloom of the vestibule is to experience a dramatic contrast of the same order as that achieved by the aria that follows the chorus. It is in the mediant key, B♭ after g minor; the orchestra is suddenly gone; the rhythm rocks softly; instead of the chromatic bass everything is diatonic, a gentle, halting confession of faith. It is sung by two boys, a soprano and an alto echoing back and forth, seeking God innocently, as though the singers were unaware of original sin. The aria, or duet rather, trills its lengthy way with much softening to the subdominant. After the mature terror of the chorus, there is double poignancy in this naïve vision.

This poignancy is emphasized by the following recitative, which sharply breaks the mood. In Metastasio's scheme, recitative is the place for the action—here not a new message or a new decision, but a new consciousness, and a new mature voice to express it, a tenor. It is the consciousness of sin, something that was terribly real to Bach, though here the hysterical grief is shown to be as partial a response as the infant hope of the duet. After Monteverdi, Bach is the great recitative writer of the baroque, and a very harrowing picture he presents of man pierced by guilt. As is conventional, the recitative prepares for a tenor aria, which seeks to resolve the sense of sin. Christ's blood will lighten the Christian's heart and fortify him against the challenge of Hell. But in spite of these words, there is no sense of peace; when the issue concerned him closely, Bach could be an accurate psychologist, and an even better dramatist. The aria is most vivid in its musical illustration of Satan's sallies, and the mood is dominated by the sorrowing image of Christ's blood "twinkling down," as the Spiritual says, in the flute *ritornello*.

Only in the next recitative, sung by the still more mature-sounding bass voice, is Christ's sacrifice met with due understanding and humility, and only in the following bass aria is real victory achieved. Episode follows episode, in rigid order. The new "action" is the contemplation of the Passion; inevitable in any case, it had been prepared for by the pointed reference to "bitter death" in the first chorus, then by the disturbed emphasis on the redeeming quality of the Blood in the tenor aria. A halo of stringed instruments appears above the clear meditation, almost as in the *Passion according to St. Matthew* for the words of Christ. The recitative culminates in an arioso wherein words and melody of the hymn are incorporated again, subtly and very richly:

> *Dies, mein Herz, mit Leid vermenget,*
> *so dein teures Blut besprenget,*
> *so am Kreuz vergossen ist,*
> *geb ich dir, Herr Jesu Christ.*

Verbal insufficiency is forgotten where music controls; here, if ever, Bach attained the Christian serenity that he repeatedly sought. The grand bass aria can now triumph, if a little simple-mindedly, over the revenge of Hell, in text and music too. In the music, victory is a matter of superb coloratura matching an irrepressible oboe line, and of a form built on the rock of resounding concerto *ritornelli*.

The three arias have entered a personal testimony which touches more deeply, if more simply, than the exhaustive, superhuman opening chorus. The process shown is essentially the dramatic process of conversion. The opening chorus never leaves our mind; and at the very end, by a simple stroke much used by Bach, its tune returns when the last stanza of the hymn is sung.

As the arias have progressed, one by one, so has the hymn by the time of its repetition. The words that matter now are "*Herr ich glaube . . .*" and the sixteen bars of the tune are sung with no adornment beyond Bach's plainest harmony. The melodic recurrence strengthens the whole as only tightness of form can; but what had been originally plunged in despair is restated in a timeless aspect. Bach transcends the subjective level of the arias to achieve a liturgical solution to the personal struggle. Arnold Schering remarks with some surprise that this final harmonization of the hymn makes no gesture to illustrate certain grim words like *verzagen, Sünd',* and *Tod.* This was no doubt deliberate. Bach knew how to paint tension in a bare harmonized hymn, as witness the end of another dramatic cantata of a very different cast: "*O Ewigkeit, du Donnerwort,*" Cantata No. 60. Instead, the plain serene close of "*Jesu, der du meine Seele*" shares the luminous quality of the ending hymn in the *Passion according to Saint John.*

The cantata shows a deep conflict, a series of increasingly real attitudes towards it, and a final solution. Every listener, I think, senses it as a dramatic form. Its anomalies, from the point of view of Metastasian opera, are certainly egregious enough; the similarities, though, may be worth emphasizing again. Within the liturgical frame of the hymn, the human drama of conversion progresses in the arias, and is articulated by their individual quality and their interrelationship. Each one presents a single emotion, stiffly; the linking recitatives give the impelling action, here the psychological action, to promote the feeling of the arias. The situation is reduced to its simplest terms. Even more than Metastasio, Bach could slough off plot to concentrate on the lyric exploration of sentiment, both because his drama is set on the abstract stage of the church and because his form could be kept so brief. Baroque composers all had trouble maintaining large forms, even Bach when he approached the Passions. It is hard to guess whether he could have preserved the dramatic rhythm through a full-scale opera libretto.

4

MUSICAL drama of the baroque has a purity and an intensity which opera could never attain again; these qualities are matched to the stately, transparent simplicity of its dramaturgy. They are still felt in Gluck, but the sophistication of later times forms the matrix for different dramatic values expressed in a different group of dramaturgical plans. The drama of Purcell and Bach, though clearly outside the two central operatic traditions, clearly derives its strength from them. We can believe that those traditions were subject to the most monstrous abuses, without believing that they were in soul so thoroughly corrupt. I suggest indeed that their main sin was a certain asceticism, a determination to do without some variety of musical expression which elsewhere was proving its contemporary vitality. Lully rejected the aria, Metastasio the chorus, each for pressing practical reasons; necessity also guided their various transformations of the recitative. Each constructed a rigorous aesthetic which showed great gaps even in the terms of the day. It is no accident, I expect, that the dramas that impress us today are anomalous exactly in filling those gaps. Purcell follows the choral plan of Lully, but adds climactic arias; Bach follows the pattern of Metastasian soliloquy, but shapes it with impressive choruses. The true potentiality of baroque music and drama, we may say, was realized less in the central operatic traditions than in the peripheral masterpieces of Purcell and Bach.

To say further that these composers chose the best from French and Italian opera would be the facile formulation, neither true to their actual procedure nor in the end illuminating as to the quality of their work. With Gluck, however, it can indeed be said. By 1760, both kinds of opera were tottering, and their limitations were apparent to composers everywhere. Gluck and his poet Calzabigi had a certain instinct for the historical moment, to say nothing of a journalistic flair and a strong attraction to the intellectual limelight. Half-instinctively with *Orfeo* for Vienna, deliberately with later operas for Paris, Gluck sought to salvage the virtues of each tradition and combine them by his own catalyst for the maturing taste of the late eighteenth century. His subjects have Lully's solemn classicism; he even set one of Quinault's librettos, *Armide*, a hundred years later, and derived three of his best operas respectfully from Euripides. *Le merveilleux* of the French opera forms a background, but the chorus, the dance, and the grand scenic effect are firmly checked to a reasonable dramatic end. And at the crises, Gluck's great arias cut through, cunningly placed, tremendously powerful. Gluck had learned the art of the aria from Italy, but the new directness of expression was his own.

Gluck also reformed the recitative, for he had to reclaim it from the workmanlike nonentity of the composers of Metastasio's librettos, and from the pretentious blankness of Lully and Rameau. Recitative was smoothed in to the imaginative level of the arias and choruses. Here Gluck's efforts brought him to the verge of an operatic solution that deserves to be called altogether new. In one form or another, "continuous opera" dominated the nineteenth century—so much so, indeed, that the values of baroque dramaturgy were misconstrued, minimized, and excoriated. Many strands led in to continuous opera; Gluck's was not the only one. During his lifetime another was gaining strength in *opera buffa*, the tradition of Italian comic opera which ranged from Neapolitan popular farce to sophisticated high comedy. Without manifestos, composers like Baldassare Galuppi, Pergolesi, Nicola Piccinni, Giovanni Paisiello, and Mozart gradually evolved a radical technique to relate dramatic action and the musical continuity. As surely as Gluck's reform, this destroyed the baroque operatic convention and prepared for the coming syntheses of romanticism.

3

Action and the Musical Continuity

T<small>HE</small> fundamental mode of presentation in drama is
action, and in musical drama the medium of imaginative articulation is music. Inevitably the relationship or interplay between these two, action and music,
is the perennial central problem of operatic dramaturgy. It has been solved in many different ways; over
the years the solutions have become, not necessarily
better, but certainly more complicated and problematic
than those of Lully or Bach. An appreciation of the
drama of Mozart and Beethoven depends on a somewhat technical understanding of their dramaturgy,
that is, of their particular set of conventions for the
mutual qualification of action and music. What is involved, indeed, is the first means by which action was
actually brought in to the musical continuity.

The new means grew up in the *opera buffa* of the
eighteenth century. As a separate genre, comic opera

appeared in Italy only after the classicizing reform of Zeno and Metastasio. One of their most successful planks was the elimination of farcical elements from what they chose to regard as an essentially heroic sort of drama; stuttering servants and lecherous tenor nurses and transvestite *castrati* had really made a dramatic shambles of seventeenth-century *opera seria*. Meanwhile comedy was forced out on to its own resources. It formed a distinct tradition, much humbler than the solemn court opera of Metastasio, bawdy, swift, lifelike, preposterous, with firm if mysterious roots in the *commedia dell' arte*. *Opera buffa* required singing actors rather than expensive *virtuosi*; its composers were the less distinguished; it fed on the *opera seria*, parodied it constantly, and made its own aesthetic discoveries. Of these the most important was a new feasible relationship between action and music. This discovery, which made possible the dramatic accomplishment of Mozart, was one of the most striking single developments in the history of opera.

The change in opera was part of a deeper change in music generally, the change from the baroque style of Bach and Metastasio to the so-called classic style of Mozart and Beethoven. This again was one of the most crucial developments in the whole history of music, for it altered the very nature of musical movement. As one listens to a Beethoven quartet after a Bach concerto, it is obvious that the even flow of baroque music has given way to a much more varied dynamic. Passages in rest alternate with passages of impulse; yet they do not simply alternate in the older fashion, but rather grow in and out of one another in a way that gives a vital impression of leading and arrival. Composers now refined these qualities, carefully calculating climaxes, tensions, and balances. Beethoven commands both a stillness and a drive which are beyond Bach's steadier pace. Moreover, the new dynamic style made it possible to join together elements in essential contrast—soon treated as elements in essential conflict: abrupt changes of feeling were at first juxtaposed, then justified and developed until a final resolution lay at hand. Music in a word became psychologically complex.

Conflict, passage, excitement, and flux could be handled within a single musical continuity, such as, most characteristically, the first movement of a symphony. At first such pieces tended to fall apart, but it is remarkable how soon they were made to cohere, to present unified impressions. The well-known sternness of classic form was a plain necessity. Finally, with Beethoven's controlled flexibility, the sense of progress could be maintained through a whole cyclic work— through the seven movements of the Quartet in c♯ minor. We may compare it, perhaps, to a "progress" in Hogarth's sense; in these terms, the four movements of the First Brandenburg Concerto show only the general unity of a well-planned room in a picture gallery.

One can show precisely the technical basis for this revolution. Sir Donald Tovey, in his unorthodox way, has explained it better than anyone else. A necessary preliminary was to strip away the ornate foliage which hid the simple trunk of baroque music; bare lines of music could emerge for fresh use, as firm and pregnant as a beech tree in Derain. The important role of tonality in modern music has been compared with that of perspective in painting, and we can say that composers now addressed themselves to tonal investigations with the preoccupation of a Paolo Uccello or a Signorelli. The very process of simplification from the baroque gave tonality a new aural clarity and hence urgency. After the opening tonic key was bluntly established, successive keys were interpreted with new force as areas of contrast rather than as formal adjuncts to that opening tonic. So automatic a relationship as that of the dominant key to the tonic was raised to a sort of musical potential or high tension; it could charge the composition for minutes, and drive complex currents. Composers also relinquished the baroque habit of stating a full idea and then working it out exhaustively at once (as in the fugue, most typically). They used different developmental methods, localized and pointed, more functional than expository. Furthermore, with a new overall simplicity of phraseology, there was a new sense of breathlessness to irregularities which the baroque had peacefully absorbed. A powerful fund of pressure and relaxation was available, in rhythmic flux, for transitions, modulations, preparations, and extensions of every kind.

Tovey called this new style, very directly, a "dramatic" one, as opposed to the "architectural" style of the baroque. For him, indeed, instrumental music was more dramatic than opera. The metaphor seems to me illuminating in both of its possible directions of application. In a Beethoven symphony, for instance, there is something exactly dramatic in the quality of the musical progression: the exposition leading at once to heightening conflict, the development of contrasts, the final resolution and achievement. And in a Mozart opera, the role of what may be loosely called dramatic symphonic technique is primary. After Haydn, Mozart first brought the classic instrumental style to realization; only a great symphonist could have written *Don Giovanni*.

The one danger in Tovey's use of "dramatic" in this context is that the metaphorical sense may grow to dominate the proper meaning of drama for the theater and the opera house. Rembrandt too can be "dramatic," but plays are not to be judged according to his techniques. In one way the strict sense of "drama" is the more limited, of course; it implies stage and time, or at least some clearly expressed action, which neither symphony nor painting quite has (even if a Bach cantata may be said to). But in another way the strict sense can be considered broader; traditionally it has come to include modes outside of any localized aesthetic system, such as that of the classic symphonic style. Drama also has its more static modes: Bach as well as Beethoven, the series of harrangues in *Samson Agonistes* as well as the mobile plan of *Anthony and Cleopatra*.

For Tovey, musical drama was impossible before the evolution of the "dramatic" symphonic style. But I have hoped to show some of the dramatic potential of the "architectural" style, as he would have used the term. The baroque musical continuity was formed by a process of unfolding rather than by dramatic development, but it was possible to arrange a grand and particularly intense sort of drama by the placing of such musical blocks. The baroque composer did not have the means to incorporate action into the musical continuity; the classic composer did. They operated with different dramaturgies and under different limitations, and unfortunately it must be said that significant musical drama was as rare in the one time as in the other.

In any case, Mozart's dramaturgy has to be approached from the standpoint of his general musical style, and this requires an understanding of the workings of symphonic "drama"—I keep the quotation marks—at its most articulate, in the sonata form. This excellently adaptable form is also the most closely dramatic of all. Even its terminology is dramatic. In the opening "exposition," the area of the tonic key is defined, the central key of the piece, perhaps after a solemn slow introduction. The musical ideas are not always very distinguished in themselves, but are curt, flexible, and open at the end, designed to lead forward rapidly. The next business is to strike the note of

essential contrast, the new key. It is to sound heightened and progressive after the tonic, and must seem
difficult to maintain; the dominant key serves well.
Transition can be accomplished in many ways. Schu-
bert sometimes uses a *coup de théâtre*, Beethoven
usually a dramatic surge, Mozart often a formal, busi-
nesslike step.

It is usual to stress the basic contrast in key by
further contrasts in musical texture, volume, and mood
—by a contrasting "second subject," conventionally
lyric in nature as compared with the more restive
opening theme. The methods of Beethoven and Schu-
bert demand this heightening of contrast more than
those of Mozart and Haydn; Haydn especially needs
only the potent change of key. The achievement of
the new key charges the composition as though elec-
trically, providing the sense of dramatic tension. This
tension is next expressed by exaggerated insistence on
the new key at the end of the exposition section, in a
passage given over to cadences. Here new melodic
ideas may enter and digressions take place, without
altering the essential dynamic.

The ensuing "development" extends the basic key
contrast by progressing to more remote regions, which
seem exciting or troubled. The section is marked by
constant modulation. It is now not a question of one
key striving to assert itself over the initial tonic, but of
many keys rushing in with no sense of stability—quite
to the contrary, they prefigure by contrast the resolution later attained by the return of the tonic. In the
development the music reaches its area of maximum
rhythmic flux; the impression is always of some sort of
close struggle, hazardous exploration, terror, uncertainty, dramatic clarification, or trial. It is usual, again,
to stress this quality of the development by reinter-
preting some of the thematic ideas of the exposition.
They are broken up or expanded, simultaneously or

successively combined in unprecedented ways—"developed" with a sense of drama unknown to the baroque. Mozart, however, sometimes foregoes this thematic intensification and relies entirely on modulation of texture and tonality for his crux.

The tension grows towards the end; signs of agitation are multiplied. Then the development reaches up to a heightened dominant chord, which at last, with a due sense of triumph or relief, resolves to the tonic and the start of the "recapitulation." Here the composer runs through the progress of the exposition again, however freely. But now its essential tension is exorcised, for now everything is presented in the fundamental tonic key. Architecturally, the long tonic area is perhaps necessary to balance the instability of the development and the bold dichotomy of the exposition which preceded it. Dramatically, the rehearsal of all the energetic gestures of the exposition, but without their impelling contrast, presents that experience in a different and superior light. As the exposition had made an issue of the dominant key, the recapitulation tends to touch its polar opposite, the quiet subdominant, to deepen the feeling of cadence or conclusion. Mere balance rarely suffices, and the recapitulation ordinarily contains some new reflection of some prior detail. This reflection seems to display in small the new ascendancy over the earlier conflict. Beethoven reserves such last words for a sizeable coda, but Mozart often uses only the simplest of inflections with as striking and as free an effect.

The whole form, finally, is coherent. That is its main accomplishment. It is not much of a task to provide conflict in art; the task is to give conflict a sense of order and rightness. In sonata form, the psychological action or "drama" is subsumed under a single musical continuity, and unified by it. Real dramatic action in the theater could be organized similarly.

2

As IN *Don Giovanni,* in the trio near the beginning of
Act II. Donna Elvira steps out to her veranda in the
romantic spell of a Spanish evening, to indulge the
most mixed of feelings towards her faithless, irresistible
libertine, who, meanwhile, below, wanting her out of
the way in order to make love to her maid, lights on
the scheme of serenading her and then delivering her
in the darkness to an only half-unwilling Leporello
disguised in his master's cloak. Elvira's initial mood is
struck by the opening violin phrase of the trio and by
her gentler reply. The music is more songlike than
usual for a sonata theme, even in a slow movement—
as it should be for a lady's private meditation. But in
certain unresolved features it shows signs of belonging
to a larger dramatic unit: the delicate, half-mocking
variation of the opening phrase and the sensuous chromatic cadence as Elvira's heart melts:

Ah, taci, ingiusto core,	Unjust heart, be silent,
non palpitarmi in seno;	My breast, your trembling halt;
è un empio, è un traditore,	Sinner is he, deceiver—
è colpa aver pietà.	To pity were a fault.

The composer can sense and develop a feeling latent
in the most unprepossessing bit of a libretto. As soon
as Elvira pauses, Don Giovanni and Leporello mutter
together on a trivial thematic tag matched to the
scurrility of their intention. The initial situation or
tableau, still in the tonic key, already hints of movement: the two more active persons are heard after
Elvira, and their repetitious phraseology has the effect
of acceleration. It prepares for Don Giovanni's main
act, a firm step to the dominant key as he steps up to
address Elvira (he stands behind Leporello, who is to

pretend to sing). Thus the essential action begins, the seduction of Elvira, its sense of peril maintained by the dominant. In this key, Don Giovanni sings to the same melodic fragments that had marked Elvira's heart-strokes, practically answering her thought. At the end, Elvira and Leporello sing the trivial second theme, so excellently designed for asides:

> (*Numi, che strano effetto . . .*)
> (*State a veder la pazza . . .*)

Because they do not hear one another, perhaps, the phrase can now overlap itself; in any case the compression gives another subtle touch of growing urgency.

This is the dramatic exposition, corresponding to a musical section analogous to the exposition of a sonata form. Now comes the development. A new phase is implied by a rich, arresting modulation in the orchestra (to ♭VI—this modulation, incidentally, always seems to crop up in Mozart's seduction scenes). As the key contrast is extended and the sense of excitement grows, Don Giovanni warms to his task in a newly persuasive, fertile lyric line. As he presses, Elvira protests more, and the struggle becomes close. She cuts him short in a sudden *agitato*—the heart-beats in the orchestra are more serious now; the music begins to modulate again, more rapidly; their phrases overlap, his increasingly ardent, hers almost a little hysterical—*pazza*, as they say many times in the libretto. Completely carried away, Don Giovanni reiterates his final plea "*Ah, credemi, o m'uccido!*" on the extended dominant, the point of highest tension. Meanwhile Leporello is unsuccessfully trying to restrain his laughter—like Don Alfonso at the farewell scene in *Così fan tutte*. Elvira falls silent, for a moment the dominant hovers, then Leporello's quiet laughter guides the music to the inevitable resolution into the tonic key.

Here the director has to contrive some sign of

Elvira's surrender (something more delicate, let us hope, than the usual gratuitous horseplay). The action itself is over, but its effect must now be gauged in an ending tableau, the recapitulation of this tiny sonata form. The three singers simultaneously speak their individual feelings, which have developed during the piece, and which naturally conflict. But they are all placed under a single musical spell, as clear and magical as the moonlight; their diversity is united by the musical continuity. Elvira, almost distraught, hardly knows what to think of her own weakness. Leporello, no longer laughing, wishes her well and blesses her credulity; he speaks for the audience. Don Giovanni says that he is proud of his amorous talent, but if we are to believe the music, it is with a mysterious humility: he is just as touched by Elvira's surrender as he had been by the death of the old man in an earlier trio. That is what makes him irresistible. The themes return all in the tonic key, held together in the orchestra as the singers smoothly harmonize almost in the background. The music moves beautifully towards the subdominant, and there is a touch of expansion to the chattering theme of the various asides.

At the very end, one element which had not been accounted for in the form comes to its fruition: Elvira's romantic chromatic thirds are repeated and repeated twice for the final cadence, while her own line has a new decoration, wonderfully delicate, tremulous, and warm. This brings the whole episode together in a flash; more, it brings a piercing new inflection—Elvira is no longer the same, or at least our understanding and sympathy have matured. In a single musical piece, action has been incorporated, unified, and interpreted. Resolved in itself, the little scene guides the total drama forward, for our sense of the total piece depends upon our realized impression of Elvira here. In an analogous way, the slow movement of a Mozart sonata, perfectly realized in itself, plays a guiding part in the composition as a whole.

3

FOR that very fine critic of Mozart's operas, Professor Edward J. Dent, this trio is the most beautiful number in *Don Giovanni*, which is practically to say in the whole of opera, and I should not be inclined to contradict him. Here, however, I have analyzed it mainly in order to show the great dramaturgical value of ensembles of this sort. Action is included within a single musical continuity, and unified by it. The situation changes, and everybody feels differently; this was never so within a baroque aria or chorus. And to have replaced some of the neutral recitative used for action in baroque opera by a genuinely musical carrier was plainly advantageous: action could now be presented on the imaginative level of music, so as to share the emotional dignity of the aria introspections. Elvira's trio has the coherence of a movement in sonata form—a coherence whose establishment occupied the best efforts of classic composers, and which became one of the most impressive achievements in all of music. The trio follows the sonata-form dynamic closely, though it is certainly simpler than the best instrumental examples. In a sense Tovey was right to maintain that symphonic form was too "dramatic" for the stage. But however this may be, a developed classic ensemble is infinitely more complex than the richest of baroque forms, such as the opening chorus of a Bach cantata, for all its fantastic accumulation of detail. In Mozart things modify their interrelation, conflicts are set, developed, and solved. No less than in a Bach chorus, if less obsessively, there is for the whole scene a single imaginative intensity, an integrating point of view.

We can also see the value, indeed the necessity, of operatic ensembles for the dramatic mode of comedy. Imagine Mozart's episode handled by Metastasio. At least three arias with linking recitative would be needed to do it at all: one for Elvira, showing her initial state of mind, one for Don Giovanni, and then another for Elvira, showing her final state of mind. The whole of Leporello's role, which wonderfully keeps the comic balance, would evaporate in recitative, to say nothing of all the delicate shades of modulation in the attitudes of Don Giovanni and Elvira *en route*. Each aria would take about three minutes . . . and this is only one brief episode among a dozen in the libretto. Eighteenth-century comedy, with its wealth of lively intrigue, demanded a newly pliant operatic scheme.

Comedy needs speed, and the ensemble provides it; Mozart's trio works on a time-scale rather faster than likely in real life (and indeed the scene would not be funny at all if he dwelt on it much longer). Comedy needs a casual atmosphere at least some of the time; characters cannot take themselves as seriously as the Didos, the Orpheuses, and the suffering Christians of the baroque dramatic world. With a musical continuity determined largely by the orchestral progress, you can have Don Giovanni muttering away in the background to a piece of musical nonsense, for this can fit excellently into the mercurial texture of a classic piece. Comedy requires a sense of surface verisimilitude; its convention cannot seem stiff. This is a relative matter, of course, but the classic ensemble technique proved admirably flexible and lifelike, certainly as contrasted with the stately artifice of Lully or Metastasio.

The dramatic flexibility of the genre can be demonstrated properly only by means of a *catalogue raisonné* of Mozart's ensembles. In form they are remarkably free, or at least the freedom might appear remarkable to those who consider classic form dogmatic. An ensemble rarely comes as close as Elvira's trio to the precise plan of sonata form, for a single dramatic action rarely falls precisely into the sonata-form dynamic. But the general principles of sonata construction, which I have discussed, are always powerfully at work in Mozart's operas. As compared with the trio "Ah, taci, ingiusto core," there are ensembles incorporating much more action, with even more humorously pointed conflicts, and with resolutions of the most varied kinds. A brilliantly complex one is the trio in the first act of *The Marriage of Figaro*, "Cosa sento!" Cherubino and Count Almaviva have in turn been flirting with Susanna, and each in turn has been forced to hide in the furniture by an inopportune arrival. The latest comer, Don Basilio, who wishes to seduce Susanna not for himself but for the Count, makes the mistake of repeating scandalous talk about Cherubino and the Countess. The trio itself begins as the Count reveals himself.

To a strong, typically symphonic "first subject," the Count orders Cherubino banished from court. Basilio unctuously disclaims any firsthand basis for his gossip. Susanna attempts to turn her embarrassment into outraged innocence; her energetic exclamations lead naturally to the dominant, where she finds it convenient to throw a faint. To a new theme denoting some concern, they convey her towards the sofa where Cherubino is hiding; with a quick change of tactic, Susanna cries rape! and it is the men's turn for embarrassment, in a subdued, subdominant version of their theme. But the Count will not relent about Cherubino, as the music makes clear by an even more forceful statement of his original subject in its original tonic key—a recapitulation. He has had earlier reasons for suspicion, and tells how he called on the gardener's daughter, only to discover the amorous page. With rare humor, Mozart used a half-solemn accompanied recitative for this anecdote, magically incorporating it into the form. And of course the Count uncovers Cherubino again, much to the satisfaction of Basilio. In a passage which has all the irony of a second recapitulation, the Count's initial indignation at Cherubino is transferred to Susanna, with his same stern theme in the tonic: *"Onestissima signora, or capisco come va."* For a recapitulation, it is best if all themes can be repeated. So Mozart had Basilio exactly reiterate his original disclaimer—a piece of insolence which Basilio would not have ventured, I imagine, if the Count himself had not been in a sarcastic frame of mind. Susanna's distress is high; a new inflection in the unifying musical web of the recapitulation. Another detail which develops the situation while settling it is Basilio's new snickering comment: *"Così fan tutte le belle, non c'è alcuna novità!"*

With *The Marriage of Figaro*, Mozart first really became aware of the possibilities of the ensemble. Writing *Don Giovanni*, he seems to have been carried away

by its power to the point of carelessness in the place-
ent of arias. Then in *Così fan tutte* and *The Magic
Flute* he subjected brilliance of ensemble treatment to
a broader dramatic end, and concentrated more particularly on the problem of extending the continuity
farther than the single ensemble.

In *Don Giovanni* Mozart's virtuosity extends from
the deadly simple stroke at Donna Elvira's first entrance, "*Ah! chi mi dice mai*," through the richness of
the trio already discussed, to the intricacy of the Ballroom Scene with its simultaneous orchestras and the
tremendous force of the catastrophe with the Commendatore and the devils. "*Ah! chi mi dice mai*" is in
the precise form of a pompous *opera seria* aria. Elvira,
who seems to be in the habit of lamenting in the
streets, goes into a long diatribe about Don Giovanni's
infidelity; but during the obligatory orchestral *ritornelli*, Don Giovanni and Leporello, not yet recogniz-
ing her, comment surreptitiously on this passionate
stranger, and Don Giovanni resolves to have her. How
preposterous this makes Elvira, and what confusion
when they realize who she is, and the music is left
hanging disconcertedly!

The casual quality of the asides in both "*Ah! chi mi
dice mai*" and "*Ah, taci, ingiusto core*" is developed
much farther in other ensembles, to the extent of making it the central dramatic device. The principle is to
have the chief musical idea in one place and the essential talk somewhere else simultaneously. The talk is
automatically informal, furtive, comic, and natural; it is
managed by a sort of low-grade counterpoint consisting
mainly of tonics and dominants. The chief musical idea
may be motivic work in the orchestra—as in Susanna's
aria "*Venite, inginocchiatevi*," in which her chatter is
overshadowed by the instruments depicting her busy
dressmaking. Or it may be sung by somebody else—
as in the sublime wedding canon in *Così fan tutte* sung

by Ferrando and the sisters while Guglielmo skulks grumbling in the background, unwilling to forget his betrayal. Or the main musical idea may be actual music played on the stage, a march or a dance or an organ postlude. In the Ballroom Scene in *Don Giovanni,* the musical continuity is provided first of all by the rigid, antiquated Minuet, a perfect symbol for the exterior formality of the occasion. But the essential business, the procuring of Zerlina and the tense intrigue of Don Giovanni's antagonists, goes on in whispered background asides. And Mozart invented an extraordinary means to increase tension by gradually jamming in two other dances heard from adjoining rooms, and each as immobile and fatuous as the Minuet. The three played together provide confused, vaguely sinister, blaring dance music against which the desperate action proceeds in an increasingly urgent undertone. The dramatic effect has not been matched, though it has been imitated in *Un Ballo in maschera, Die Fledermaus, Boris Godunov, Tosca, Wozzeck, Peter Grimes,* and elsewhere.

Discussions of the operatic ensemble always stress its value for presenting conflicting emotions at one time, with some of the participants perhaps unaware of others. The famous example always cited is the quartet from Verdi's *Rigoletto;* the trio in *Otello,* in which Otello overhears the conversation between Iago and Cassio about the handkerchief, shows the force of the device especially well by contrast with Shakespeare. But the presentation of simultaneous feelings is the simplest of Mozart's effects, and was not beyond the means of the baroque, as one can see in Lully and in those Bach cantatas which personify Fear and Hope. The sophistication of the classic style allowed the much richer possibility of *altering* such emotions within the musical piece in response to action—as does not happen in Bach or in the quartet from *Rigoletto,* though it certainly does in the trio from *Otello*. With Mozart such development is the rule. All in all, the variety of dramatic effect available to the ensemble is confined only by the imagination of the librettist and composer.

4

THE LARGEST and most ambitious ensembles were those at the ends of acts, the "finales." In these, more action and more intricate action was absorbed into the musical continuity, and eighteenth-century composers stretched the span of musical coherence, as they could control it, to the limits. It was even theoretically possible to construct a whole opera as one long ensemble; but this would have been beyond the limits.

Classic *opera buffa* still kept the matrix of *secco* recitative inherited from *opera seria*. Most of the action, indeed, proceeded on the level of recitative, in chatter that was at least amusing, if old-fashioned in style. But the important action was reserved for the higher musical level of the ensembles. Arias were also included, of course, some of them light and humorous and probably rather trivial, some of them serious; like Purcell and Gluck, Mozart and the other composers of *opera buffa* appreciated the power of a small number of arias well placed in the total form. The importance of the ensemble, however, cannot be overemphasized, even with composers who used it slightly. Conventionally ensembles were employed for the beginnings of acts, where vivid exposition was needed, and particularly at the ends of acts, where the plot reached its maximum complexity and brilliance. The temptation was to absorb more and more of the end of the act into its finale. Already in *The Marriage of Figaro* Mozart included something like half of Act II in an immense finale; in *The Magic Flute* the music of the second finale continues uninterrupted through several climactic scenes.

In what sense are these long ensembles unified? Since it was the age of Mozart and not the age of Mahler, there were serious temporal limitations: a single musical continuity lasting twenty-five minutes was inconceivable even to the most long-winded of composers. The procedure in a finale was to tack together a series of distinct ensembles and even little arias, changing key, tempo, and mood, in all probability, at the arrival of each new character. We may speak of a "composite ensemble." Mozart's librettist wrote amusingly and simply enough of the finale:

. . . every style of singing must find a place in it— *adagio, allegro, andante, amabile, armonioso, strepitoso, arcistrepitoso, strepitosissimo,* and with this the said finale generally ends.

This eminently theatrical prescription is adequate to most of the examples known to or written by Lorenzo da Ponte. Still, however dimly, we sense in Mozart's late finales something deeper than this "effectiveness."

Just what holds them together is admittedly hard to say; this is as taxing a critical problem as that of articulating the coherence of the four movements of a Mozart symphony. In both opera and symphony, the unity seems to be rather more than just one of key or style. It is not a thematic synthesis, for Mozart never tried the simple-minded, strangely prophetic scheme invented by Piccinni, whereby melodic ideas recur during some successive sections, in the manner of a loose rondo (an example is in the last finale of Cimarosa's once-popular *Il Matrimonio segreto*). With Mozart, it is a matter of the subtlest modulation of moods; though the wide range of action in the finale does not require or receive the same binding as a single scene, it is all brought together with a sense of balance and inevitability. To substitute a section of a finale from *The Marriage of Figaro* in *Così fan tutte* would be as unthinkable as to exchange movements between the "Linz" and the "Jupiter" symphonies.

Compared with Mozart, Beethoven always has a warmer relationship among musical sections, whether symphony movements or parts of composite operatic numbers. The end of *Fidelio* shows as clearly as any classic opera the integrity to which the composite finale tended. The assertion of a single view over all the action was of especial dramatic value here; to be sure, less action is involved than is usual with Mozart, though still enough to require four sections. *Fidelio* is a short opera, and no comedy, and even its modicum of action is too much for some critics. In the previous dungeon scene, Leonora has finally rescued Florestan, and Pizarro has rushed off in confusion on hearing the trumpet-signal for Don Ferrando's arrival. At last husband and wife come together in an ecstatic duet, and though it is unclear how the plot is to come out, there is a clear feeling that the worst is over. The finale runs concurrently with the entire last scene, in the bright daylight above the dungeon. Libertarian villagers are there to cheer Don Ferrando; they hope he will prove to be an emancipator, and indeed his first words bode well. Pizarro's defeat is met by a hymn-like section of relief, followed by general jubilation and praise of Leonora. The whole progress of the finale, then, tempts a composer to pull it into a single unity, transforming the generalized hope at the start through the central uncertainty to well-founded rejoicing at the end.

Beethoven's first section is a brilliant march in C major for Don Ferrando's entrance, turning into a chorus to greet him. The march builds up more tension than the chorus actually releases, for the latter is ingeniously left incomplete; the crowd's hushed ref-

erence to the dungeon provides Beethoven with a natural means to break the expected formal fullness. After
Don Ferrando speaks in free arioso, still in C, the choral
praises are echoed, tentatively and expectantly. As
the good-hearted gaoler Rocco pushes through the
crowd to denounce the villain, the music shifts to
the minor and modulates *poco agitato* into an *andan-
tino* in A major, the second section. Here the inner
coherence is not that of a simple march, but that of a
complicated motivic web; its mood is of tense unravel-
ing. The recognitions and exposures are accomplished
to considerable modulation, with a sally to f♯ minor as
Pizarro is condemned. But Don Ferrando resolves the
situation firmly back in A.

As he guides Leonora to unlock Florestan's irons,
her flood of emotion is such as to sweep the music
suddenly into F. The third section, *sostenuto assai*,
is governed by a heavenly tune in the oboe, against
which Leonora and the others can only utter half-
phrases in the background. "*O Gott, welch' ein Augen-
blick!*" The technique is Mozart's, and the effect is an
intensity of feeling so true that at first the persons
have no way of articulating it in words. If we smile at
the librettist's horrible fancy for *Augenblicke*, we shall
be smiling, I hope, through tears. The passage has
some kinship to the ethereal scene of forgiveness at the
end of *The Marriage of Figaro*. The singers gradually
join the orchestra, until they comprehend and dominate the emotion at the end.

After a moment's hush, the great emphatic celebra-
tions begin as a last section in C. In this section the
heightened cadences *alla Cherubini* which have marked
the opera come into their own, the off-beat accents
that enter Beethoven's style around this time make
their strangely spiritual effect, and there are similarities
of word and tone to his later setting of Schiller's *Ode
to Joy* in the Ninth Symphony:

Wer ein holdes Weib errungen
stimm' in unsern Jubel ein . . .

Da Ponte's *"strepitosissimo"* follows in due course. The whole tonal dynamic is instantly impressive as it rarely is in a Mozart finale: the original C major victoriously restored at the end after the double step to the subdominant, C–A–F. The articulateness of this final chorus, a matter of musical technique as well as of the dramatic situation, has grown magnificently out of the fragmentary, somewhat vague cheering at the start. The finale is experienced as a dramatic unity with its own progress and resolution.

This enthusiastic conclusion to *Fidelio* seems to me closely beholden to the end of *Egmont*, where Goethe, determined to snatch triumph out of the tragedy of a tyrannous execution, demanded that Egmont's ringing last words dissolve into a great "Symphony of Victory." What music he could have been thinking of in 1775 I cannot imagine, but thirty-five years later Beethoven wrote it for him in his incidental music for the play: a violent, ecstatic, very loud piece informed with the almost intolerably fierce sincerity of his so-called second period. Then, as an overture to *Egmont*, Beethoven composed a tragic sonata-form movement capped with an entirely fresh section as a coda—the identical "Symphony of Victory" which is to cap the play later in the evening. Beethoven always had a tendency to get the whole progress of a play into its overture. Goethe's vision of a "Symphony of Victory" as climax to a dramatic struggle suited Beethoven's needs in *Fidelio*; something of the kind appears as a resolving musical section in all the overtures that he wrote for the opera, as well as at the end of the opera itself.

Indeed the vision haunted Beethoven all through his second period, during his thirties. One can trace it most characteristically in the symphonies: already in the *"Eroica"* to some extent, most literally in the

Fifth, through a cloud in the Seventh, and from a religious standpoint in the Ninth. Just as the sections of the *Egmont* Overture and of the composite finale to *Fidelio* grow together, so do the movements of the symphonies. The intimate relationship between the last two movements of the Fifth Symphony shows the same necessity as the relationship among those sections. Beethoven achieved his final synthesis in the late quartets, where seven movements could progress together as a single dramatic continuity unmatched in other music. Both the Fifth Symphony and *Fidelio* can be seen to point the way; and, conversely, their own unities are illuminated by Beethoven's later solutions.

5

In the aria, finally, Mozart and Beethoven were able to incorporate "psychological action" by means analogous to those of the ensemble.

From the time of Pergolesi, composers of *opera buffa* had easily managed to write gay comic arias, providing lively characterization and often matching musical to verbal wit. They also saw possibilities of parody on various levels, by employing sententious *opera seria* techniques in the casual context of comedy. To be sure, critics do not necessarily agree on just where solemnity ends and parody begins; the case is rarely so clear as with Elvira's entrance aria—actually an ensemble—"*Ah! chi mi dice mai,*" where other characters on the stage laugh at her *opera seria* pretensions. Is there perhaps a note of parody in Donna Anna's heroic "*Or sai chi l'onore,*" which has no explanatory accompanying asides? In *Così fan tutte,* Mozart and Da Ponte must have mocked Dorabella's love-sick fury in "*Smanie implacabili*," with its invocations of the Eumenides and its *suono orribile*; and, more sadly, Fiordiligi's monumental self-reproach in "*Per pietà*," with its fantastic vocal range employed to stress the most incongruous, dramatically ironic words of the poem. In *The Magic Flute*, a divine parody or parallel of Pamina's despair (her great g-minor aria "*Ach, ich fühl's*") echoes in the later interrupted suicide of Papageno (the g-minor ending of his song "*Papagena! Weibchen! Täubchen!*").

However, the central problem, and a very interesting one, was to write an entirely serious aria on the same level of consciousness as that of the ensembles, either in a comedy when a serious moment was needed, or in a melodrama like *Fidelio*, which employs the musical style developed for comedy. This style was in essence progressive; an introspection, an aria, is appropriately static. Baroque music worked best in arias; classic music worked best in ensembles involving action. Arias do not ordinarily include any physical action at all.

Even without pressing action into the aria, Mozart could achieve considerable psychological subtlety thanks to the ability of his musical style to encompass, modulate, and harmonize sharp contrasts. Thus, in the space of a concise piece, Donna Anna's steely passion for revenge and the torture of her remembrance of her father's corpse are brought together and justified—as certainly as contrasting themes in a symphony are justified, and by analogous, if not identical, musical means. Now in the Metastasian aria it was not only possible but indeed conventional to portray two different "affects." First one of them was exposed at length, then the next, then the first one was resumed in a literal repetition or *da capo*. But the difference between such literal repetition and recapitulation in the classic manner is crucial: a recapitulation section grows inevitably out of the earlier ones and shows the original material in a quite new light, whereas the baroque *da capo* merely juxtaposes sections. The baroque scheme is, as always, rigid and intense. In the classic style, Mozart discovered means to a more flexible and natural presentation of the complexity of multiple feelings.

Furthermore, Mozart experimented with the idea of bringing psychological action into the aria; he implied emotional development by a composite aria form comparable to that of the larger ensembles. He went farthest in this direction, perhaps, with the great aria for the Countess in *The Marriage of Figaro*, "*Dove sono.*" Again, Beethoven provides the richest example. Florestan's aria in *Fidelio* has three separate sections, if we count the integrated recitative at the start. As the curtain rises on Act II, a long, oppressive introduction in f minor suggests his miserable state in almost tragic terms. This modulates beautifully to a new section, the famous *cantabile* in A♭, wherein Florestan steadily considers his devotion to duty, his strength against imprisonment, darkness, and hunger. Suddenly, like Egmont, he has a vision of Leonora as the principle of freedom; the music slips back to F major for a faster third section, an ecstatic climax through which the premonitory apparition seems to soar in a rapturous oboe line. Though chained and solitary, Florestan is led through a clear progress from suffering to solace to hope; he even faints, to an altogether suitable orchestral accompaniment, before the musical continuity ends. This composite aria is, mysteriously, a single work of very great force. It has never occurred to anyone to doubt that Florestan is worthy of Leonora's rescue; if it did, the drama would collapse (as *Tosca* does). Yet Florestan sings little. The heroism and pathos of the one aria sustain him magnificently for the rest of the opera.

This accomplishment of Beethoven's, however, is really less in the spirit of Mozart's dramaturgy than prophetic of a later one. Beethoven looks back to the classic period of Haydn and Mozart, but he also looks forward to the romantic era of Wagner. The idea of disclosing emotional progress in a drama without the intervention of actual dramatic action might have been suggested to Beethoven by another Janus-like figure, by Goethe, in the treatment of Orestes in *Iphigeneia in Tauris*. In opera such progress would have been impossible without the "dramatic" classic musical style. But the idea came to its fruition (not only for opera, but also for German drama as a whole) in the huge scene at the beginning of Act III of *Tristan und Isolde*, during which Tristan, rooted to his couch, pulls himself from profound despair to an almost religious ecstasy in preparation for his death. Wagner, in his turn, had met the perennial problem of operatic dramaturgy, the relationship or interplay between action and music. His solution—not necessarily better, but certainly more complicated and problematic than Beethoven's—was contingent on new principles which were only dimly evidenced in classic music.

4

Mozart

THE late eighteenth-century solution to the problem of action and the musical continuity, through the ensemble and the "dramatic" symphonic technique, found its consummation in the operas of Mozart. These works, or at any rate the best-known ones, occupy a rather remarkable position in the current estimate of opera as drama. To a significant and sensitive section of the opera-going public, Mozart is a genuine dramatist, while the other great opera composers seem to fall short. Wagner, who enjoyed similar prestige years ago, is badly out of fashion now; Gluck is lost with Monteverdi and the rest of baroque opera; Verdi, while showing some signs of coming into his own, is still viewed equivocally and will continue to be so until we rid ourselves of the notion of an "Italian opera" embracing Donizetti, Verdi, Puccini, and now Gian-Carlo Menotti. As for the modern writers of opera, they are beset by the cloud of contemporaneity that hides today's art from us with the force of a neurosis. *Boris Godunov* is admired, and so latterly is *Wozzeck*; for the rest, Mozartian comedy provides our time with its clearest vision of the dramatic potential of opera.

To write in the hope of expanding this vision is argumentative enough. Only with Mozart can one feel that no special plea is necessary. The plea was made by Edward J. Dent in his book *Mozart's Operas,* as long ago as 1913. Dent's rare blend of insight, authority, practical understanding, and sense must have spelled victory from the start; for although criticism hardly determines musical taste, it can sometimes articulate it with an inspired sense of prophecy. Newly imaginative operatic productions preceded the book, and many more followed it, allowing Mozart's drama to make its effect on generations which for one reason or another were ready to receive it. Meanwhile Dent's "Critical Study" remains one of the best things ever written about opera or about Mozart, and a model for the proper place of historical studies in musical criticism.

Today, more clearly than when Dent first wrote, Mozart's reputation as a dramatist can rest (as it must) on general appreciation of all his music. Devotion to Mozart is a strong feature of contemporary taste, uniting musicians and amateurs of very diverse tendencies. I am inclined to think, moreover, that this fashion is truer than most. By and large, Mozart is loved for what he really is. It is now two hundred years since he was born; one wonders whether any striking new evaluation will emerge from the mass of festivals, appreciations, and monographs which the anniversary has promoted. Will someone perhaps trigger a reaction against Mozart—as Dent himself essayed with Beethoven in 1927? But Mozart is less shadowed with misapprehensions and sentimentalities than Beethoven, even to the present day. Certainly Mozart needs as much reflective attention as we can bring; if an anniversary is required as pretext, it serves its purpose. The hope is always to deepen our understanding of his virtues, at the same time as we recognize his limitations and failures more frankly. We may turn to the operas with this hope, and analyze, through whatever prism, the narrow flame of musical drama which Mozart keeps alive.

2

ORDINARY opinion is not wrong to regard *The Marriage of Figaro* as Mozart's first great opera. It is the first opera of his maturity. *Idomeneo* and *Die Entführung aus dem Serail* are beautiful works, and it is with some pain that I pass them by, but they can neither of them be called fully developed products of Mozart's imagination—nor can so many beautiful early instrumental compositions, like the violin concertos, the Divertimento-Sextet in D, some of the sonatas, and the Bb and "Haffner" symphonies. Though Mozart's phenomenal sensitivity was very early in evidence, his vision and his sorrow did not grow to meet it until after 1782. He first took full artistic responsibility in the six great quartets dedicated to Haydn, the unfinished Mass in c minor, the Viennese piano concertos, and then in *Figaro*. The emotional maturity reflected in these works came evidently out of several crucial events of a few years earlier: Mozart's escape from Salzburg to independence and struggle in Vienna, his rupture with his father, and especially his marriage to Constanze Weber. In this new atmosphere Mozart faced up to Haydn and Bach, and found his own

certain, complete voice. Vienna also meant a widening
of intellectual horizons. In *The Marriage of Figaro*,
for the first time, Mozart addressed himself to a dramatic problem with full insight and understanding.

For Mozart, *Figaro* was also an initiation in theatrical sophistication. He was working with Lorenzo da
Ponte, not with a Varesco or a Stephanie. An operatic
version of *Le Barbier de Séville* had just made a
success in Vienna—a bright, innocent play, innocently
composed by Giovanni Paisiello, who was a leading
opera buffa composer of the day. But Beaumarchais's
sequel, *Le Mariage de Figaro*, was politically and morally so suspect that it could not be staged at all without
the sugar-coat of music. *Opera buffa* at that time was
gingerly turning towards adult themes, libertarianism,
genuine wit, and humanity; Mozart and Da Ponte must
have half-realized that they were creating living comedy out of the traditional simple farce of Pergolesi,
Piccinni, and Paisiello. Goldoni had done something
similar with the *commedia dell' arte*. Everything about
Figaro is exceptional, advanced, brilliant, alarmingly
real; it was much too clever to succeed in Vienna. Mozart's sense of cleverness, power, and exhilaration remains an actual aesthetic quality of the piece, one that
will always fascinate the connoisseur. Most recently,
Siegmund Levarie has performed an exhaustively
wrongheaded analysis of the opera, glorifying its every
musical detail. The principal glory of *Figaro*, however,
is the central drama which binds the details.

Writing *Figaro*, Mozart first grasped the dramatic
force of the ensemble, and more generally, the dramatic possibilities of the classic musical style. In a
word, he found his characteristic dramatic stride. The
way Mozart transformed the rather simple-minded
technique of the *opera buffa* is absolutely astonishing;
Paisiello's *Il Barbiere di Siviglia*—one of Mozart's
models—may stand as a superior example of the genre,

but its dramaturgy seems childish next to that of *Figaro*. The dramatic strength of *Figaro* stems directly out of Mozart's realization of values latent in the Italian comic-opera style. This fact is clearest of all from the opera's resolution, the reconciliation between the Count and Countess before the final curtain.

Mozart built this into a large finale; so would any other composer, but no other would have turned the peculiarities of the form to so trenchant a dramatic end. In this finale, complexity of plot becomes almost painful, and is heightened by complexity of musical structure: the sections flow into one another with elaborate musical conflicts, parodies, and asides, rapidly developing the action on various planes within the musical continuity. The intensity of intrigue is matched to the intensity of musical feeling. Even the décor is strained: the darkness, the summerhouses where everybody hides, the sardonic formality of the rococo garden. Count Almaviva, who has made an assignation with the maid Susanna, makes love to his own wife dressed in the maid's clothes; Figaro pretends to make love to "the Countess," actually his Susanna in disguise. When the Count overhears this last maneuver ("*Ah, senz' arme son io!*"), he summons torches and prepares a scene of public humiliation. Susanna (for the Countess) acts out a frantic plea for mercy, as do Figaro and the assembled courtiers, but the Count is adamant—until the real Countess appears and throws aside her disguise: "Perhaps my entreaties may prevail." Suddenly all gaiety is gone from the music. At once the turn in the action is reflected: an abrupt movement to the minor mode, a tense rhythm, whispers, a nervous staccato scale-figure in the violins, a newly serious harmonic progression. This brief section changes the mood drastically to prepare for an even greater modulation as the Count begs and gains forgiveness from the Countess. The new section is *andante,* with an altogether unprecedented stillness, half hymn-like, without Mozart's ordinary glitter:

[WITHOUT BASSES]

The complexity of the finale prior to this moment has been criticized as excessive. But the point is surely that its very excruciation plays wonderfully into the serenity of the resolution; the musical technique itself emphasizes the essential articulation of the plot.

The plot in turn illuminates the characters by its dénouement. This is a moment of realization, almost an epiphany, for the Count, who shows an unsuspected capacity for contrition, with none of the breast-beating of the mock-pleas by Figaro and Susanna a moment before. The Countess has never been more lovely and true to herself, or less caught in the artificialities of her existence. Even the Basilios and Cherubinos are touched. And the characters themselves illuminate the central dramatic idea: the scene uncovers a core of decency under all the shabbiness which the comedy has exposed and tried to rationalize in laughter. All this is possible because *musically* it is a climax, because the music at this section has a seriousness and a new clarity of feeling. Unimpressive in itself, the section depends for its effect on the rest of the finale, with its striving hilarity, and grows out of it, and yet transcends it completely. Mozart here foreshadows the later vision of *The Magic Flute*.

The Marriage of Figaro would be a lesser work if this sublime note were introduced at the end without prior warning or articulation. Actually, strands tending to it have appeared clearly all through the piece. Act I is devoted to comic intrigue, but the first appearance of the Countess, at the start of Act II, moves the drama to a new plane. More or less scurrilous talk about this Countess had dominated Act I; the Count has revealed his colors; we wonder about her. Even though we could safely anticipate that a composer would present a person of more profound emotion, her *cavatina "Porgi amor"* is breathtaking, always. (It was predictable also that an *opera buffa* would have its *"parti serie,"* but no one before Mozart had been willing to assume the responsibility of this serious-ness.) The Countess, living in the world of comedy, wears the mask of the court for conversation and in-trigue. But in soliloquies we see the real woman—and the court sees her too when she unmasks at the final reconciliation. What is more, this reconciliation has been prepared by another: in Act III, when Don Bartolo and Marcellina discover that Figaro is their long-lost bastard and happily get married at last, with no more thought of the marriage contract between Marcellina and Figaro. Thanks to Beaumarchais's sense of bur-lesque, it is a hilarious scene; thanks to Mozart's music, also a strangely beautiful one. The touching, comic ecstasy of the old people at finding their "little Ra-faello" is set against Susanna's misunderstanding and the Count's exasperation, and in the last section of the sextet, warm harmonies suggest a serenity in hu-man relationships which had never been indicated be-fore. As personalities, Bartolo and Marcellina are

sketched only lightly—just exactly as firmly as was
necessary to make Mozart's essential dramatic point,
which was to give a strong hint, as early as this, of salvation for such separated people as the Count and
Countess.

The sextet also opens up a significant subplot by
showing the first signs of friction in the little love-nest
of Figaro and Susanna: when she sees him embracing
Marcellina (*"sua madre? sua madre!!"*) she flares up
and boxes his ears, in her best *commedia dell' arte*
fashion. The subsequent development of this theme
does more than provide extra comic situations and
complicate the dénouement; it supports the central
drama by setting up a manifest analogy between Figaro
and Susanna on the one hand, and the Count and
Countess on the other. Susanna sings *"Deh vieni,"*
confirming Figaro's worst fears by her ambiguous
phraseology, not so much because she wants to make
him jealous, but because Mozart did. (In Act IV, before the finale, the composition of *Figaro* got to be
rushed, as always happened with the ends of Mozart's
operas. The dramaturgy is a little clumsy, the music
less interesting.) Complementary pairs of characters
are a regular feature of Mozart's operas: Belmonte-
Constanze *vs.* Pedrillo-Blonde, Ferrando-Fiordiligi *vs.*
Guglielmo-Dorabella, Tamino-Pamina *vs.* Papageno-
Papagena. The pairs are always carefully parallel, and
in *Figaro* the analogy is stressed by having the two
women actually pose as one another.

It is of some importance for Mozart's conception to
contrast Figaro-Susanna and the Count-Countess in
the entire complex of love, desertion, jealousy, suspicion, and forgiveness. With the servants, the causes for
jealousy are only imaginary, and their feelings are more
or less trivial: Susanna slaps Figaro, twice, and he
generalizes anger at her "betrayal" into a conventional
diatribe against womanhood, *"Aprite un po' quegli*

occhi." Their reconciliation is correspondingly superficial, for they are safely behind their *commedia dell'
arte* masks when all is forgiven in the charming duet
(within the finale), "*Pace, pace, mio dolce tesoro.*"
But with the Count and the Countess there certainly
has been betrayal; the Count has a regular squad of
panderers. Instead of jealousy the Countess reveals
poignant grief. His fury when his schemes are thwarted,
and especially when he thinks her unfaithful, is intense and extremely unpleasant; Almaviva is Mozart's
most savage creation. Yet in spite of high injury and
high feelings, their reconciliation is deep and true, the
most beautiful thing in the opera. They are able to
meet on terms that we had never dreamed were still
available to them. The doors of Wisdom, Virtue, and
Love are not far away.

Beaumarchais's play had social significance in its day,
and it is said that Mozart's opera too, in its exaltation
of the servant classes, sets forth a cunning criticism of
the *ancien régime*. But surely Mozart intended nobility
of station as the clear symbol for nobility of spirit.
The court may smirk, but the Count and Countess
interest us more profoundly than any court intrigues.
She is not strong, he is not good, and even their servants can show them up as pathetic or ludicrous—with
the help of Mozart's and Da Ponte's instinct for
comedy. But the Count and Countess are conscious;
they feel their feelings through, and there is a ground
of sympathy between them which Figaro and Susanna
cannot ever comprehend. Cruelty and shame have
their place in Mozart's picture of human fallibility;
particularly in this context, his drama reveals a view
of life that is realistic, unsentimental, optimistic, and
humane. Probably no one has left a performance of
Figaro without reflecting that the Count will soon
be philandering again. But just as surely there will be
another reconciliation, another renewal as genuine on

both sides, as contrite and as beautiful. Clever Figaro
and Susanna are not actually so secure.

Finally, it should be emphasized that the drama of
The Marriage of Figaro is Mozart's, not Beaumarchais's
or Da Ponte's. Music here does not merely decorate
what playwright or librettist had designed; Mozart's
music creates a drama that they never suspected. In
his serious treatment of the Countess, Mozart transcends anything in Da Ponte's verse or in operatic tradition as he knew it, and with the Count, Cherubino,
and Susanna he performed famous miracles of characterization (I have not said much about this, only
because I believe that it is better understood than
Mozart's central dramatic idea). Then at the reconciliation between Bartolo and Marcellina, Mozart actually departed from Da Ponte and Beaumarchais
rather than simply expanding on them. The original
Bartolo chafes at the awkward turn of events, and this
feeling is even left in Mozart's recitative; but in opera
we trust what is musically forceful, and Bartolo's tender
joy in the sextet is instantly, unshakeably convincing.
Most important, of course, is Mozart's transformation
of the ending of the play. With Beaumarchais, the
reconciliation is nothing—worse than nothing, it suggests fatally that the intricate plot had beaten the
author, and that clemency was the only way he saw to
unravel it. As for Da Ponte, here is his contribution:

COUNT:	*Contessa perdono!*	Forgive me, Countess!
COUNTESS:	*Più docile io sono,* *e dico di sì.*	I am more gentle And answer you "yes."
ALL:	*Ah tutti contenti* *saremo così.*	We all are delighted To have it end thus.

With this miserable material before him, Mozart built
a revelation, and saw how it could be supported by
other elements in Beaumarchais's scaffolding. In opera,
the dramatist is the composer.

3

THE SUCCESS of *Figaro* was compounded of genius, skill, ingenuity, good luck, and time. The last two of these ingredients were lacking for Mozart's next two operas; neither *Don Giovanni* nor *Così fan tutte* has the dramatic consistency and force of *Figaro* or the later *Magic Flute*. In fact, the two middle operas present an object lesson in the range of frustration that librettos can cause a composer. Da Ponte was of course a superior librettist, and his collaboration with Mozart was enormously fortunate, whatever went wrong. But the trouble, as I guess, was that he was too confident and facile and famous a writer for Mozart to control, as later he was to control Emanuel Schikaneder in *The Magic Flute*. In any case the libretto for *Don Giovanni* was not written well enough, and that for *Così fan tutte* was written too well. Mozart was equally at a loss.

Even the most devoted Mozartian will have to admit that there is something unsatisfactory about *Così fan tutte*. Certainly it is Mozart's most problematic opera, a fact which is reflected by the curious history of the critical attitude towards the story. Romantic critics considered it outrageous, improbable, immoral, frivolous, unworthy of Mozart; the last two charges are true enough, and will not be evaporated by our pious horror, today, at the naïve remedies attempted in the nineteenth century—such as adapting the music to a French version of *Love's Labour's Lost*. Today we insist on our works of art just as they were originally presented; we feel that if we can only experience them with enough historical impartiality, they must be all right. Lorenzo da Ponte's libretto must remain, and it must be rationalized too. This is always done with

an air of injured ease, but I have never seen an explanation of any "convention" that makes sense both of
the action, on whatever level or levels, and also of the
remarkable expressivity of some of the music. Nothing
is settled by concluding that Da Ponte gave Mozart a
frivolous book, whereupon Mozart took parts of it seriously, and on them lavished beautiful music. You can
say the same about *The Marriage of Figaro* and *Don
Giovanni*; the real question is, what is the result of
this strange blend? The artistic nature and the degree
of success of the two earlier operas are quite different
from those of *Così fan tutte*.

Most fundamentally, its plane of reality differs from
that of *Figaro* and *Don Giovanni* on the one hand,
and that of *The Magic Flute* on the other. Mozart
and Da Ponte had unresolved differences about it; the
confusion is in the piece as well as in the minds of the
audience. Dent does not dispel confusion by his remark that the four lovers are puppets expressing an
amazingly wide range of emotions. They are certainly
silly, dear children, and easily led by the nose, but their
actions and feelings are logical, true, and dramatically
arresting. This would seem sufficient reason for us to
grant them the courtesy of the usual metaphor, and
consider them "real people" rather than marionettes.
"Don Alfonso so obviously pulls all the strings that one
begins to wonder if he is not really Don Lorenzo or
Don Wolfgango." It is important, though, to distinguish the roles of these three manipulators.

Don Alfonso is the clearest of them, and the least
aware of any essential problems. He explains his attitude unmistakably when he recites an *ottava* to the
boys as a moral sentence, near the end. This piece
comes as close to an aria as anything that Don Alfonso
sings, and incorporates the title of our opera, together
with music that had already figured in the overture:

Everyone censures women; I excuse them
If every minute fresh love seems to start.
Some say it's habit, others vice; say I—
The necessary instinct of the heart.
Deluded lover, do not place the blame
On someone else's, but on your own part;
    For women young and old, and fair and foul
    (Now come repeat with me) THUS DO THEY ALL!

Mutability is a *"necessità del core."* Alfonso does not deny feeling or oppose it; he wishes to show only that it does not last. So he does, and wins his bets, though it is not clear that anything else has been gained.

Don Lorenzo's task was to pull this play-within-a-play into a total drama. There is really no question that his libretto is technically first-rate, the intrigue smooth and elegant, the construction masterly, the verse delightful. It begins with an amusing picture of the silly lovers exhibiting sentiments demanded by convention: the two girls going into raptures over locket-portraits, the boys demanding satisfaction when Don Alfonso doubts feminine fidelity. This satisfaction is a bet that the girls will succumb to the charms of the boys absurdly disguised as Albanians and under strict orders of Alfonso, who is abetted by the chambermaid Despina. For some time, conventional refusals meet conventional lovemaking by the Albanians. But then, one after the other, the girls capitulate.

As might perhaps be anticipated, it is the asymmetries in this highly symmetrical plot that provide the dramatic drive. Dorabella falls at once, but Fiordiligi puts up an unexpected struggle, around which the second act comes to revolve. Da Ponte arranged different reactions from the boys, too, when they learn of their betrayals: Guglielmo spiteful, Ferrando emotional and hurt. Then at the end the masquerade is revealed to the girls, and with much embarrassment they return to their original lovers. The pairing-off at the end is not specified, but it seems quite clear that the original *status quo* is to stand.*

The thing is watertight—and that is what caused Mozart trouble. Only a prude will object to people changing their feelings, in whatever possible frame of reality (though it may seem odd that the boys remain faithful while the girls waver.) Only a pedant will object to the compression of the action into a single day or to the fact that the girls do not recognize the Albanians (why should they have known the other boys well at all, or, for that matter, even their own lovers?). It is even pompous to complain of the implied psychology, because the play is firmly posited on the view that emotion is essentially trivial—a legitimate comic exaggeration. Here Da Ponte goes farther than Don Alfonso, for whom feeling is transitory but real enough while it lasts; for Da Ponte it is really false through and through. We have to believe that the girls' feelings about the Albanians are as trivial as their original feelings about their lovers; that it has really been a lark in Despina's sense; that they have been as cold-blooded in giving in to the Albanians as the boys were in consenting to the masquerade. Otherwise, of course, they could hardly go back to their first lovers with so little pain. It took Fiordiligi three arias and a duet to change the first time, and if there was any depth to her feeling, she would require some parallel dramatic development

* Three reasons: first, a remark of Alfonso's as he tells the boys to marry the girls in spite of their fickleness: "Basically you love these plucked chicks of yours"—"*In fondo voi le amate, queste vostre cornacchie spennacchiate*"—and the boys ruefully agree. Second, returning to the original lovers is the "correct" thing; as everybody acts on convention until pressed, any wrench from the usual would have to elicit some explanation. Third, the second switch is dramatically necessary; otherwise the whole finale lacks point—it must do more than just tease the girls, it must in fact teach them a lesson reflected by action. And very funny it is, at the end, when the girls swear eternal fidelity just as they had at their first appearance, in Act I, scene ii.

to change back. But true feeling must have been far
from Da Ponte's mind. He wrote a clever comedy
which is satirical, witty, superficial, and unworthy of
Mozart—and I say so not on the basis of any Victorian
sentimentality about art and artists, but on the basis
of what happened when Mozart came to set the libretto. His approach to the action was neither that
of the cynical Da Ponte, nor that of Don Alfonso the
"*vecchio filosofo.*"

For there are more things in heaven and earth than
are dreamt of in Alfonso's philosophy. Don Wolfgango,
inevitably, took emotion seriously. Da Ponte should
have known by this time that Mozart would pounce
upon any feasible emotional matter, in however dry a
book, and turn it to account. For a long time, Mozart
valiantly parodied everything as Da Ponte wished. For
the ensembles he developed a special arrangement,
whereby the lovers sing in parallel thirds and sixths
or else parrot each other's music closely. This gives the
ensembles of *Così fan tutte* a curiously different quality from any others in Mozart: the characterization is
neutral for the lovers, though as vivid as ever for Don
Alfonso and Despina. The girls' three duets are almost
indistinguishable in feeling: "*Ah guarda, sorella,*" expressing love for the original boys, "*Ah! che tutta in
un momento,*" registering sorrow at their departure,
and "*Prenderò quel brunettino,*" announcing readiness
for flirtation. Even recitatives tend to be sung in
in thirds.

This initial neutrality of characterization determines
the primary plane of reality in *Così fan tutte*. Obviously, musical parallelism was a convenience to Mozart; but I am sure that he adopted it primarily in
order to show the lovers less as serious individuals than
as anonymous representatives of their sexes. For that
is all they are to Don Alfonso. Anonymous representatives can have only conventional feelings, and such feel-

ings, as Mozart knew, are all of about the same quality. So the paleness, the sameness, and the unintelligence which we feel in *Così fan tutte* are appropriate enough dramatically, and before dismissing the convention as uninteresting, we must consider Mozart's rich modulation of it in the second act. The full-blooded realism of *Figaro* would have been as out of place in this opera as in *The Magic Flute* or *Idomeneo*. Furthermore, Mozart constantly parodies the arias; it is very hard for these unintelligent characters to gauge their emotions, as it is for convention-bound people in actual life. In Act II, it is even very hard for the audience to understand these characters, for their truest feelings are automatically expressed in sentimental, "operatic" terms. The audience, however, has no doubt as to the superficiality of the girls' arias in Act I. So far, it is an artificial comedy after Da Ponte's heart.

But as the libretto allows the characters to slip out of their neutrality, Mozart with an excellent sense of drama fires their individualities. Convention veils these people in the company of their sisters or companions or original lovers, whom we cannot take seriously; in later soliloquies, though, and most particularly in the two seduction duets, some of the veils begin to drop. This is so even with Dorabella, whose main function is to serve as a shallow foil for Fiordiligi. Her exquisite duet with Guglielmo seems frigidly contained, with its heart- and locket-symbolism. But when he touches her, there is a sudden flash of feeling in a modulatory passage, and in the recapitulation (or resolution to this tiny drama) the divided phrases are as eloquent as the tremulous new orchestral figure. As for Fiordiligi, the more solemn sister, we cannot shake off the impression of sorrow in her second aria, *"Per pietà,"* for all its preposterousness; and her duet with Ferrando has always been understood as the expressive center of the opera, as it is the dramatic center. No theory of

Così fan tutte will do that does not take full measure of this wonderful piece. Fiordiligi is closer to emotional truth here than anyone anywhere else in the play.

And what of Ferrando in the duet? He has just sung of his fidelity to Dorabella in the *cavatina* "*Tradito, schernito*," but Mozart never works on a double standard, and certainly means to tease him here just as he teased Fiordiligi when she swore eternal fidelity in "*Come scoglio*." If ever an operatic lover was sincere, it is Ferrando in the duet with Fiordiligi—with its mysterious echo, too, of his lovely aria in Act I, "*Un' aura amorosa*." (It may be objected that Don Giovanni also seems utterly sincere in each of his affairs; but Ferrando has none of Don Giovanni's experience in amorous dissimulation.) Certainly Ferrando shows no affection for Fiordiligi later—and, incidentally, no further grief at Dorabella's infidelity. But for this we blame the libretto. In opera we trust what is most convincing in the music.

Mozart's music clarifies and damns Da Ponte's cynicism, and so spoils his immaculate play. It was worth it. Where Da Ponte left room for personal sentiments under the actual stress of action, Mozart was too good a dramatist not to take them at face value: the girls' reactions to the Albanians and to their own distressing instability, the boys' attitudes towards their betrayals. Don Alfonso wanted to show that feelings change; Da Ponte wanted to expose them as meaningless; Mozart wanted to define their quality, whether they last or not. So in the end it is a wry joke on Da Ponte: fickleness seems irrelevant and relatively unreal; Mozart's point is that emotions touch anyhow, even if soon they alter. Don Alfonso's triumphant demonstration does not concern the central problem as Mozart saw it—the mystery of feeling itself. With Fiordiligi, indeed, it is not a matter of changing love, but of finding it. Our main impression in the duet with Ferrando is of her new capacity for genuine feeling, even—or perhaps, particularly—in her capitulation. Ferrando, after all, is obviously the better man.

As articulated by Mozart, then, the opera seems to show a pair of rather unconscious couples tried and drawn a little way out of their conventional shells of sentimentality, proffered suicides, lockets, and parallel thirds. Everything is very funny, and their progress is admirably dramatic, and we are pleased to discover that we feel for them after all. But then, as a conclusion, everything snaps back to the original state of affairs; emotion is eradicated in Lorenzo da Ponte's final jest. Fiordiligi's experience goes up in smoke as she turns blankly back to Guglielmo, whose insufficiency has meanwhile been made only too clear by the action. The *volte face* was witty enough in Da Ponte's scheme, but in Mozart's it is simply an anticlimax. In the last analysis it is improbable and immoral. For the first time we realize how tired we are of the singing in thirds and sixths; it has been a long evening. The lovers are back in their original anonymity, without any explanation for the abrupt lowering of the imaginative level. That is quite undramatic. There is no ultimate epiphany, as in *The Marriage of Figaro*, and there really could not have been within the range of this excellently calculated libretto.

4

THE LIBRETTO for *Così fan tutte* was too nearly perfect, in its soulless terms, for Mozart to deal with it properly in his. But the libretto for *Don Giovanni* left much to be desired—more than a composer could supply.

Now the critical attitude towards *Don Giovanni* has really changed as much as that towards *Così fan tutte*, though in just the opposite way. The Romantics worshipped it as a unique masterpiece, the only opera in which Mozart touched the daemonic roots of reality. From E. T. A. Hoffmann and Kierkegaard to Bernard Shaw and Richard Strauss, Don Giovanni has been idealized into a Faust or a superman, a shining knight of the *ewig Weibliche* if not the life-force itself. Only in the twentieth century has historical scholarship labored to interpret the opera as an ordinary farce with supernatural additions, clumsily grafted together and blessedly over-composed. Apparently the story was well known in *opera buffa*, and indeed discredited, fit for the provinces. If Da Ponte had not known that Mozart would be sure to spruce it up, he probably would never have touched it. The speed with which the piece had to be written explains certain of its crudities; Da Ponte was busy with two rather more fashionable composers, and had time only to expand an earlier libretto for Mozart. Since *Don Giovanni* was ordered for the city which loved *Figaro*, the authors set out to duplicate the winning features of that opera. Once Dent has pointed it out, it is easy to see that *Don Giovanni* was originally laid out in the unusual four-act scheme of *Figaro* in order to include much action; that it exploits the same social complex of masters and servants; that it has the same baritone preponderance and three women, having been designed for the same company; and that many arias echo numbers in the earlier opera. "I know this thing only too well!" says Leporello when Don Giovanni's band plays the latest hit from *The Marriage of Figaro*.

The dependence runs deeper. The success of *Figaro* in Prague must have gone to Mozart's head as well as to his heart, and *Don Giovanni*, written less than a year later, shows wonderful signs of his eagerness to develop his artistic gains. *The Marriage of Figaro* is re-markable for its graphic realism, which was unprecedented in *opera buffa*, and which Mozart must have stumbled upon under the influence of Beaumarchais's admirably realistic play. He applied and deepened the same quality of realism in *Don Giovanni*; but it was really rather thoughtless to have done so with this picaresque, supernatural, and not at all contemporary story. (Mozart never attempted such realism later, with *Così fan tutte* or *The Magic Flute*.) Almost accidentally, we may suppose, he had discovered in *Figaro* the serious possibilities inherent in comic opera. His enthusiasm for pressing this discovery is everywhere apparent in *Don Giovanni*; he is ready to take anything and anybody seriously. To Mozart in this frame of mind, Donna Anna was a priceless gift from the poet: a full-fledged Metastasian heroine, but for once in a vivid, naturalistic context! Beside her, *Idomeneo's* Electra and *Tito's* Vitellia seem pale and orderly. Mozart, now intoxicated with the dramatic power of the ensemble, left the greatest of all examples of this quintessential form in *Don Giovanni*. He rejoiced in *tours de force*; one dazzling effect follows another; the drama gets out of hand. If *Figaro* was an extremely clever work, *Don Giovanni* is magnificently brash. Perhaps it had to be, with that hoary subject matter. *Don Giovanni* is Mozart's richest score, and the dearest of all his operas to the musician, as it is to the opera-going public today.

In *Don Giovanni* the sense of drama on the detailed level (though not on the largest level) is even more vivid than in *Figaro*. No praise is too high for the famous first-act introduction, where in a sudden rush of impression we see Leporello pacing the street, Donna Anna wrestling with Don Giovanni, the abrupt duel, and the Commendatore's death—and then the scurrilous chatter of Leporello again, in the recitative which interrupts the cadence. Three things are indelibly established: the tone of violence, speed, and passion; the clashing mode of comedy, thanks to Leporello; and the peculiar beauty which Mozart sounds in this opera, thanks to the moonlit trio as the Commendatore dies. Don Giovanni here does not exactly regret the death, but he is taken aback by its suddenness and unthinkingness. He might have wished for something else, if he ever took the trouble to think. Another perfect touch is the trio of the conspirators, with the woodwinds, inserted into the tense action of the first-act finale; a quite unrealistic fragment which has the effect of a chorus comment, and which deepens the solemnity of the intrigue. I have spoken previously of the extraordinary Ballroom Scene later in the finale, and of several of Elvira's ensembles. "*Là ci darem la mano*," one of the simplest-sounding things in the score, is also one of the most carefully calculated, with its gradual bringing-together of the two voices, Zerlina's nervous checks, and Don Giovanni's gently increasing pressure. Their next encounter, during that same finale, "*Tra quest' arbori celata*," is even more beautiful, especially in the larger dramatic context.

Mozart's developing sense of musical means for drama is illustrated by his reworking of one small detail from *The Marriage of Figaro*. In the sextet of Act II in *Don Giovanni*, the modulatory shock of the conspirators, when Leporello throws off his disguise and explains that they have not caught Don Giovanni after all, is parallel to, but even better managed than, the musical reaction of the court at the end of *Figaro*, when the Countess throws off her disguise. Yet we cannot help noting, at the same time, the triviality to which the device is turned, as compared with the situation in *Figaro*. Dramaturgical perfection is not the same thing as fine drama.

Can Da Ponte's libretto as a whole support Mozart's

sense of drama, his graphic realism, his profundity of insight and expression? The question will not arise for those who, like Dr. Johnson, regard opera as an irrational and exotic entertainment. But it certainly will for those who look at other Mozart operas, and find that they are entirely rational and not exotic in the least. Certainly the libretto to *Don Giovanni* "works" on the large level; Da Ponte was an excellent theatrical craftsman, and his knowledge of dramatic rhythm did not desert him here. But on many levels the piece shows deficiencies more severe than any in Mozart's other great operas. The libretto is full of improbabilities: to cite only one of the first, furious Elvira stands patiently listening to a servant sing a long, insolent, suggestive aria about her betrayal. Whereas the improbabilities of *Così fan tutte* are carefully chosen and witty, those of *Don Giovanni* are fortuitous and clumsy; while *Figaro*, of course, does not show any improbabilities. It always takes a modicum of care to arrange arias in a libretto, and in *Così fan tutte* it is always elegantly done. In *Figaro*, four arias are inserted into Act IV stiffly enough, but though they strain our patience, they do not strain our credulity. The way in which the last act of *Don Giovanni* is distorted to provide arias for Anna and Elvira, however, can only be called dramatically cynical, whether they enhance characterization or not. And these faults in *Don Giovanni* are especially glaring in its context of passionate naturalism.

As far as characterization is concerned, Mozart's wonderful picture of the three women has always been rightly admired, if often wrongly interpreted: steely Donna Anna, innocent (yes, innocent) Zerlina, and especially Donna Elvira, the first of Mozart's developing heroines, a type more systematically worked out with Fiordiligi and Pamina. But rich personalities do not automatically make for true drama; the study of characterization was the primrose path of older dramatic criticism. What is one to say of the mysterious Don himself? He is an unaware person for a Mozartian hero, though his charm, largesse, ingenuity, and reasonableness are not left in doubt. The singular fact is that until the end almost all of the action and musical expression goes to illuminate the people with whom he is involved, not Don Giovanni himself. This seems to me a dramatic mistake, and one that was fatally compounded when Da Ponte began to build the second act around Leporello. Even the scene in the graveyard, which certainly should involve Don Giovanni and the Statue, turns out to be mostly about Leporello. Like Faust and Peer Gynt, Don Juan goes through a series of loosely joined adventures. It was clever and dramatic of Da Ponte to have succeeded in relating them so well, but this very cleverness led him into an impasse which Marlowe and Ibsen avoided—the adventures assume more interest than the hero. To say that Don Giovanni's lack of involvement is precisely the strongest element of his personality is to argue *ab vacuo*; in opera we trust what is done most firmly by the music. The very blankness of Don Giovanni's characterization, indeed, must have been what especially attracted romantic critics. Their daydreams and idealizations could sprout and flourish in Mozart's relative void.

Finally, though, Leporello is pushed under the table as the Statue pulls Don Giovanni down to hell in the great finale. Mozart composed this *con amore*; another godsent opportunity to be serious and intense. The eighteenth century may have been used to treating Don Juan in terms of farce with supernatural additions, but under the influence of Mozart's setting of the catastrophe, we cannot shun its implications. Inherent in the legend is the conflict between the glamour and the irrevocability of sin. The opera merely enlarges this conflict—an expression of the "daemonic,"

or else a weakness in the central conception, according
to taste. Up to the end, our sympathies have been
enlisted for the hero in countless ways; then Mozart
shows him damned in a scene whose terror suddenly
dominates the drama. As the action touches Don Giovanni at last, he rises magnificently to the occasion,
fearless and true to himself in a crisis which is past
pride. In what way, then, does he deserve his damnation? what does Mozart think of his doom? what does
Don Giovanni himself think—for presumably by this
time he will be open to some introspection? Honest
and subtle equivocation would be a dramatic possibility, but instead we have accidental and unformed
ambiguity. Either Da Ponte was unaware of all the
questions that he conjured up along with his devils,
or else he deliberately pushed them under. Certainly
the epilogue answers none of them; it only goes to
show how drab life is without the Don.

It is no use speculating on what might have been.
Mozart, who transformed other dramas, might have
transformed this one, but Da Ponte is mostly responsible for the weakness. After all, nobody believes in
ghosts and devils, least of all Don Giovanni; such things
can assuredly be put on the stage, but only on the
strict condition that the convention and the attitude
are clearly established. This is what everyone else has
done who has dealt with Don Juan or any of his dramatic brothers. But Da Ponte failed to rationalize the
action. One rather suspects that he lacked the intellectual force to cope with it.

Kierkegaard first spoke of a magic "marriage" be-
tween the genius of Mozart and the subject matter of
Don Juan, and many have followed him in this view.
I could not disagree more completely; the whole basis
of the Don Juan legend seems to me curiously out of
Mozart's intellectual, ethical, and metaphysical style.
Very few people nowadays see Mozart as a "daemonic"

composer, even if they think of music as a daemonic art. In a work like the g-minor Quintet, we sense an exquisitely constrained pathos, in the Piano Concerto in c minor a controlled foreshadowing of Beethovenian tragedy, in the Requiem Mass a certain frustration strikingly symbolized by its noncompletion. As an opera composer, Mozart had dwelt more profoundly than anyone else on man in relation to other men and women, never in relation to God and the universe. Then suddenly theology was thrust on him at the end of *Don Giovanni*—right at the end, when things were getting rushed, as usual. He did his best, a very wonderful best, but everything we know or feel about Mozart should assure us that the inflexible view of sin and death set forth in the legend must have been distasteful to him. Mozart never saw man's will as inevitably opposed by the will of God. He conceived an essential harmony expressed by human feelings; his terms were brotherhood and sympathy and humility, not damnation and defiance. The magic marriage is *The Magic Flute*.

And with *The Magic Flute* anyone might be tempted to echo Kierkegaard about the consuming desire of Genius for Idea. What an extraordinary subject, after all, as compared with the traditional claptrap of Don Juan. No mystique is necessary to comprehend the opera, though. Says Dent: "The initial idea of *Die Zauberflöte* was to be more or less as follows: the hero makes the acquaintance of the fairy queen, who gives him a portrait of her daughter and sends him to rescue her from captivity in the castle of the wicked magician, which he will be able to do by the help of the magic flute. For some reason which has never yet been satisfactorily explained, the whole plot was completely changed at this stage." I should think that this change can be explained very simply and very happily on the assumption that Mozart himself insisted on it, and

thereafter strictly supervised the libretto. The opera
as we know it, then, would have been determined not
by any Magic or Destiny, but by a conscious intellectual decision on Mozart's part. For the first time, at
long last, Mozart appears to have been in charge; he
really learned to bully his librettist; maybe he was responsible for the participation of the shadowy Carl
Ludwig Giesecke. Unlike *Don Giovanni*, *The Magic
Flute* is unified in conception, and everything about it
matches the temper of Mozart's genius. All the diversi-
ties—of musical style, action, tone, and mood—are
perfectly controlled to a single dramatic end.*

The Magic Flute is the least problematic of Mozart's
operas; nobody can miss or misinterpret its humane
message. In a hundred years the only real change in
critical attitude towards it is that now we take it seriously. Mozart's view of destiny is rather mystic than
Manichaean. In Sarastro's realm sin merits neither
glamour nor damnation; it is simply checked as inevitably as day follows night:

> Die Strahlen der Sonne vertreiben die Nacht,
> Zernichten der Heuchler erschlichene Macht.

Lying is met by a temporary padlock on the lips,
lechery by a beating, deceit by rendering the rebels

---

* There is of course no external proof for the change in plot,
and the inconsistencies that this change is supposed to have
occasioned have been exaggerated. The Queen of the Night
and her Ladies are first represented as forces for good, but this
only corresponds to Tamino's opinion; his own later reflection
and better understanding are matched by that of the audience.
It has been objected that the magic flute and bells, as gifts
from the Queen, should not become agencies of good; but in
fairy tales magic items are always morally indifferent. And one
of the not-so-subtle aspects of the action is that Tamino wins
through his own character and through Pamina's love, not essentially by magic. In the scene of the lovers' meeting Pamina
explains at considerable length that the flute was mysteriously
shaped by her father; the flute then is in some sense hers, and it is
Pamina who guides Tamino through the Trials. Magic and
deceit are the Queen's powers. Sarastro's are deeper, more lasting and human.

impotent. Virtue is attained by an esoteric but demo-
cratic and hospitable ascent, in which Tamino, Pamina,
and even Papageno can all share in various ways. Tamino, ready at first to fall in love with images, takes
the Queen of the Night at her word, just as the audience does. He learns to doubt, to seek a higher reality,
and to submit to the Ordeals. Pamina learns love,
despair, and freedom from parental despotism. For
both of them, a deeper love is the last step, and they
stand together before the Fire and the Water. Pamina
assists Tamino; what the supposedly misogynic Free-
masons thought of this, I cannot say, but Mozart made
it the center of his drama. Pamina is by far the fullest
person in it, and her progress, by way of Mozart's
greatest aria, *"Ach, ich fühl's,"* is the most emphatically articulated. (One need only imagine the opera
without her—it could "work," after a fashion—to realize how valuable her role is.) Through brotherhood
man achieves Wisdom, Virtue, and the Love of God,
and brotherhood is not restricted by sex. Nor by intelligence; Papageno, who is generally unconscious and
afraid, can gain his salvation too if he will keep good
cheer and not lie. The gods are as humble as men.
Sarastro suffers gently with his novices, and all the
Priests and Spirits and Armed Men are their brothers.

Since the underlying conception is so single and
pure, the almost crazy variety of musical styles which
Mozart dared bring together can harmonize as beautifully as the solemn animals of the Peaceable Kingdom.
There is no stress of stylistic contradiction, as there
is in *Don Giovanni*, though the elements are in actual
fact much more disparate: *opera seria* arias and *opera
buffa* ensembles, panpipe scales and an overture with
a real fugal theme, Masonic fanfares and a Lutheran
chorale which sounds like Bach, Viennese street-songs
and (as Shaw said) the only music yet written fit
for the mouth of God. All these seem to be subsumed

into the particular "Magic Flute style," the style of Mozart's last months. There is a new serenity, a new sense of control over basic processes, a distillation of technique to the purest essentials of the art. Mozart can hardly resolve a dominant seventh chord now without shedding on it a light that no other composer has ever comprehended:

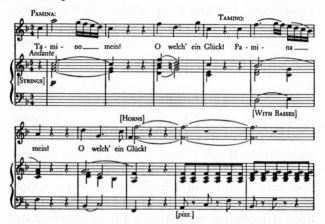

These sublime accents were foreshadowed by the climactic scene of reconciliation at the end of *The Marriage of Figaro*. They recur now in works like the Clarinet Quintet, the Clarinet Concerto, the last Piano Concerto (B♭, K.595), the Rondo for Musical Glasses, the Fantasy for Mechanical Organ, and sometimes in *La Clemenza di Tito* and the Requiem Mass.

Little needs to be added to Dent's analysis and appreciation of the overall dramatic structure of *The Magic Flute*. Everything progresses calmly but firmly and clearly, the pacing is immaculate, and at every point the music sums up the dramatic situation and illuminates it. From the very opening scene, which is in its quiet way as perfect as the introduction to *Don Giovanni*, we see that the virtuosity of the earlier opera has given way to effortless assurance; this is especially striking in the treatment of the ensemble. Music defines the marvelous dramatic illusion, the fairy-tale world which exposes Mozart's vision of human perfectability and the vanity of evil. Planes of reality merge in this music, and all the diverse lines of action converge to one resolution: the grave, tranquil, unearthly march heard as the initiates go forward to suffer the Ordeals. This still climax, with flute and drums and quiet brass, is surely the most extraordinary in all opera. If Gluck had written it, we would complain that it has no counterpoint; if Mozart had written it anywhere else, we could rightly call it senseless. For the avenging Statue, Mozart had been able to paint a Triumph of Death which has probably been the despair of later composers. Now he shows the Queen of the Night's defeat, in her last ensemble *"Nur stille, stille, stille, stille!"* as a painless, almost organic process. Her agent Monastatos is innocent of trombones, chromatic rows, and d minor; at his first appearance he is practically equated with Papageno, and he always sings approximately in Papageno's comic style. And the coloratura of the Queen herself can mislead only the unitiated or the unthinking, children or children in spirit. It had seduced Mozart in *Die Entführung*.

You can hear it said that *The Magic Flute* is a supreme work of art entirely on account of its wonderful music and in spite of the foolish accompanying plot. That is the "pure-music" view of opera. But the truth is that its adherents would not tolerate fully a third of the music of *The Magic Flute* in the concert hall, outside its dramatic framework; think of Papageno's folk songs, or Tamino's great recitative with the Orator, or the unimaginably bare march for the Ordeals. Other critics, and especially Germans, have admired voluminously its combination of beautiful music and noble ideals. Such honors are dubious, though, unless the nature of the alloy can be defined; plenty of

Metastasian operas have put beautiful music next to noble ideals without being canonized. The strength of *The Magic Flute* is that its philosophy or its binding dramatic idea is consistently molded by the dramatic form, in which music is the essential element, as always in opera. Something of what Freemasonry meant to Mozart is indeed fused into articulation here, and musical drama is the refining agent. Ideals can be cheapened, and doubtless they are by Schikaneder's doggerel. Ideals can also be raised to a unique personal incandescence, and that they are by Mozart's drama.

The four great operas of Mozart all show music's great power to determine dramatic form. *The Magic Flute* and *The Marriage of Figaro* show further how such dramatic form can articulate a consistent, profound action. In these masterpieces, all of Mozart's eloquence and strength, his faultless response to action, his control over the dramaturgical wealth of the ensemble, his sensitivity to character in the aria, his famous ingenuity, sympathy, delicacy, and humor, his superb sense of artistic form on every level—all this is fired to cast a single dramatic conception. One cannot very well describe such a conception without lapsing into platitudes; one can find words more easily for operas like *Don Giovanni* and *Così fan tutte,* wherein the dramatic ideas are half-formed or unresolved, despite very great beauties. But where the dramatist has been successful, the idea cannot be defined except as the work itself. The meaning of a complete work of art will be manifested only in the medium that realizes, consummates, or creates it. The vindication of opera as drama comes in such occasional, unique triumphs; and among these, Mozart has left our most precious examples.

5

Otello: *Traditional Opera and the Image of Shakespeare*

THE spoken theater serves as a court of appeal, or at least of analogy, where the dramatic efficacy of opera or any other non-verbal medium is likely to be tested. The test, then, becomes something of a polemic necessity, and the plea may as well be entered as broadly as possible. On a rather general plane, one can draw convincing parallels in dramatic rhythm, technique, convention, and so on, among various genres of musical and literary drama. Indeed, the nature of certain Greek and certain Elizabethan plays has been explained on the basis of a "musical" structure—musical in a modern rather than in a Greek or Elizabethan sense. On a more specific plane, one can examine critically the evidence of good operas which are evolved carefully from good plays. Comparison shows the play and the opera to be analogously dramatic, rich, and significant; contrast sets into convenient relief the particular techniques and intentions of each. In the present chapter and the next, I shall try this comparative method with Verdi's *Otello*, derived closely from Shakespeare's *Othello*, and with Debussy's *Pelléas et Mélisande*, derived even more closely from the play by Maurice Maeterlinck.

Such close derivations are rare in the seventeenth or eighteenth centuries. *The Marriage of Figaro* is rather the exception; opera was content with its own highly stylized forms. But in the nineteenth century, opera, especially in Italy and France, developed a strong inclination to adapt itself to the form of the play. The preoccupation with "continuity" in opera, so characteristic of the middle of the century, may be seen as a tendency towards the more even flow of literary drama; once this had been achieved, the way was open to the influence of the Naturalistic theater, the *verismo*. Many details of structure in nineteenth-century opera correspond to fundamentally literary effects and devices. Symptomatic is the large number of important operas derived from plays. With Verdi, for instance, a list of the sources for his librettos reads like a dramatic anthology: Hugo's *Hernani* and *Le Roi s'amuse*; Schiller's *Die Jungfrau von Orleans*, *Die Räuber*, *Kabale und Liebe*, and *Don Carlos*; Byron's *The Two Foscari* and *The Corsair*; Shakespeare's *Macbeth*, *Othello*, *The Merry Wives of Windsor*, and (a hope for many years) *King Lear*. To be sure, the relationship between opera and play is insignificant in the early works, up to and including *Macbeth*. But *Luisa Miller* and *Rigoletto*, the operas in which Verdi first stretched hard the stiff form inherited from Rossini and Donizetti, are modeled rather seriously on plays. The formal fluidity of *Otello* and *Falstaff*, at the end of his career, certainly reflects the influence of literary models. As for Debussy, he carried the tendency to its logical conclusion. *Pelléas et Mélisande* incorporates the original play whole; the form of the opera is practically that of the play.

Now this is not true of *Otello*. As compared with Verdi's *Macbeth* of 1847, his *Otello* of 1887 has a flexibility of structure, to say nothing of a seriousness of conception, due to the spoken theater; but the form of *Otello* is not the form of a play, nor certainly the form of the particular play of Shakespeare. The drama is still articulated primarily by large lyric numbers—handled now with new subtlety and force, and blended in to the rest with new art. *Otello*, in other words, preserves the essence of the classic tradition of Italian opera. Verdi was proud to continue this tradition, and took a dim view of operatic reforms. Yet Verdi was less of a conservative than he liked to make out; the stress between a desire for a more "literary" flow and the demands of the tradition caused him serious problems in the middle years. Only in *Otello* did he reach a consistent, viable balance. The balance necessitated a unique transformation of Shakespeare's play.

Arrigo Boïto, who wrote the libretto and persuaded old Verdi to take it, was a distinguished literary man and composer with a strong interest in transalpine culture. He was well aware of the stress in later nineteenth-century opera. He had tried to meet it in *Mefistofele*, the most high-minded Italian opera since the days of Gluck; if he failed, he did so because of his insufficiencies as a composer, not because of any lack of boldness, skill, or understanding of the problem. Two principles, then, guided Boïto's transformation of his Shakespearean model. The first, a tendency towards naturalism, is revealed most deeply by his underlying conception of the story, to which I shall return later. It is also revealed in his evident wish to condense an untidy plot into something striking

for the audience of the well-made play. This would
not have occurred to an Italian composer of an earlier
century, who might actually have found Shakespeare
too classical for his episodic taste. But an Italian composer of any century would have shared Boïto's second, actually contradictory principle: that of crystalliz-
ing emotional situations regularly into lyric sections or
tableaux in which music can take its own time and
contribute most strongly and unequivocally to the
drama. Situation by situation, Shakespeare was bent
to this two-sided conception of the musical theater.

2

THUS at the very start, Shakespeare's storm (Act II,
scene i) was strengthened out of all proportion to
make the opera's opening tableau. No doubt it was a
foregone conclusion that Boïto would omit Shakespeare's Act I, the Venetian act—as Dr. Johnson had
prophesied:

Had the scene opened in Cyprus, and the preceding incidents been occasionally related, there had been little
wanting to a drama of the most exact and scrupulous
regularity.

Verdi even skipped an overture. His initial chorus is
the most thrilling *temporale* in Italian opera; the violence and terror at once strike the pitch characteristic
of the opera throughout. Shakespeare, as Granville-
Barker says, "makes his storm out of poetry," but
verse is not so evocative as music in mood-painting
of this sort. The sense of pervasive disorder is thrust
home to the emotions in musical terms, and when
Otello finally appears, his triumph over the elements
is magnificent. He merely sings two lines and goes off
to bed, but a good tenor can make this the most un-

forgettable entrance in all of opera. Iago and Roderigo
are introduced, on a much lower emotional level; they
have much to explain, and the end of their talk is
drowned by preparations for the victory celebration
(the fireside Chorus "*Fuoco di gioia!*"). As soon as
this ends, Iago can smoothly begin plying Cassio with
drink, and all proceeds as in Shakespeare up to the
drunken duel and the return of Otello, followed then
by Desdemona. Thanks to the force of his original
entrance, Otello remains in the imagination all through
the act, and his dominating appearance to quiet the
brawl is excellently prepared.

Verdi further scaled the storm to the drama by
passing from thunder and lightning to firelight, and
afterwards to the cloudless night of the love-duet,
which ends the act with the words "*Vien—Venere
splende.*" In Shakespeare, the understated verse-temp-
est looks back on an intermission uneasy with thoughts
of sea-travel, battles, and a father's curse, and looks
forward to Desdemona's anxiety. Both of these elements are missing from the libretto, for the storm is a
bald preface to the action, and Desdemona is carefully
reserved until after the brawl. Then her first appearance
demands some decisive utterance, such as Shakespeare
had provided in his first act. Verdi met this necessity
with the love-duet, a lyric crystallization not indicated
directly in the play, as the storm was. With Shakespeare, the reticence of the relationship between
Othello and Desdemona is of the essence of the
drama. With Verdi, the immediacy and frankness of
their love, expressed in this supremely beautiful duet,
is also of the essence—but of a different drama. The
one affectionate dialogue in the play (II, i, 184) comes
out of the excitement of their first meeting after the
storm; the opera gains a special sense of peace and
stability by placing the dialogue (as the duet) later,
when they have been roused from their bed by the

drunken brawl. An apt moment for reminiscences; Boïto has been admired for "occasionally relating" here something of the tale of Othello's wooing, from Shakespeare's Venetian act. The duet is a triumph of Verdi's newly flexible and expressive lyric art. At the climax, music surges up in the orchestra, for the first time, rather than from the singers, who now have only broken phrases: "*Un bacio*—"; "*Otello!*—." The powerful orchestral melody associated with the kiss recurs twice at the end of the opera as an all-important means of dramatic organization.

Only when the curtain falls after Act I does the music actually come to a clear stop. There have been no pauses for *secco* recitative, no cadences for applause, no sudden changes in the musical flow. All the incidents are blended together, just as they are by the uninterrupted verse of the play; *Otello* is of course a "continuous opera." Operatic continuity was a universal ideal of nineteenth-century music, and *Otello* and *Falstaff* are the finest realizations of its non-Wagnerian variety.

* * *

On the face of it, continuous opera seems to differ radically from the "stop-and-go" opera of the eighteenth century. Everything is handled on the musical plane, without breaking the mood abruptly and regularly for recitative or spoken dialogue. The tendency towards the establishment of a single convention for all the action, rather than a double one, is literary in spirit, and in an important sense naturalistic. Also highly romantic, in its implication that all elements of the plot should be treated with equal seriousness. But none of the composers of the nineteenth century (Debussy always excepted) was quite willing to sacrifice the emphasis of fully rounded musical numbers. Various balances were struck, but lyric high-points are

still apparent, however carefully the edges are blurred
—one can say the same of Shakespeare's "continuous"
poetry. Defeating the artificiality of the old dichotomy
of aria and recitative meant obscuring the frank, convenient contrast between plot detail and lyrical introspection. This fact defined the reformers' main problem: the stress of which Boïto and Verdi were still
painfully aware.

Gluck had determined to raise action part way towards the level of the arias by dignifying all his recitative. This he did by orchestrating the accompaniment,
and sometimes by binding it motivically or harmoni-
cally. In so doing, he found that he had to limit himself to action that was worth dignifying; on this account action in *Orfeo* is reduced to a minimum. His
later operas have more plot, necessarily, and wisely
cling to the passionate action of Greek models. But
they are perilously high-minded, and such few operas
as were written under Gluck's influence—Spontini's
La Vestale, for instance—are insufferably so. Mozart,
on the other hand, following the *opera buffa* composers, dignified action by taking it out of recitative
and working it into genuinely musical sections, into
ensembles. Essentially this was a more radical procedure than Gluck's, but it was less conclusive in that
Mozart applied this technique only to the most important parts of the action. The rest he was content
to leave in *secco* recitative or plain speech; as a writer
of comedy, he had no wish to eliminate all low-grade
intrigue.

Italian opera in the first half of the nineteenth century was as resolute as a hundred years before in its
reliance on recitative and aria. Some of the techniques
of Mozart and Gluck which tended towards continuity
were incorporated, in a frightfully debased form. Recitative, for instance, was always accompanied by orchestra—a fact that made things if anything more stilted

than ever, inasmuch as librettists could not restrict
recitative to appropriately solemn sentiments. To Rossini goes the credit for establishing some *opera buffa*
devices in "serious" Italian opera. The immediate result was that the levity of *The Barber of Seville* could
be extended to Shakespeare's *Othello*, which Rossini
set to music in the same year, 1816; but the innovation
was useful, and later composers could better control
tone and technique. By the time of Verdi's *Otello*, the
subtlety of the Mozartian ensemble had been recaptured for Italian opera. And Verdi gradually reduced
the extent of the recitatives and blended them into
a more continuous texture. In *Rigoletto*, we are no
longer conscious of a dichotomy, but of a continuum;
in *Otello*, of a remarkably subtle continuum. This was
accomplished partly by approximately Gluckian methods in recitative, but chiefly by a new technique known
at the time as "*parlante*."

This was in fact a new solution to the problem of
action and the musical continuity. The principle was
to hold together a considerable passage of advancing
dialogue by means of a systematic motivic ground-plan
in the orchestra; the voices chime in with low-grade
counterpoint as best suits the verbal phrase and sentiment. *Parlante* can slip very easily into an aria or
chorus, thanks to the musical organization in the orchestra, and also just as easily into recitative, thanks
to the essentially declamatory vocal lines—"*parlante*,"
"talking." The orchestra provides the musical coherence to lift the dialogue towards the imaginative plane
of the fully musical numbers. Once again, something
of a precedent can be found in Mozart and Gluck, by
way of Rossini. As I have pointed out previously,
Gluck's climactic recitatives are often lent weight and
direction by repeated organizing figures in the bass.
And Mozart's ensembles often include sections in

which the discussion is surreptitiously in the background, while motivic work in the orchestra determines the musical continuity. At the little crisis in *The Marriage of Figaro* during which the Count questions Figaro about Cherubino's commission, the situation is unified and characterized by tight modulatory shifting development of a single theme in the orchestra, while sporadic talk defines the action. Resolution into the regular scheme of the ensemble occurs when Figaro triumphantly comes up with the answer. We have seen a similar technique at the dénouement of *Fidelio*.

Such refinements, however, do not elevate the early nineteenth-century Italian *parlante*. Everything is stereotyped, predictable, and actually organized lyrically. Where Gluck is driving and angular in his treatment of an orchestral motive, where Mozart and Beethoven adopt the tense dialectic of a clearly directed sonata-form development, Rossini and Bellini and Donizetti do their best to construct little instrumental arias. The orchestral motives are slick; they arrange themselves inconspicuously into the standard pattern; the dialogue moves forward, but the orchestral accompaniment stands still. Even in a technique which purports to treat dialogue in a continuous, "dramatic" fashion, Rossini works as closely as possible in the terms of his simple-minded arias.

Verdi's *parlante* is always more excitable, but in early works it is bound in the same way. Soon the technique became genuinely dramatic. Regularity could still be of use: to indicate the ominous patience of Sparafucile in *Rigoletto* or the metallic gaiety of the parties in *La Traviata*. Irregularity in the *parlante* could create such astonishingly naturalistic effects as Violetta's outburst leading into "*Amami, Alfredo*." In the duel between Cassio and Montano, Act I of *Otello* contains a highly complex example which shows how

Verdi could blend the texture into other elements of a scene. After Iago's Drinking Song ("And let me the canakin clink, clink"), a formal strophic piece in b minor enlivened by Cassio's increasing drunkenness, Montano enters to a few bars of recitative. The succeeding section is developmental, organized by a clear harmonic movement and by rather insignificant motivic material—which has however excellent dramatic interest in that it is derived from the Drinking Song. Disjointed comments and cries from the duellers, Iago, and the chorus harmonize as best they can.

The music moves in a somber circle of fifths by steady four-bar phrases: from F♯ to D, using a two-bar arpeggio motive begun by a triplet sixteenth-note figure; then from D to F, using a compressed version of the motive. As Iago tells Roderigo to rouse the town, the bass starts to move up tensely, supporting a chromatically descending scale motive related to the original one through the triplet. Both triplet and scale come out of the Drinking Song, and are snake-like sounds characteristic of Iago. The key is stabilized towards F♯ with new derived themes; the thematic

and modulatory complexity gives the effect of confusion, urgency, intensity. Then Otello's entrance to
the words *"Abbasso le spade!"* carries splendid authority by taking the F♯ up to G, rather than by resolving
it back to b minor, the key of the Drinking Song. A
new section is obviously in order; by means of the
deceptive resolution to G, it is smoothly yet dramatically worked in.

The section for the duel is integrated with the rest
of the scene as meticulously as a section in Mozart—
as meticulously as the section of Figaro's interrogation
is joined into the total ensemble. Notice also how the
stiff strophic outline of the Drinking Song is eased into
the following action. Passages of *parlante* are introduced in *Otello* with the greatest cunning to shade
the edges of the highly charged arias and ensembles.
In addition, the texture is used for its own sake in
longer and longer passages.

Some recitative is kept for properly unemotional
details—"How now, Roderigo?" "I like not that,"
"Prithee unpin me." But again, recitative must absolutely blend in soon with sections of *parlante* or
arioso; it must never go on for long; it develops interesting orchestral background material at the least
provocation, so that recitative is scarcely to be distinguished from fully musical sections. The continuum
is amazingly flexible. If the librettist could not feed
this style by making all conversations turn passionate
at the first possible occasion, so much the worse. With
the initially very dry recitative between Iago and Roderigo near the beginning of Act I, for instance, there
is really no pressing reason why Iago should keep flaring up into arioso (*"Se un fragil voto di femmina,"*
"Ed io rimango," etc.). As he does, he takes on at
once an aspect of particular pent-up violence. Verdi
may not have quite sensed the danger of over-emo-
tionality latent in this treatment of recitative.

3

Acts II and III are Iago's. Shakespeare presents him obliquely, by means of his conversations with Roderigo, Emilia, Cassio, Othello, and Desdemona; Verdi follows him here, and characterizes Iago musically with great skill according to the mask that he presents to his partner in conversation. But when there are stronger means available, recitative and arioso cannot carry the primary force. Verdi's essential method is blunter: he sweeps together Shakespeare's four or five little soliloquies into a single great aria near the start of the act, Iago's "Credo." It is the most sensational number in the score, and rightly; the listener is jolted enough to sustain two acts of Iago's dissimulation to follow. There is none of Shakespeare's curiously inconclusive "motive-hunting" in Verdi's "Credo," but instead the villain direct, complete, and terrible. Now starts the tempting and goading of Otello, a less subtle and gradual process than in Shakespeare. Though Verdi had to compress the plot, he was also careful to dwell on certain of its emotional climaxes, and the result is a progress quite different from Shakespeare's, in spite of the ingenuity with which much of the original dialogue is maintained.

The following will recall Shakespeare's arrangement in Act III, scene iii:

(1) Iago begins: "I like not that"; Othello pays no heed.
(2) Desdemona pleads for Cassio; Othello, delighted with her, means presently to comply.
(3) Iago plants the suspicion. "I see this hath a little dash'd your spirits"; Othello is certainly taken aback.
(4) Yet when Desdemona enters: "If she be false, O then heaven mocks itself! / I'll not believe't." Desdemona has no reason to be seriously disturbed as yet. They leave after she drops the handkerchief.

(5) Emilia and Iago and the handkerchief; and very delicately an era passes while Desdemona and Othello are off-stage.

(6) Now only, Othello returns infuriated. What has he remembered? "Thou hast set me on the rack . . . Farewell the tranquil mind! . . . Othello's occupation's gone!" The attack on Iago, the "proof" of Cassio's dream, and the vow of vengeance.

Things go faster in Verdi, and ways had to be devised to take up the strain on the credibility. Before Desdemona pleads for Cassio at all, there is a scene combining stages 1 and 3 of Shakespeare's Act III, scene iii; but although Otello actually has *less* cause now, he is considerably more than taken aback; he is already on the rack, ready for violence. It was, then, even more important for Verdi to brake the progress here (stage 4). However, it is not Desdemona who manages this, but instead Shakespeare's musicians of Act III, scene i, sea-changed into Cypriot sailors and peasants with *fanciulli* and mandolines, come at Cassio's bidding to serenade the mistress of the isle. Whereas in the play Othello's doubts could be quieted by the appearance of Desdemona, in the opera Otello has gone farther, and requires more appeasement; nothing less than a lyric interlude, in fact this serenade. Its function is made manifest by Otello himself: "*Quel canto mi conquide.*" The more ordinary thing would have been to have Desdemona sing an aria here. But what could this Desdemona have sung without sentimentality— after the love-duet, before the quartet? Verdi preferred to have the chorus symbolize her beauty and purity; their act of affection, and the sweetness and naïveté of their song, characterize Desdemona as she could not have done herself. It is one of the most original things in the score.

Only now does Desdemona plead for Cassio; that puts a different complexion on the matter as compared with Shakespeare's subtler placement of this

scene (as stage 2). No wonder Otello repulses her
with un-Shakespearean violence when she offers to
bind his head, and no wonder Desdemona now feels
the sting so deeply as to sing a long grief-stricken
melody—Shakespeare's inarticulate Desdemona! (Compare the original: "I am very sorry that you are not
well.") This melody is the basis of a rather old-
fashioned quartet, essentially Desdemona's piece; Verdi
will not leave her feelings to chance here, any more
than in the expository first act. It is her sorrow that is
expressed by the passionate tune, while simultaneously
Otello mutters "Haply, for I am black . . ." (taken
from Shakespeare's stage 3) and over on one side
Emilia and Iago bicker over the handkerchief. An economy, this; but there was a reason for Shakespeare's
ostensibly clumsy stagecraft with this fragment of his
scene. After the women are sent off, Verdi stays close
to the play. The act ends with the oath of vengeance,
a carefully rounded, strophic duet, rousing, melodra-
matic, blustery—and once again, thoroughly appropriate; Otello, and Iago matched to him, ought to be
"operatic" at this juncture, just as they are in Shakespeare. The music is all inflated metaphor and grandiose gesture, down to the last snarling chords.

In accordance with their two guiding principles for
modifying the original play, Boïto and Verdi recast
Shakespeare's scene in order to have it move in hard,
certain lines, and interposed a series of strong lyric
sections to stress its dramatic goals. On this account
Act II of *Otello* may be said to be the most conventionally operatic of the four. But Verdi was manipu-
lating old resources with the greatest awareness: the
principle "numbers"—the "Credo," the serenade, the
quartet, and the duet—are set in place with a wholly
fresh exploitation of their conventionality. Iago's aria
electrifies the action for two acts and characterizes
him so particularly that he can control the plot while

others are in fact more articulate. The chorus gently speaks for Desdemona while she herself is much better silent. The duet reveals with terrible force the new hysteria of Otello and the hypocritical bombast of Iago. It is easy to see that these numbers satisfy certain clear demands of the tradition in which Verdi wrote. The point is not, however, that the baritone needed an aria, or that a place had to be found for the chorus, which was on salary, or that a "Duet of Friendship" makes a sure-fire curtain. The point is how wonderfully well Verdi knew how to turn these necessities to a dramatic end.

* * *

He gained this knowledge painfully, and only at the end of his career—a career twice as long as those of Rossini, Bellini, and Donizetti, his best predecessors. The depraved state of opera in their day can be compared only with that of Italian opera at the end of the seventeenth century, before the reform of Metastasio. As at the earlier time, opera was blessed with the services of many good melodists and was dominated by the idea of lyricism; this in itself was not a fault. The fault was in the abysmal lack of integration of lyricism into a sensible dramatic plan. The disparity reflects sharply the confusion of early romanticism, its disruption of the stable order in the interest of new and as yet unsatisfied ideals.

Romanticism required a certain emotional immediacy, which composers supplied by drastic simplification of the aria form. They abandoned the formal subtlety and elaboration of the eighteenth century and provided instead something more popular. Composers now wrote "tunes," not "compositions"; whereas the eighteenth-century aria had been able to serve as model for the sonata, the nineteenth-century aria was modeled on the folk song. The composers of Metastasio's carefully diverse lyrics had been able to handle idealized feelings of all sorts in the same rhetorical, discursive fashion. Immediate feelings, though, were harder to treat under the technical conditions of the nineteenth century; the conditions of simplicity meant limitation as well as instant comprehensibility. Limitation, practically speaking, to a faint, sentimental melancholy, and to a polite, spirited enthusiasm—both equally unintelligent, for with extreme simplicity of form goes blankness. Yet arias had to be distributed recklessly throughout a score. What could possibly be done? Sentimental farce would work, and in *opera buffa* Rossini and Donizetti produced, if not serious comedy in Mozart's sense, at least works of some sort of aesthetic integrity. But for romantic melodrama their emotional range was simply inadequate.

Romantic melodrama was what the times demanded and what the wretched librettists found themselves supplying. How badly Rossini missed a Metastasio, a poet to define a bold convention suited to at least some of the strengths of contemporary music! But no stable tradition existed in that era of transition, and the tendency was away from convention in the old sense. Rarely, and almost by accident, does an aria in one of Rossini's serious Italian operas suit the situation. The last act of his *Otello* is fortunate in the "Willow Song"; Rossini could produce a beautiful, folk-like melody whose gentle nostalgia serves well enough (though Shakespeare and Verdi did better yet without any sentimentality!). But the following duet shows the full fatuity of Rossini's dramatic conception. Desdemona first offers her breast to Otello's scimitar with a peaceful melody accompanied by a dully repeating figure that we recognize from Basilio's aria in *The Barber*. When it is Otello's turn with this melody, he observes that her lover has been killed; he has the air of a shopkeeper showing her a bolt of silk. Desdemona listens politely, for she knows that the tune has one more time to repeat. "Yes," sings Otello (and the graceful coloratura does not help), "Iago has assassinated him."

Verdi, of course, attempts nothing in the way of a formal lyric number at this place. The whole duet is set in menacing, furious *parlante*.

One of the best scenes in Donizetti is the final scene of *Lucia di Lammermoor*. A graveyard is just the place to heighten susceptibilities, and Edgardo sings a touching, melancholy aria. As Lucia's funeral procession bears into sight, the movement quickens to a new aria, in which the dear, emptyheaded lad pours out his whole heart. It is very pretty indeed, and in itself dramatic; but nothing could be more grotesque than suicide at this elegiac juncture. Metastasio, after his earliest works, never risked an unhappy ending.

If in this tradition lyricism was to be turned to full dramatic use in melodrama or tragedy, two developments were necessary. First, Verdi had to learn to be merciless with the singers and with himself in restricting arias to emotionally appropriate positions. Second, he had to extend the emotional scope of the aria of Rossini, Bellini, and Donizetti; he had in fact to re-complicate the form, though of course from a new standpoint. These two processes required a good deal of self-understanding. To be sure, they complemented one another, for as the emotional range of the aria was extended, it became easier to find good dramatic places for it. The aria for Iago is excellent in Verdi, because Verdi could handle the sentiment in musical terms; the same placement would have been wasted on Rossini.

Verdi's growing understanding may be traced in his changing attitude towards the *cabaletta*, one of the worst lyric conventions of early nineteenth-century opera. This *cabaletta* was a fast, vehement aria or duet of extremely crude form and sentiment; it always came after a slower, quieter piece for the same singer or singers, and served to provide a rousing curtain. The form was strophic, and of the simplest pattern (*aaba* or *abb*); the accompaniment consisted of a mechanically repeated polonaise or fast march rhythm. Between the slower aria and its *cabaletta*, a passage of recitative or *parlante* served to present some sort of excuse for the singer to change his mind. The whole complex, indeed, is a simplification and stereotyping of the older composite aria of Mozart and Beethoven. Instead of the rather subtle interrelation of one sentiment and the next, and a sense of flux between them, there was now a formalized break into two crude, self-contained pieces. Though Rossini still employed composite arias for the most part, Donizetti arranged for half a dozen *cabalettas* in every opera.

Verdi's use of the *cabaletta* is still conventional in
Rigoletto, an opera that in many ways marks his decisive advance. At the start of Act II, the Duke sings a
gentle aria, *"Parmi veder le lagrime,"* lamenting the
absence of Gilda; when the courtiers tell them that
she is in the castle, he sings a heady *cabaletta* (*"Pos-
sente amor mi chiama"*—this is always cut in modern
productions). The whole complex is superfluous and
worse, for the Duke should be neither gentle nor genuinely excited. A little later, after Gilda and Rigoletto
sing their tender duet, Verdi goes to the extraordinary
subterfuge of leading in Monterone and his guards on
the way to prison, simply to spur Rigoletto on to the
concluding *cabaletta* of vengeance, *"Si vendetta."* In
La Traviata, on the other hand, two years later, the
cabaletta for Violetta is much more imaginatively arranged. At the end of Act I, touched by Alfredo's
previous avowal, Violetta wonders whether she can
find lasting love, in the aria *"Ah fors' è lui."* Then,
quite abruptly, she puts the self-indulgent thought
away from her, and sings the slightly hysterical *cabaletta "Sempre libera"*; she must be free, and think only
of day-to-day pleasure. After her first stanza, Alfredo's
voice is actually heard under the balcony, but Violetta
continues her next stanza (or rather, repeats her first
one), more resolute than ever in her new frame of
mind. This is a good dramatic use of the aria-*cabaletta*
complex; but *"Sempre libera"* is still coarse in sentiment compared with other utterances of Violetta's
during the course of the opera.

Gradually, and as it seems reluctantly, Verdi cut
down more and more on *cabalettas*. The later ones are
almost all duets, where things can be made more flexible. The last real example is in Act III of *Aïda*, *"Sì:
fuggiam da questa mura,"* marking the point at which
Rhadames resolves to flee with Aïda. Verdi ingeniously
cut off the second stanza with an emphatic return to

the original melody of the scene, *"Pur ti riveggo, mia dolce Aïda"*; but the elementary boisterousness of the *cabaletta* still sits strangely in this scene, which is in any case the least satisfactory in the whole opera. Some years after *Aïda*, while Verdi was working on his revision of *Simon Boccanegra* for Milan, he wrote to his publisher on the subject of *cabalettas*:

But the whole second act has got to be done over . . . Musically speaking, we could keep the women's *cavatina*, the duet with the tenor, and the other duet between father and daughter, in spite of the *cabalettas*! (Open, earth, and swallow us!) Anyway, I have no such horror of *cabalettas*, and if a young man were born tomorrow who could write any as good as, for instance, *Meco tu vieni o misera*, or *Ah perchè non posso odiarti*, I would go to hear him with all my heart, and let the harmonic fancies and the refinements of our learned orchestration go. Ah, progress, science, realism! Alas, alack! Be a realist as much as you please, but . . . Shakespeare was a realist, only he did not know it. He was a realist by inspiration; we are realists by design, by calculation. And so, after all, system for system, the *cabalettas* are still better. *

After having delivered himself of this blast, Verdi eliminated one *cabaletta* altogether from the revised *Simon*, and cut two others to the bone. *Cabalettas*, after all, did not fit into his new continuous, "realist" opera.

And yet a trace, just a trace of the *cabaletta* is left in the great duet of vengeance at the end of Act II of *Otello*. This duet does not stem from any formal slow lyric number, but it does serve to ring down the curtain, and does maintain the old driving rhythmic accompaniment; and it carries the conventional vehemence to extremes of violence and decision which make the shouts of Rigoletto or Rhadames sound dull indeed. The piece even has a backbone of the old strophic *aaba* form, but the pattern is quite trans-

* From *Verdi, the Man in his Letters*, as edited and selected by Franz Werfel and Paul Stefan; translated by Edward Downes (New York, L. B. Fischer, 1942), pp. 360–1.

formed to fit the necessities of the drama. To the accompaniment of orchestral thunder, Otello trumpets out the first magnificent stanza: four bars a to the tonic, four bars a to the key of $\flat$III, b with bounding sequences—but before he can round things off, Iago breaks in: "Do not rise yet!" Again in the tonic, Iago begins stanza 2, and we realize that Otello had not really sung the tune at all, but an upper counterpoint to it, a descant. Iago calls the tune. He sings it now: a to the tonic, a this time to the key of iii, and after b a vicious modulation interrupts for stanza 3. This they sing together, melody and descant; at last (after a shrewd extra bar in b) a free final a arrives to complete the anticipated *aaba* form. In a strophic piece, cadence is reserved for the climax of the final strophe. Formal freedom of this sort led to a new extent of expressivity in all the numbers of *Otello*. However, freedom operates not to countermand the lyric tradition, but to refine it.

Lyricism is Verdi's chief power as a dramatist; not only his chief power, but also the greatness that sets him off decisively from all his followers. Verdi's tunes and melodic phrases never reveal the fatal sentimental softness of his followers'. At worst they lapse into the hearty blankness of Donizetti, never into vulgarity, if one can except the Frenchified *brillantes* of Oscar, Preziosilla, and the like. And nothing lapses after *La Forza del destino*. It is certainly unfortunate that Bernard Shaw, in the very act of defending Verdi from the charge of Wagnerism, had to help perpetuate the equally wild libel that the late operas show "inevitable natural drying up of his spontaneity and fertility." The quality of sheer beauty in Verdi's lyricism developed as much as his awareness of its proper dramatic use. He refined his art to make each melodic phrase interesting and vital, to break away from schematic forms that checked his highly romantic genius, and to control the sumptuous flexibility of such long lyric complexes as those in the love-duet of Act I of *Otello* and the ensemble ending Act III. Here Verdi sustained larger, ever-expanding, freely evolving melodic arcs with a new emotional intensity. Perfect Wagnerites were unused to such purely melodic ambition.

4
———

THE PRELUDE to Act III is built out of the striking fragment of arioso previously heard when Iago, suddenly confidential, unctuous, and most melodious, warned of the green-eyed monster. "Beware, my lord. . .":

> *E un' idra fosca, livida,*
> *cieca, col suo veleno*
> *sè stessa attosca, vivida*
> *piaga le squarcia il seno.*

As the curtain rises and the prelude is due to end, it is interrupted by a rich quiet chord in the full brass, to which Titian hue a Herald announces the impending arrival of the Venetian Ambassadors. But Otello has no mind for affairs of state, and after he dismisses the Herald, the music of the hydra calmly returns to fulfill its interrupted cadence. When he turns to Iago and says "*continua,*" the orchestra has already indicated their subject of conversation. Coming as it does after an intermission during which Iago's poison has worked with frightful surety and the symbolic enormity of the lost handkerchief has fully dawned on Otello, the prelude acts as a specifically musical translation of the sense of "continuation" that Shakespeare obtains by starting his fourth act in the midst of a frenetic dialogue between Iago and Othello. For the moment, all that Verdi takes from Shakespeare's long scene (Act

IV, scene i) is this initial mood and the subsequent agreement to eavesdrop on Cassio's talk of Bianca. It is not really time for Otello's fit, for although Iago has told him about the handkerchief, Desdemona has not yet denied its loss. This she does in the succeeding duet *"Dio ti giocondi, o sposo,"* which combines Shakespeare's Handkerchief and Brothel Scenes (III, iv, and IV, ii). Though the compression gains smoothness and immediate force, it loses something of Shakespeare's disjunct crescendo and the credibility that goes with it.

The duet is a marvelous piece of characterization, with its binding musical recapitulation capturing exactly the horrible forced jest of Shakespeare's

> I cry you mercy then.
> I took you for that cunning whore of Venice
> That married with Othello.

Naturally, the piece is less continuously lyrical than the love-duet of Act I; but Verdi did not neglect to incorporate a passionate arioso for Desdemona, *"Mi guarda!"* again registering her feelings with un-Shakespearean completeness. As for Otello, he moves from tight-lipped civility to rage; this parallels a progress that we have already seen twice in Act II, and are to see twice more in this act, reaching a higher pitch each time and culminating in the epileptic fit. Otello now sinks into noble anguish, *"Dio! mi potevi scagliar,"* but works himself up to a fury again; at the climax of this great arioso he is spurred on by the sudden appearance of Iago announcing the presence of Cassio. This *coup de théâtre* might seem objectionable if it were more organic. The eavesdropping trio, in which Otello's asides are rationalized, is one of the finest numbers in the score, with its joshing arpeggio theme of Cassio's laughter disembodied as words escape the eavesdropper, and then transformed on a fierce diminished seventh as he recognizes the handkerchief in Cassio's hand. Certainly this is also the plainest improvement over Shakespeare's more awkward arrangement. It is an ensemble with all of Mozart's subtlety, and its ending stretto captures perfectly the sense of the handkerchief's grim, delicate, dramatic magic. "Sure there's some wonder in this handkerchief."

From this point on the action is shadowed by the splendor of Venice, and with it the image of the "lion of St. Mark," the noble Moor. Trumpet fanfares are already ironic as the noble Moor plots Desdemona's murder to their accompaniment; the subsequent choral shouts of *"Evviva Otello!"* are more profoundly so, recalling as they do Otello's first entrance after the storm, with news of his and Venice's victory. The coming of the Ambassadors had been presaged (with the brass) at the beginning of the act, and the final humiliation of Desdemona, as Boïto arranged it, was to take place in their public view. But after Otello has insulted her in front of them and thrown her to the ground, Verdi's Desdemona, instead of escaping, rises to the occasion with another long, explicit song of self-expression. In fact a huge ensemble in the old style, with seven soloists and two choruses, is constructed downwards from her superb lament.

This piece has been deprecated, and Verdi himself shortened it for the Paris production, but I find it admirably dramatic in its place. The very grandiosity of the score sets exactly the tone of vanity in the pageantry of Venice to mirror the transitory glory of the Lion, who is significantly silent. What is more, the finale provides a wonderful backdrop for Iago, whose power has been growing steadily for two acts and who now seems to control the whole ensemble. He is the one *dynamic* singer; first he arranges for the various murders with Otello, then marches across the stage to give Roderigo his orders. All this is under the spell of

Desdemona's melody, which is the more poignant for its subtle echoes of the love-duet in Act I. It was essential, in Verdi's scheme, for Desdemona to have her say. Though this blaze of sound would have made an effective curtain, Boïto passed it by for something better, and introduced Otello's fit now, at the climax of things—a stronger place for it than in Shakespeare. Iago, still in command, clears the stage as ironic cries of *"Gloria al Leon di Venezia!"* from the unknowing crowd outside, sound around Otello's prostrate body. Music and scene combine to make a suitably violent symbol of Otello's descent: the former man publicly celebrated as the noble general, while the present man is spurned beneath Iago's heel in literally insensate fury. *"Ecco il Leone!"*—and the musical equivalent of the jackass kick.

After the rapidly moving third act, Act IV seems architectural, austere. It is concerned not with Iago's intrigue and Otello's degradation, but with the grim simplicity of catastrophe. The first half of the act is effectively a monologue for Desdemona, opening with the scene in her bedroom with Emilia (Shakespeare's Act IV, scene iii), pared down to the Willow Song— the best gift a composer ever received from a literary source. As Emilia leaves, a prayer for Desdemona gives Otello time to suppose that she has fallen asleep. The second half of the act shows Otello: his entrance *di una porta segreta*, the murder, Emilia's explanation, and the suicide.

Here, for once, the composer takes less emotional stock of his man than the playwright. Nothing replaces the great poetry of Othello's final speeches in which Shakespeare and Othello try to summon up his old self; *"Niun mi tema"* is by comparison tentative in expression. In his anxiety to be "realist" and gripping, Verdi employed more and more orchestral organization: not arias or big ariosos, but long musical sections in dialogue, and passages of his most furious *parlante*, all more highly charged than usual with thematic references and development. Several motives for this use are introduced during the pantomime following Otello's entry, which I have already mentioned in a more general context, and illustrated (page 11). Otello enters making the decision, not already resolved, as Othello is in Shakespeare's great speech "It is the cause." The famous orchestral passage beginning with the double-basses follows the conflict of love and fury in Otello's spirit.

As in Shakespeare, Otello kisses the sleeping Desdemona. Verdi expanded this kiss into a major symbol; he had "planted" it with its music in Act I, at the climax of the love-duet, where it made an impression that three acts do not dim. After the fury, this music returns once more at the very end:

> I kiss'd thee ere I kill'd thee. No way but this—
> Killing myself, to die upon a kiss.

As in Verdi's conclusion neither Otello nor Lodovico speak of the past, this love-music carries the full reference to the noble Otello who is fallen now. Its repetition pulls the whole drama together with shattering pathos.

* * *

The repetition of musical fragments with some sort of symbolic intent is not unknown in early opera; examples can be found in each of Mozart's four great operas, to say nothing of Monteverdi's *Orfeo*. But thematic repetition as a dramatic technique could not realize itself until the advent of continuous opera in the nineteenth century. Recurring themes force the listener to relate one moment in the drama to another, force him to think past rigid boundaries between numbers; they are truly continuous in effect. They have been used best in the operas of Verdi and Wagner, but in ways that are very different and characteristic of each composer's individual operatic solution.

Whereas the Wagnerian leitmotive is a small, flexible figure designed for frequent detailed reference and for spinning into a complicated symphonic web, Verdi much prefers the stronger emphasis to be obtained by the climactic repetition of fuller phrases. Such effects lose their force if the music is used more than two or three times; leitmotives scarcely deserve the name unless they appear much more copiously. The phrases that Verdi repeats are usually lyric, and among his most striking melodic inspirations; Wagner uses instead flexible cellules of harmonic or rhythmic interest. And in their symbolic nature, Verdi's themes are less various and less problematic than Wagner's. Generally they do not identify persons or ideas, but recall a previous occasion in the opera, and with it the sentiment experienced there. We may say that instead of serving to remind the audience, they remind characters in the play.

As regards recurring themes in opera, Verdi learned little from his immediate predecessors, who were quite literal-minded about it. The most familiar usage was to have a group of soldiers, nuns, or revellers sing the same music on several different occasions, with the effect of self-identification rather than reminiscence. Furthermore, during scenes of "*delirio*" or "*sogno*" or "*sonnambulismo*" a demented or dreaming character often recalled previous music. The right tune might restore him (her, usually) to sanity. But since the person may be supposed actually to "hear things," this usage should also be considered literal—the literal representation of an abnormal state of mind. The best-known instance is of course the Mad Scene from *Lucia di Lammermoor*; another opera inspired by Sir Walter Scott may provide the earliest example, Rossini's *La*

Donna del lago. Though Verdi occasionally employed this cliché (luckily not in Lady Macbeth's Sleepwalking Scene, however), his best repeated themes are more genuinely imaginative. A person in his right mind is brought by the pressure of some extraordinary circumstance to remember an earlier occasion, and his feelings then. The music is used for imaginative reminiscence, and almost always in some climactic context.

Rigoletto provides the first impressive example of this technique, as of so many others in Verdi's maturing style. Four times in Act I, scene ii, Rigoletto remembers the curse of Monterone, and mutters the words "*Quel vecchio maledivami!*" to the same music. The musical phrase itself is especially apt, for all its simplicity; and I am inclined to think that much of its grisly effect stems from the fact that it is not identical, but only similar, to the actual music sung by Monterone in Act I, scene i. The phrase forms the substance of the opera's terse prelude. In Act II Monterone returns (gratuitously) to reiterate his curse, approximately; Act III makes no musical reference to this particular curse-music, but there is another link: Rigoletto ends both acts I and III with the same words and music, "*Ah, la maledizione!!*" The original title for the opera, objected to by the censor, was *La Maledizione*. Verdi seems to have formed the vague idea of using music to unify the opera around the curse—as though to spite the censor! The Italian critic Gino Roncaglia speaks of the "*tema-cardine*" in Verdi, the "hinge-theme," a recurring fragment around which the entire drama is made to revolve. Such themes are sometimes crude enough: in *Ernani*, *La Battaglia di Legnano*, and *La Forza del destino*. They are first used well in *Rigoletto* and *La Traviata*.

Indeed the central use of thematic repetition in *La Traviata* makes *Rigoletto* seem almost diffuse. In Act I, Alfredo's avowal "*Di quell' amor*" returns very surprisingly and very beautifully during the course of Violetta's aria "*Ah fors' è lui*," as she recalls the earlier moment. Then her *cabaletta* is interrupted by Alfredo actually singing the phrase under her balcony. The librettist (less obliging than he had been with *Rigoletto*) suggested no further recollections; the orchestral restatement of "*Di quell' amor*" in the final act, as Violetta reads the letter and then as she dies, was an inspiration of Verdi's. So was the exquisite modulating extension to the phrase in the latter situation. A sentimental moment, perhaps, but Violetta is just such a sentimental creature, and the drama depends on the conflict of sentimentality and reality. At least we are spared a thunderous orchestral rendition of "*Amami, Alfredo*" for the final curtain, *alla Tosca*.

In *La Traviata* the principle of thematic recurrence crossed with one of Verdi's greatest lyric techniques. Many of his finest arias consist of a section in the minor mode blossoming out into the major for a concluding period of especially striking melody. With Violetta's aria "*Ah fors' è lui*," which is in f minor, Verdi hit on the further plan of using the *maggiore* consummation as a repeating theme; the crowning passage in F major, the echo of Alfredo's phrase, is sung or played on four other occasions. Melodically analogous passages are among the most memorable in *Un Ballo in maschera* and *La Forza del destino*: "*Consentimi, signor, virtu*" in E major, sung by Amelia to end her e-minor trio with Ulrica and Riccardo, and "*deh! non m'abbandonar, pietà, pietà di me, signore*" in F♯ major, sung by Leonora to end her f♯-minor aria "*Madre, pietosa Vergine*." Both are prayers, both make great play with the beloved Italian vocal appoggiatura, typically from sixth to fifth degree, and both phrases recur elsewhere during the operas, in the orchestra. In an instance from *Aïda*, significantly, the *minore* beginning is much reduced, leaving more interest to the *maggiore* conclusion that is to recur: "*I sacri nomi*" (a♭ minor) and "*Numi, pietà*" (A♭ major).

Technically speaking, these pieces are forerunners of the music for the kiss in *Otello*, entirely orchestral though it be. Although in this case the melody is never sung by the heroine, still it clearly belongs to her. The opening *minore* section is entirely transformed, into the long orchestral passage of Otello's entry; but the wonderful sense of expansion and soaring release caused by the *maggiore* is more affecting than ever. As in *La Traviata*, Verdi here had hold of a real "hinge-theme," and seems to have been more conscious than ever of the full dramatic power latent in the device. Otello's love for Desdemona, the crux of "kiss and kill," is central to Verdi's dramatic conception in *Otello*. The musical reminiscence, a heightened reminiscence, unifies the opera musically and psychologically by a single stroke, penetrating in its grand simplicity. The technique of musical repetition in opera reaches its ultimate refinement.

In fact the only musical passage that one can compare with it is the concluding "*Liebestod*" of *Tristan und Isolde*—which is not in the spirit of the leitmotive at all, but is a large-scale repetition of the climax of a previous love-duet. Wagner is more ingenious, perhaps; he changes the aspect of the passage even in close recapitulation, and naturally he takes at least five times as long. But dramatically the "*Liebestod*" is no more masterful than the ending of *Otello*.

5

FOR more than fifty years Verdi gradually refined every element of his dramaturgy: the *parlante*, the lyric aria and duet, the repetition of lyric themes for the purpose of reminiscence, and many others that I have not attempted to trace. All of these elements are essentially in the classic tradition of opera which began with Monteverdi. It is nicely symbolic that the story of *Aïda* is actually derived from Metastasio, and that *Falstaff* finally reinstates the consciousness and clarity of Mozartian comedy. *Otello*, far from being a reflection of the Wagnerian reform, as used to be said, is more relevantly a fulfillment of Rossini's venture at the beginning of the century. By the time that Verdi came to compose *Otello*, his control of dramatic technique and his sensibility in dealing with a momentary situation would seem to have been sufficient for any end that he might have had in view.

Verdi brought traditional opera to its perfection; but as a dramatist, of course, he was entirely a man of the nineteenth century. In basic dramatic conception, *Otello* is as different from Shakespeare's *Othello* as it is in the matter of dramaturgy. Knowing Shakespeare, we may not entirely like this conception, but we shall have to admit its characteristic romanticism, and admire its directness, consistency, and force.

Let us see how Verdi treated the three main characters and their interrelationship. Iago is the clearest case; he was altered from Shakespeare's very complicated human being into that perennial operatic standby Mephistopheles. Or one can say that the Mephistophelian quality that Goethe discerned in Iago was magnified and almost everything else abandoned. As with all the people in the opera, Iago's talk and action is beautifully characterized; but, as usual, our strongest impression of him comes from his "numbers," in particular his tremendous soliloquy. Though Iago's theology is somewhat muddled in the words of his "Credo," the music strikes unequivocally the tone of blasphemous bravado proper to the Black Mass. Iago's Drinking Song recalls Mephistopheles in Auerbach's cellar, and minor corroboration is found in certain un-Shakespearean references elsewhere: *"Ti spinge il tuo dimone / e il tuo dimon son io"*; *"aiuta Sàtana il mio cimento!"* Boïto, composer of *Mefistofele*, wished to call this opera *Iago*. The simplification of Iago's personality actually relieved him of the whole vexatious matter of motivation.

Perhaps no nineteenth-century Italian could have been satisfied with innocent Desdemona, and the transformation of her role must have been even more deliberate. Expanding her role meant making her more articulate. The first surprise is at her first appearance, in the love-duet of Act I. Desdemona sings without any reserve on an equal plane with her Otello; they share and echo each other's phrase, music, and sentiment. It was clever of Boïto to have incorporated here some information about Othello's wooing; but it is very different to have Othello give this information to the Duke when accused of sorcery, than to have the husband and wife reminiscing about it intimately and sympathetically together. In fact I can scarcely credit the one remark of Iago's telling us that Verdi's couple are newly wed. As in the original Italian *novella* by Giraldi Cinthio (which Verdi incidentally seems to have known something about), they must have been happily married for some time. Otello cannot be significantly older than his wife, though to be sure she must be older than Shakespeare's girl; there has been nothing "unnatural" about the match; there is no reason for Otello to be black.

As the opera continues, Desdemona becomes more and more mature, conscious, articulate, and (practically) indignant. Her complaints in the great ensembles of acts II and III are expressions of one who feels a hurt and faces it. In her discussions with Otello, the strong note of passion and resentment may not be apparent from the libretto, with its deceptively close translation of Shakespeare's "is't possible? . . . is't true? . . . In sooth, you are to blame . . . I understand a fury in your words . . . Alas, what ignorant sin have I committed?" and so on. But it is apparent from the accent that music, doing the actor's work, supplies to these exclamations. And at the end of the incomparable "Willow Song," that incomparable cry of "*Ah! Emilia, addio!*" comes from a person who lives through her emotions in style. Verdi's Desdemona is a creature of the colorful and not notably innocent romantic Renaissance of Symonds, De Sanctis, and Gabriele d'Annunzio; she is as capable of adultery as she is of passion in the grand manner.

Meanwhile the expansion of her role led, perhaps less deliberately, to a cutting-down of Othello. I have indicated how his nobility, as well as his degradation, is conveyed by the powerful structure of Verdi's Act III; but over the four acts this nobility is not so convincing, in the absence of so many of Shakespeare's safeguards—the Venetian act, for instance, which solidly grounds the personality of the tragic hero, and the pedestal erected for Othello by Shakespeare's Desdemona. Most critically, at the end, Verdi sacrificed the tragedy of Otello for the pathos of Desdemona. So much attention is directed towards her that Otello cannot be allowed to recall his former self in any capacity save that of a lover. His love is recaptured and even intensified; the repetition of the music associated with the kiss is the most eloquent passage in the opera. But this music is as much Desdemona's as Otello's, and in the great wave of pity for her we are left in doubt about our man. The grave postscript of Lodovico is missed here, as is also any other echo of the State.

Finally, the conception of the hero suffers because,

throughout, Otello finds it so hard to control his emotions. From the time he quiets the drunken brawl, one is uneasy about his temper; Shakespeare's

> Now by heaven
> My blood begins my safer guides to rule

may be a portent, but Verdi takes it as a stage direction and writes it in the music. The orchestral passage at Otello's entrance in the last act represents his irresolution and instability. True, Othello is one of the most emotional of Shakespeare's tragic protagonists. He is also the most volatile of Verdi's tenors, in his least artificial opera, and that is too much.

Verdi's instinct was to transfer more and more of the play to Desdemona, and fitfully she was made to occupy the center of things at Iago's, and especially at Otello's, expense. But in this Verdi was actually hindered by his close reliance on Shakespeare. Desdemona's actions, or rather her lack of actions, no longer match the person whose maturity and spirit are set forth by the musical expression. Especially in the murder scene we have an anachronistically Shakespearean Desdemona; the notable rhythm of her growth in adversity is arrested here. For that matter, Otello in his Shakespearean role as "executioner" is also rather unconvincing, for the record of his tragic fall is weakened both before and after. If we cannot believe unflinchingly in Othello's greatness the relevance of the drama becomes problematic; Desdemona's relationship with Othello becomes more trivial, and Iago's virtuosity loses its terrible force. Yet this Iago is ostensibly the Fiend himself.

In *Otello*, Verdi glances forward to the *verismo* theater as surely as he peers backward to the Elizabethan. His deepest instinct of all, I suspect, was to make something more understandable and naturalistic than Shakespeare's cryptic tragedy. Like many students of Shakespeare, Boïto and Verdi seem to have wished to harmonize the irrationalities in the play. No other Shakespeare tragedy can show so lively a critical history, in the range of repulsion, attraction, perplexity, and exasperation recorded over its web of conflicting meanings. But all critics except the most exasperated admit the deep center of truth that Shakespeare has touched and half released. The motivations of evil, the tragic contradictions latent in nobility, the ambiguity of innocence, the cruelty of coincidence—it is hard to know where we can sense these more profoundly than in *Othello*. Verdi's opera does not present exactly such insights, or raise such drastic questions, or cause such a thrilling strain on the artistic imagination. Boïto was careful to explain, in his last few lines, the etymology of Des–demona, Shakespeare's "ill-starr'd wench":

Pia crëatura nata sotto maligna stella.

It is the evil star and the fallen angel that cause the havoc; this is dramatically candid and at the same time reassuring. Verdi has written the "credible" *Othello*, the drama to appease (yes, and to vindicate) Thomas Rymer and his friends. Motives are brought to the surface, sympathies are clearly directed; the central action has been aereated as thoroughly as the foul imagery of Iago, the jibes of Othello in the Brothel Scene, and even one innocent line of the "Willow Song." Verdi's is a decorous, rationalized, powerfully romantic *Othello*.

6
___

THE SENSE of a total drama—in this Verdi's development was neither so constant nor so instinctively certain as in his dramaturgy and his sensibility to person and situation. So much depended on lucky chance with the librettists; and Verdi seems never to have worried them enough. It is true that his letters to the librettists are full of trenchant corrections, firm demands, and excellent suggestions. But these are never fundamental enough, and never touch the central failures of each of the works between *La Traviata* and *Otello*. *Les Vêpres siciliennes*, *Simon Boccanegra*, *Un Ballo in maschera*, *La Forza del destino*, *Don Carlo*—let us forget *Aroldo*—are works that the connoisseur wants to hear again and again, but he can hardly blame the public for stinting its interest. Not one of these operas makes a satisfactory dramatic whole, and the man in the balcony can readily tell you why. Why Verdi allowed himself to set such librettos is another question. That he was a mature artist is excellently clear from countless musical and dramatic details; he was a man in his forties and fifties, famous, wealthy enough, who could afford to insist. He had time, for he was composing only one piece every three or four years. Indeed he spent time rewriting no fewer than three of these operas some years after their original performances— almost a tacit admission of failure. But he was no more thoroughgoing in his revisions than in his original efforts. The pieces were never improved enough.

Rigoletto, in spite of lapses, has an old-fashioned consistency and fire about it, thanks largely to the splendidly operatic play by Victor Hugo. One feels that Verdi's sensibility at the time was exactly suited to the play. *Rigoletto* in 1851 was far and away his most original work, a decisive stage in his evolution, as I have already suggested. Yet its success did not stop Verdi from glorifying the bad old style two years later in *Il Trovatore*, a magnificent demonstration of unprincipled melodrama. Yet—in the same year *La Traviata* turned out to be one of his most homogeneous and meaningful dramatic works. It has been suggested that this particular libretto may have had secret significance for the composer, whose liaison with the good Giuseppina, not yet regularized, was scandalizing the countryfolk of Busseto. Was *La Traviata* perhaps the one opera prior to *Otello* that Verdi really thought deeply through? The succeeding operas, as the man in the balcony knows, contain arias, scenes, and whole acts that make most (not all) of *La Traviata* seem childish: the scene on the heath in *Un Ballo in maschera*; the Prologue even in the early (1857) *Simon Boccanegra*, and the magnificent Council Scene by Boïto in the later (1881) version; the duets between Don Alvaro and Don Carlo in *La Forza del destino*; the entire third act and much more in *Don Carlo*. But none of these works has a genuine dramatic focus, as *Rigoletto* and especially *La Traviata* have. None of them can be taken seriously as *dramma per musica*, or ever has been.

The last opera before Verdi's collaboration with Boïto, in the revised *Simon Boccanegra* and in *Otello* and *Falstaff*, was the carefully planned Egyptian grand opera *Aïda*. *Aïda* is a special case. It has a good libretto, with a simple, credible, clearly shaped plot and all motives accounted for. In fact, it has recently been discovered to be a Metastasian plot—this is a real curiosity of operatic history: it stems from Metastasio's *Nitteti*.* The stiff conflicts of love and patriotism, the exoticism, the princes, priests, warriors, and disguised slaves are all delightfully typical of the schematic drama of the eighteenth century. But unfortunately this was exactly the wrong sort of "good libretto" for Verdi, who was striking out into unformalized, immediate, present-day emotions and approaching the psychological precision of the spoken

* See F. Pérez de la Vega, *La Prosapia de Aida* (Mexico City, 1950), or (more accessibly) *Opera News*, vol. 20, no. 8, Dec. 26, 1955.

play. "Real" life, "realist" life, will not fit into so conventionalized a separation of deeds and feelings; you
might as well give Bertolt Brecht the plot of *The
School for Scandal*. The result in *Aïda* is, in my opinion, an almost constant disparity between the particular
glib simplicity of the libretto and the alarming complexity of the musical expression—for of course Verdi's
technique had never been so rich. Only Amneris comes
to life; Aïda is thoroughly confused; Rhadames seems
like a throwback, if not to Metastasio, at least to Rossini. It goes without saying that some pages, numbers,
and scenes are beyond praise, reason enough for this
opera's great popularity. Nevertheless, there is a curious falsity about *Aïda* which is quite unlike Verdi,
and which recalls Meyerbeer more disturbingly than
the grand-opera apparatus of triumphs, consecrations,
and brass bands.

I would not hesitate to give Boïto much credit for
the unparalleled dramatic unity of *Otello* and *Falstaff*.
The poor man never had the musical art to compose
Iago's "Credo," which malicious whisperers actually
claimed was his, but on the other hand, Verdi had
never before exerted the dramatic control shown in
Otello. The credit of course is irrelevant; the important
thing is that between them Boïto and Verdi took the
only course that could lead to success: they fashioned
Shakespeare to suit Verdi. The dramatist is the composer. They did not leave *Othello* as Shakespeare left
it, or press it into a Metastasian mold. The dramatic
figures and the dramatic conflicts were translated into
nineteenth-century figures and conflicts that Verdi
could grasp and bring to life. In this opera Verdi seems
to have been working with a sense of aesthetic honesty
which can only be compared with that involved in *La
Traviata*. By now, however, his dramatic technique
was altogether prodigious.

Shakespeare provides a severe enough context in

which to view the integrity of opera as a dramatic form. Verdi's *Otello* is in fact a unique, independent transformation of the play, both in exterior form and in underlying conception. As to form, Verdi and Boïto made an ingenious, flexible, powerful compromise between the demands of the lyric tradition and strong new pressures for a more literary flow in opera. As to the basic dramatic conception—if this appears, perhaps, limited, let us at least understand that such limitations are not due to any "necessities" in the medium of musical drama. Verdi himself kept defeating limitations, as is especially evident from his last opera, *Falstaff*, composed six years after *Otello*, when he was 79. The musical technique is further refined in extraordinary ways, but it is the dramatic sensitivity, principally, which is so much more subtle than before, so much more conscious and clear. In his greatest and most paradoxical masterpiece, Verdi transcended Shakespeare as emphatically as, forty years before, he had fallen short in *Macbeth*. Opera is not necessarily blunter than literary forms. If more evidence is wanted, we have it in the great operas of Mozart, Mussorgsky, Wagner, Alban Berg, and Stravinsky. And in *Pelléas et Mélisande;* an opera which not only preserves the subtleties of a play written first for the spoken theater, but which also justifies and deepens them all.

REFORM

*

6

Opera as Sung Play

Fʀᴏᴍ certain works of art, we get the impression of an almost magical convergence of the artist and the subject matter: from the *Iliad* and from *Don Giovanni*, according to Kierkegaard. This impression is certainly too strong to be denied, even though we recognize that the formulation treats clumsily the whole complicated question of the artist's spirit in relation to artistic content and form. For unfortunately no amount of passionate sympathy for the theme can automatically solve the artist's basic formal problem. Kierkegaard's mistake—a philosopher's mistake—was to view in isolation a content which is actually definable only in terms of its formal realization; his regard for *Don Giovanni* was based on little understanding of Mozart's drama as such. To make possible the ultimate success, the subject matter must match the opera composer's dramatic vision and technique, as well as his temperament, his time, and his particular musical powers. Some such matching accounts for the special incandescence of *The Magic Flute*, of Gluck's *Orfeo*, of *Tristan und Isolde*, *Boris Godunov*, and *Wozzeck*, as well as for the limited glow of a work like *La Bohème*.

With operas derived from plays, the aesthetic problem becomes even more involved; for in question are not only the artist's predilection and operatic form and subject matter, but also the prior work of art which molds the subject matter from another standpoint. In *Otello* Verdi tended to ignore that previous synthesis, though doubtless this opera is his "ideal" work in any case: here at last, we may say, Verdi dealt centrally and at the height of his dramatic awareness with jealousy, the theme that haunted him in *Ernani*, *Il Trovatore*, *La Traviata*, *Un Ballo in maschera*, *Aïda*, and later in *Falstaff*. But in *Pelléas et Mélisande* Debussy ignored no aspect of Maurice Maeterlinck's prior literary effort. Of all the ingenious, fortunate, magic convergences in the history of opera, *Pelléas* is surely the most extraordinary. The composer found his unique material not in an idea or in a literary source which he then bent to his use, but complete in the model play. What struck Debussy was not merely the story of Pelléas and Mélisande, or any idea about it, but Maeterlinck's whole system of aesthetics and metaphysics as embodied in the play.

This fact explains the very unusual relationship between the opera and the play, a relationship altogether different from that between Verdi's *Otello* and Shakespeare's *Othello*. The play is enveloped whole into the opera—literally so: there is no separate libretto; Debussy took the playwright's scenes just as he found them, with scrupulously few cuts. He never expanded the sentiment of a moment into an aria or a "*Liebestod*," or changed the dramatic tempo into something more convenient for a musician, or constructed strong musical forms to counterpoint literary ones. The whole play is set in reticent declamation over a shadowy musical continuum; the word, the literary element, is humbly preserved. At no point did Debussy transform the play musically, as Verdi did when he came to set *Othello*, to say nothing of *Macbeth* or *The Merry Wives*. Music supports the play, never trying to do more than clarify it or make it more vivid or credible. *Pace* Maeterlinck, the play is all there, in its own essential literary terms.

Debussy did not construct elaborate theories of operatic reform, but the radical nature of his method may be apparent already. In his opera, the primary dramatic articulation is literary rather than musical— in contradiction to the principle repeated so many times in the course of this study. To put it another way: when Debussy found his ideal material in Maeterlinck's play, his solution to the opera composer's "basic formal problem" was quite simply to keep that play in its literary form. The delicate question of operatic continuity and literary flow, which had preoccupied Verdi, was resolved in a way that would have horrified Verdi. Debussy's extreme method has had as profound an effect on later operatic dramaturgy as Wagner's almost diametrically opposed method. Wagner and Debussy, in fact, may be said to stand at opposite poles of the celebrated nineteenth-century operatic "reform."

Now it is something of a simplification to speak as though Maeterlinck's *Pelléas et Mélisande* inspired Debussy's operatic scheme. That is only one side of the story. This play, and only this play, made Debussy into an opera composer; yet it is also true that before he had read Maeterlinck he had formulated an operatic ideal closely prophetic of his actual procedure with *Pelléas et Mélisande*. But without the right inspiration, the ideal would have remained theory. In connection with Monteverdi's *Orfeo* I had reason to suggest two good ways of looking at the opera composer's relationship to his text. The text brings out or directs latent tendencies which the composer could not otherwise have realized—in the beginning the libretto is the inspiration. On the other hand, the composer brings his particular powers and ideals to the text, and can only succeed with such elements in it as really suit him—in the end the libretto is the limitation. What is so remarkable is that no elements in this play failed to suit Debussy's particular, unusual, limited powers.

That Debussy could find any play at all amenable to his operatic ideal is remarkable enough. The peculiarities of Maeterlinck's *Pelléas et Mélisande* that allow, even encourage Debussy's peculiar method also explain the quality of the opera. For in a sense, the opera *is* the play. With this opera, for once, the right critical procedure is to enter into the "libretto" first, by itself, and only then to approach the music.

2

MAETERLINCK'S Mélisande is a mysterious, beautiful young creature who suffers quietly, asks nothing, and never acts. On men she exerts an inexorable fascination: Maeterlinck and Debussy, it seems, are as susceptible as Golaud and young Pelléas, and their grandfather Arkel the old King of Allemonde. They know nothing of her past beyond what is evoked by a golden crown sunk in a well. Golaud first comes upon her weeping by the well while he is lost on a hunting trip in a great forest; fascinated by her, he brings her home as bride—for Mélisande has no will to resist. Yet he knows that he can never penetrate into her consciousness or share her special intuition of reality. Gradually, without the faintest impetus on either side, Mélisande becomes romantically involved with Pelléas, who is as innocent of will or conscience as she is herself. Golaud finds that she has lost her wedding ring; he comes upon her with Pelléas in a possibly compromising situation; he warns Pelléas off and tries crudely to eavesdrop on one of their silent meetings. There is nothing to do, for the young lovers move, or rather, continue to exist, as though in a dream. Golaud reaches the point at which he swings Mélisande back and forth by her hair, locks the two of them out of the castle, and, on discovering their tryst, kills Pelléas. Mélisande receives some sort of wound on this occasion, and later she dies too, after childbirth, forgiving, but explaining nothing. She makes no attempt, indeed she can conceive of no attempt, to communicate with the now penitent and crushed Golaud.

Stripped of its shadowy motivations and accomplishments, this is an oddly conventional plot, recalling the French tradition of bourgeois melodrama; so does the manner of its construction. The *crescendo* is faultlessly well made. Act I clears up the exposition, ending with the most delicate intimation of interest between Mélisande and her new brother-in-law. Act II charts the beginning and the end of the first real incident, the loss of Golaud's ring in a second well, "Blindman's Well," while Mélisande is with Pelléas. Act III shows more serious, but still not quite unequivocal, intimacies; only by Act IV do the lovers recognize their situation and arrange the meeting that leads to their death. The progress of Golaud's attitude is even more carefully arranged. The action of Act I subtly suggests his constitutional incompatibility with Mélisande, which is then expressed in Act II by unformed premonitions of trouble. We learn that Golaud's horse

shied psychically at the moment of the dropping of
the ring; when Golaud notices its absence from Mélisande's finger he becomes irrationally angry, but
ironically sends her out to seek it with Pelléas. Faced
with the facts of Act III, Golaud first tries to shrug
them off as mere adolescent games, but then betrays a
subconscious wish to attack Pelléas when they are alone
in the castle vaults. After warning Pelléas in an older-
brotherly fashion, Golaud shows (or shows farther) the
ugly side of his personality in his frustrated eavesdropping with the child Yniold. Brutality and murder
mark Golaud in Act IV.

Now all these characters can be rationalized, as
Golaud keeps trying to rationalize Mélisande. But to
do so is to misinterpret Maeterlinck entirely; Golaud's
attempt is a signal irony of the play. Maeterlinck's
main idea is the dominance of gentle, irrational fate,
and he expresses it with Wagnerian fanaticism on every
possible level: the plot, characterization, dramaturgy,
symbolism, imagery, and diction. Mélisande is the "heroine" because intuitively she grasps and accepts the
conditions of fatality, offering no vain resistance. She
goes with Golaud, drops the ring, accepts the beating,
and lets the love-affair run its fateful course. Old Arkel
preaches a wise resignation grown out of long experience of the pointlessness of life, will, and action. If
by mistake he does allow himself to do anything, it
invariably works out for the worst. Golaud is the "villain" because he will not accept this view of life
(though he seems not unaware of it). He is the one
person who acts: he hunts, complains of the famine,
inspects the foundations of the castle, and struggles to
save his marriage. Golaud's main effort is to understand and rationalize Mélisande—to comprehend the
incomprehensible, to rationalize irrational fate. His actions, all thoroughly frustrated, lead to more misery
than anyone else's. In Act V he is a broken man, and

by his standards genuinely penitent, but ironically he pursues his quest for understanding up to the very moment of Mélisande's death agony. The experience has brought him no closer to Mélisande or to a true acceptance of fate. Golaud will still fight; that is Maeterlinck's supreme irony.

The pointlessness of action is a paradoxical theme for dramatic treatment, to say the least. It defeated Maeterlinck, I think, but not before he had worked furiously to create the illusion of purposelessness on every level within a secretly purposeful dramatic frame. Pointlessness is expressed by details of dramaturgy as well as by the overall scheme of well-made plot for nebulous matter. Each of the short scenes gets something done, but their effect is of a "slice of life" with a drabness and incoherence characteristic enough of ordinary living. Naturalism was well suited to Maeterlinck's stratagem, for actual life *is* undirected, at least in its details: persons do not ordinarily sustain action in a properly dramatic fashion. Hence Maeterlinck's famous evaporating lines of thought, his *non sequiturs,* understatements, silences, and absent-minded scene-endings. (He is disingenuously absent-minded about Geneviève, who silently drops out of the play unnoticed after Act I.) The scenes are carefully arranged to appear to follow one another haphazardly, but actually they contribute to the whole by a sort of *montage* method. Indeed the plot as a whole, as I have described it, is a good deal less original than the detailed technique.

Maeterlinck's wish for an apparently powerless surface hiding great dramatic pressures led him naturally to heavy symbolism and imagery. The play is hugely symbolic, of course. These bourgeois figures with their conventional triangle represent universal life in the fairy-tale Kingdom of "All-the-World"; Maeterlinck could only get to the universal through the fourth wall.

Every detail—a child looking for his ball—is invested with a grandiose significance which plays in to the main theme. The little deeds and situations, seemingly nonchalant, have been sifted and gathered together with relentless care. Dreamlike, they all reflect the general frustration. Emotion itself is futile; so the diction is as egregiously plain as everyday French conversation. In spite of this, the dialogue is made to carry an enormous amount of imagery, cleverly arranged to appear "natural" by the involvement of items that are literally close at hand—the dark forests, infinite caves, vanishing ships in fog, and dark stirring wells. Maeterlinck's "poetic prose" is as densely imagistic as most verse, and this imagery, perhaps more strongly than anything else, makes palpable the central vision of fatality. Makes it palpable as a *mood*, which is almost "musical" already. Yet at no point does anyone utter a poetic word beyond ordinary emotional proprieties.

By now we are in a position to understand the uncanny appropriateness of this play to this composer— to Debussy the musician as he actually was, and to Debussy the theorist with his ideal of opera as sung play. Poetic prose was precisely suited to someone as sensitive to prosody as Debussy, who hated to tamper with the precious accents of French prose, let alone verse. Highly rhythmic diction is necessarily transformed when musical setting superimposes musical rhythms. But music does not destroy verbal imagery; it can support it, as already the madrigalists and Bach and, most recently, Wagner had demonstrated. So while the play did not embarrass Debussy with verse rhythms, which he could only have ignored or distorted, it did supply a mass of rich, "poetic" images for musical development. Dark forests and vanishing ships—these could be presented to the musical ear; and it is exactly such effects that Debussy knew how to manage so wonderfully. *La Mer, Jardins sous la pluie, La Cathédrale engloutie, Voiles, Brouillards* and the rest are evoked superbly in his instrumental compositions, again and again. What Debussy does with external objects or scenes is capture the moods that they convey. So does the impressionist painter, for all his naturalism. So does Maeterlinck, who is not interested in the genus of the trees or the velocity of the ships, but in the feelings they can stir, poetically, in the audience. Debussy's dramatic method matches Maeterlinck's; impressionism is primary.

And this primacy of mood is crucial. In the play, the sense of fatality is projected first by dialogue and action, which Debussy left alone, and second—more strongly—by the poetically induced mood. Debussy could induce mood better than Maeterlinck or anyone else. By abandoning himself to mood-painting, his greatest strength, Debussy not only preserved Maeterlinck's guiding dramatic conception, but deepened it in directions unknown to verbal imagery.

How hard it is to imagine Debussy writing any other opera! His subsequent search for a second libretto seems somehow fantastic. Unlike most of the other opera composers discussed in this book, Debussy was not a man of the theater at all. He came to opera from the outside, fastidious and high-minded, making no quick concessions and asking no quick success. Gluck and Wagner could afford such idealism only after years of humdrum practice; Verdi, again, would never have understood. *Pelléas et Mélisande* was Debussy's one serious operatic attempt, and he fussed over it for a decade. And nurtured a hothouse flower, with all the incredible perfection, the isolation, and the exquisite arbitrariness characteristic of the genre. But not every hothouse product can bear the outside air so well—the cold draught of the theater, and the moving current of time.

3
―――――

A LITERARY form of drama continuously supported by
music; this brings to mind the classicizing experiments
of the Florentine *camerata* at the end of the sixteenth
century, and indeed, Greek drama itself. Peri, Caccini,
and, a little later, Monteverdi formed an ideal of
musical declamation on the musical translation of the
diction of a great actor. And as one tries to define the
actual dramatic function of Debussy's declamation, one
can put it in the same terms: music fixes the inflection
at every point, doing the actor's work. More purely,
perhaps, than anyone else's recitative, Debussy's follows the cadence of the momentary word, as a great
actor might be imagined to speak it, without any aspiration to purely musical coherence.

The difference between Debussy and the earliest
opera composers in this respect comes simply from
their utterly different concepts of what constitutes
great acting. For Monteverdi, acting meant a highly
stylized, affective, passionate, exaggerated delivery, and
so his recitative tried to capture the inflections of great
heroes at points of emotional extremity. For Debussy
and Maeterlinck, good acting was essentially naturalistic; for all its symbolism, the play purports to record
the quiet, reserved dialogue of contemporary life. Debussy tried to catch literally the accents of French day-
by-day speech, and in his understated way certainly
succeeded as well as Monteverdi.

His vocal line is a delicate, murmuring thing, with
much monotone recitation, few sudden rhythms, an
ordinary range of very few notes, and a horror of
strongly emotional melodic intervals. By means of
the slightest deviations of pitch and rhythm, Debussy's line indicates precisely how the speaker raises his

voice, hastens his speech, hesitates, allows himself a touch of feeling, and then lapses into polite emotional anonymity. Almost all these inflections, be it noted, stem subtly from the speaker's subconscious. The result in *Pelléas et Mélisande* is quite exquisite—if sometimes as slick as the original dialogue itself; for Maeterlinck's shadowy quality does not obscure his reliance on conventional nineteenth-century dramaturgy. In Act II, scene ii, for instance, where Golaud questions Mélisande about her sudden unmotivated tears, the pacing of her answers is almost too ingeniously controlled by the composer. Golaud's first general inquiries are met by slow, halting replies, separated from his questions by rests in the music. Characteristically, Golaud the realist then suggests that it must be some person who has made her unhappy; and from the speed of her answering "no's" he seems to sense that he is right. Is it the King, or Geneviève—or Pelléas? only now does Mélisande answer "no," practically on top of his last note; the rhythmic arrangement speaks guilty haste. Next Golaud asks whether she wants to leave him, and again, in the rapidity and intensity of her denial, Mélisande betrays feelings of which she herself is not fully aware, perhaps. In the play, it would take a certain intelligence on the part of actress or director to bring this out. With Debussy's setting, they cannot go wrong.

More poetic is the conception of Golaud's speech a moment later as he tries to comfort Mélisande. "Can you not fall in with the life we lead here? Is it too sad here? True, this castle is very old and somber, cold and deep, and all who live here are already old . . ." The rich sober lyricism of the vocal line reveals suddenly that Golaud too feels the oppressive gloom of the Castle of All-the-World. That is his tragic predicament; though by no means insensitive to the pathos of existence, he tries vainly, ironically, to combat it.

If Golaud were all *petit bourgeois* there would be less play. Once again, the delivery of a great actor would achieve this central fact of Golaud's character. Debussy guarantees the result.

In spite of all Maeterlinck's attention to dialogue, however, dialogue is not his primary tool; nor is declamation Debussy's primary dramatic means. The main thing is the mood which defines the encompassing sense of fatality. What dense imagery does for the poet, background music does for the composer, both in general, and also in a detailed manner which is in close analogy to a literary technique. Indeed Debussy's orchestral web beneath his naturalistic dialogue is the element that rescues his opera from the stony ideal of sung play. Deliberately, I am sure.

Generally, pervasively, ever-changingly, the orchestral continuum in *Pelléas et Mélisande* fixes with great exactitude the unforgettable emotional atmosphere. This continuum is an imponderable thing compared with that of Verdi in the late operas, for example. With Debussy, nothing very much coheres musically, in the mysterious succession of fragmentary motives (some of them leitmotives) and brief figures which are too slight to be felt as motivic; of half-articulated progressions and waiting chords; of rustling *ostinatos* and quiet sections of suddenly striking, iridescent orchestral color. The mood is all, and the mood is trapped perfectly. It may be hard to do critical justice to the musical effects discovered by Debussy during the present time of their vulgarization; but the vulgarizations will lose their force, and time will show again the beauty of Debussy's own use of "impressionistic" musical devices. In time his highly original attempts to organize purely musical forms will also become clearer. But that is another matter, and one that does not concern *Pelléas et Mélisande*. Here Debussy never wished to organize his music so strongly that it would make a full emotional effect in itself. Music suggests, and so supports the play.

By means of musical interludes flowing in and out of Maeterlinck's brief scenes, Debussy linked the scenes all together within the acts. (The first two acts contain three scenes each, the next four, the next really four; Act V is a single scene.) This procedure, of course, significantly preserves and deepens the mood, for the audience is allowed no let-down between the scenes, as they are in the play. To be sure, the composers of *Otello* and *Tristan und Isolde* also hold the audience's attention despotically through whole acts—but only by arranging those acts as single long scenes; this artificiality of construction was foreign to Maeterlinck's naturalism and to his paradoxical dramatic depiction of the purposelessness of action. Wagner, when he used orchestral interludes between scenes, often demanded a "transformation" before your very eyes; characteristically, he wanted to impress the eye as well as the ear . . . the darkened theater is especially impressive in *Pelléas et Mélisande*. In Debussy's interludes, the music naturally comes as close as it ever does to speaking in its own terms. Its reticence is still great, and it concentrates on the dramatic task of modulating the mood from one scene to the next.

For each scene may be said to have its own subtle variant of the overall mood. This is another delicate addition of the composer's. Each scene employs an individual theme which is all its own, and which tends to set it off from the others. Often the theme is introduced during the prelude or interlude prior to the scene, recurs to mark a few notable points in the action, grows with it, and closes the scene as the curtain falls. I am frankly uncertain as to how much real organization Debussy meant to establish by means

of these motives. At best it seems slight, and at worst
esoteric. Act I, scene ii, the Letter Scene, is in every
way the filmiest in the opera; it is bounded by an un-
obtrusive set of sixteenth-note arpeggios on wind instruments, heard only at the very start and at the very
end of the scene. In the next scene, however, when the
lovers first come together, the "organizing theme" is a
clear one, haunting and tender:

Permission to reprint excerpts from Debussy's PELLÉAS ET MÉLISANDE
granted by Durand & Cie., Paris, France, copyright owners.
Elkan-Vogel Co., Inc., Philadelphia, Pennsylvania, Agents.

This recurs many times, often on a solo violin. The
fact that it is a variant of the chief leitmotive of the
opera does not alter its function in this scene as a
kind of musical mortar. The leitmotive as such has
not yet established itself in the listener's mind, and
only in retrospect can it possibly be related to the
love of Pelléas and Mélisande.

If musical organization is at its most unsubstantial
and theoretical in the Letter Scene, it is most defi-
nite in Act IV, scene iii, the scene of the child Yniold.
Here the music actually starts to congeal, motivically
and rhythmically; if any part of the opera could stand
by itself and make sense without the words, this would
be it. The musical certainty corresponds to the unproblematic, touchingly certain world of the child, as
contrasted with the frustration of the adults. But even
here, characteristically, the musical organization soon
peters out, and as poor Yniold gets lost like all his
elders, his music becomes less and less coherent. All
that remains at the end is a mournful inversion of
what had been a fairly optimistic motive:

One dramatic purpose is to extend the range of help-
lessness: age (Arkel), graying maturity (Golaud),
youth (Pelléas and Mélisande), and now childhood
(Yniold, who cannot retrieve his golden ball behind
the great rock—"it is heavier than me"; who cannot
understand where the sheep are being conducted,
though it is certainly not to the stable—"where will
they sleep tonight?"; who cannot quite grasp his own
sensations—"I shall go and tell someone something
about it. . . ." At the last minute Maeterlinck even
managed to add infancy, conveniently provided by
Mélisande's new baby, to his chain of the ages. "Now
it is the turn of the poor little one" is Arkel's final
apothegm). Yniold's scene serves another dramatic
purpose by relieving the tension between the castiga-
tion of Mélisande and the climax of the lovers' tryst
and the murder. Most appropriately, the music all but
gains contour, a lyric interlude between two intense
scenes.

In addition to themes whose main function is to
organize scenes, *Pelléas et Mélisande* contains leitmotives essentially in the Wagnerian tradition—short
flexible fragments recurring very many times, associated with a person, an idea, or a mood. Even more

clearly than the cluttered operas of Wagner, *Pelléas*
reveals the analogy between the musical leitmotive and
the poetic image or, more precisely, the recurring image used many times. Maeterlinck's play is fairly loaded
with such recurring images, which gather force as the
piece proceeds. To mention only one: the half-peaceful,
half-sinister image of the blind man, *l'aveugle*. Ironically, wise Arkel is nearly blind, and the lovers' meeting-
place is called "Blindman's Well," though it no longer
heals blindness. In Act II, scene ii, Golaud says that
his horse shied like a blind man (but which of them
was blind?); in Act III, scene iv, he cries out that he is
like a blind man seeking his treasure at the bottom of
the ocean; in Act IV, scene iv, Pelléas compares himself
to a blind man fleeing his burning home; in Act V
Golaud says that he is going to die as a blind man.
At the first mention of the word, its effect may be
slight, but at each successive repetition the listener
half-consciously recalls all the others, so that rich associations and inter-associations are set up in the
imagination. Add to the image of blindness all the
related images: the ship disappearing into the fog,
Mélisande's eyes which never close, the darkness which
descends on Yniold and his sheep, and so on and so
on—painstakingly the poet evokes a pervasive sense of
the blindness of humanity in the face of binding fate.

A leitmotive acts like a recurring image, with this
difference: that whereas the verbal symbol has some
specific meaning, however limited, at its first appearance, the musical symbol has at best mood, and can
only absorb conceptual meaning by association. This
is something that Debussy understood better than
Wagner, and he arranged his leitmotives to clarify
themselves very gradually in the consciousness. As an
example we may take the most prominent leitmotive in
Pelléas et Mélisande, usually spoken of as "the theme
of Mélisande"—a frightful simplification, for the mean-

ing of a leitmotive is nothing less (or more) than the whole complex of all the associations, dramatic and musical, that attach to its every appearance. Analysts may point to the motive in the prelude before Act I, scene i, but it has little symbolic significance there. Later the listener may realize, perhaps as he hears the variant that organizes Act I, scene iii (quoted on page 184), that this musical idea has been with him from the start. Perhaps he notes that the sad little wisp of melody is completely absent from the one half-happy scene in the work, the one in which the lovers meet at the well (Act II, scene i). But only in the next scene does Debussy come forward with the leitmotive in a fairly emphatic way. After Mélisande has comforted Golaud for his hunting accident, Maeterlinck makes a sudden *non sequitur* as she begins to cry for no apparent reason. It is a moment of some dramatic force, and Debussy introduces it by a self-conscious pause, during which the motive sounds all alone in the orchestra:

The motive has to do with the sadness that accompanies Mélisande and spreads to everyone who deals with her. It is used impressionistically, not literally. With many telling melodic and rhythmic modifications it grows imperceptibly in the succeeding scenes; most impressive is its transformation into the measured knell of Act V:

Of course Debussy cannot have expected every shade
to be evident in the theater, any more than Maeterlinck
can have with his blind man. But each time the leitmotive is heard, it makes its subliminal effect, and can
mean more and more. It can be fully apprehended
only at the end of the opera, cumulatively. At one
of its very last appearances, Arkel comes closest to
interpreting its meaning. Mélisande dies; the motive
is poignant on the oboe: "But the sadness, Golaud,
the sadness of everything we see!" Gentle gloom
was a good deal more important to Maeterlinck than
the personality of Mélisande, who was only a counter
to project his vision of futility. Her leitmotive, the
chief musical thematic idea in the opera, represents
the overall mood rather than the person. Yet another
detail of musical dramaturgy is brought to bear on the
central dramatic idea.

Every single musical device, in fact, suits the play
marvelously and subtly emphasizes its quintessential
features. Once again, the contrast with Verdi's bold,
personal transformation of Shakespeare's *Othello* is
striking. Even the quality of Debussy's themes is true
to the universal pointlessness. The tiny motive of
Mélisande and sadness is sweet and static, returning
weakly on itself. That of Pelléas seems to start with a
little youthful vigor, but lapses into an indefinite oscil-
lation. Wagner's motives are entirely different; even
the shortest of them, such as "Fate" in the *Ring*, have
ominous, repressed harmonic energy. Golaud's leitmotive is the most exquisitely pointless of all. It is
merely a rhythmic flurry, but the implied action gets
nowhere; the melody cannot rear itself past the in-
terval of a second:

4
———

C'est magnifique, mais . . . this play, this opera, suffers from the chronic disease of dramas constructed
essentially out of ideas instead of persons and their
progress. I leave out of the question Maeterlinck's
strange view of fate as gently pathetic, rather than
outrageous. However conceived, fate extinguishes the
play. As Mélisande never acts, she never comes to life
dramatically, and dies without gaining or providing any
illumination. She is exasperating, not simply because
she is that sort of person, but because she is arbitrarily
given so much dramatic responsibility. And she never
really earns the sympathy that she receives from Arkel,
speaking at the end for the poet and the composer.
Their *ingenu* Pelléas doesn't exist at all; Don Ottavio
is flesh and blood beside him. Especially in this company, Golaud attracts much sympathetic interest; the
portrait is drawn with great psychological aplomb and
with little sentimentality. But Maeterlinck's fatal fal-
lacy was his insistence that Golaud should not progress
or draw any insight, mental or emotional, from his rich,
terrible experience. Perhaps if he did, that would have
meant a hope, a denial of purposelessness. Though the
dramatic skill merits admiration, ultimately Maeterlinck was defeated by his paradoxical effort to convey
dramatically the meaninglessness of action. Not only
are human deeds and emotions shown to be futile,
but the dramatic action itself is turned to no account.
Action is meaningless; and melodrama is not made
more interesting by providing it with metaphysical
justification.

The paradox caught Maeterlinck sooner, and more
painfully, in the matter of his symbolism and imagery.
Bourgeois Allemonde is, I am afraid, ludicrous, and

the attempt to charge plain, naturalistic conversation
with all that imagery soon reaches the breaking-point.
The play needs the distance of verse; Debussy provides something analogous by adding music. If texture
were all, the composer would have saved the play, for
music establishes its own convincing imaginative plane
in place of Maeterlinck's equivocal naturalism. The
poetic imagery does not seem exaggerated in the opera,
as it does in the play, because imagery takes second
place to the music, and the music is certainly not
de trop. Debussy had learned his grim lesson from
Wagner's excesses, even if Maeterlinck had not.

It is hard to guess what more Debussy could have
done, if he had been prepared to let music take a
greater part. At the one point in *Pelléas et Mélisande*
where he seems to have been tempted to expand musically, the whole illusion begins somehow to cloud tenu-
ously—I refer to the love scene between Pelléas and
Mélisande in Act IV.* It is a rare opera in which the
love music is the least effective. Still, I should not be
prepared to say finally that this scene disturbs Debussy's
consistent texture. This composer had a refined sense
of his own limitations, in addition to a set of intransigently literary theories about opera. Taking a play for
which he had an almost miraculous sympathy, he
matched it in musical terms perfectly; he enlarged it
only in the slightest degree. Yet only with that enlarge-
ment is the play presentable at all. The final paradox
is that Debussy succeeded with *Pelléas et Mélisande*
exactly to the extent that he defeated his ideal of opera
as sung play. Operatic ideals, perhaps, are made to be
defeated.

The opposite ideal was Wagner's: opera as symphonic poem. This was not attained either, luckily,
though the tendency towards it is powerful in *Tristan*

* Interestingly enough, this was the first scene composed, ten
years before the whole opera was ready.

und Isolde, and basic to Wagner's highly un-literary dramatic convention. *Tristan* is in many ways the obvious model for *Pelléas,* with its gloomy tale of adulterous love subdued to an obsessive idea, a vision of fatality which sweeps all before it. Wagner had the true dramatic instinct. His opera hinges on Tristan's growing awareness of this reality—on Tristan's conversion, if one cares to think of it in religious terms. Tristan, like Golaud, struggles against fate and suffers; unlike Golaud, he progresses and triumphs. The idea of an all-encompassing fate is a regular component of great tragedy, but when it dominates to the extent that Maeterlinck wished, when it stultifies action, the form ceases to be dramatic, let alone tragic. Here was a play that needed transformation—much more than *Othello!*—and in a very real sense dramatization too. Debussy's respectful, reticent method could not do quite enough.

7

Opera as Symphonic Poem

WE COME at last to Wagner, the man who arrogantly pre-empted to himself the very concept of opera, and wrote *Tristan und Isolde* and the *Ring* to stake his claim, and managed in doing so to shake the musical world into alignments that are still in evidence today.

Only quite recently, I think, has it become possible to view the old redoubtable wizard with some impassivity and with some clarity. In our century Wagner has been the most problematic of the great composers: criticism has been stultified by the furious partisanship that first idolized him and then exorcised his spell. By now, however, the fervor of the original Wagnerians seems fairly remote, and the incantation of the anti-Wagnerians too seems less and less real with time, less forceful and obligatory. Since Nietzsche and Debussy, many have set out to expose the chicanery, while many more have declared that the magic vision of Bayreuth has simply faded away. But as high feelings and self-interest abate, *Tristan und Isolde* remains; and Richard Wagner remains a name to conjure with.

In recent years the legerdemain has been carried on with better sense and skill, and with increased (if not yet sufficient) illumination. Following the lead of Bernard Shaw, Eric Bentley in *The Playwright as Thinker* sets up Wagner and Ibsen at the poles of the nineteenth-century dramatic tradition which is our immediate heritage. Jacques Barzun, our polyhistor of romanticism, has produced a study of *Darwin, Marx, Wagner*. In *The Idea of a Theater*, Francis Fergusson sees Wagner with Racine in a longer perspective—the "theater of passion" as against the "theater of reason." Thomas Mann had three major essays put together, not altogether fortuitously, as a book entitled *Freud, Goethe, Wagner*; and Mann's novel *Doktor Faustus* is the most impressively Wagnerian work of our time. On the composer himself we can now consult Ernest Newman's monumental biography, which must come to mind for any account of recent Wagner literature. With Wagner, more than with any other opera composer, the musician's insight is to be enriched with others; the *Gesamtkunstwerk* calls loudly for its *Gesamtkritik*.

The plain musician, accustomed to thinking along relatively direct evolutionary lines, would probably write on *Beethoven, Wagner, and Schoenberg*. When opera is in question, he has traditionally pitted Wagner against Verdi, and discoursed of Italian lyricism, German orchestral technique, leitmotives, arias, and the like. But as far as the basic principles of operatic dramaturgy are concerned, it is actually more enlightening to consider Wagner in contrast with Debussy. Wagner and Debussy took the extreme opposite positions; this is true in spite of everything

that Maeterlinck willingly and Debussy unwillingly
learned from the formidable earlier master. Wagner
tended towards the ideal of opera as symphonic
poem, Debussy towards the ideal of opera as sung
play, and although neither ideal was attained, the
results were imposing and far-reaching. *Pelléas et
Mélisande* is the more refined, self-conscious, constrained, freakish work; *Tristan und Isolde* is much
the more radical, the more imaginative, and the more
difficult to come to terms with. Both of these operas
must be encompassed in order to understand the
scope of the famous operatic "reform" of the nineteenth century.

As Mr. Bentley insists, *Tristan und Isolde* is not
a tragedy. Wagner never intended it to be. It is a
religious drama. Anti-religious, fascist, bogus, cry Wagner's enemies; but the form of the opera is that of
religious drama nonetheless, however we may be inclined to value its message. Whether *Tristan und
Isolde* is bogus or not depends only on its artistic
truth or success, and this depends on an appreciation
of its dramatic intention (for Wagner intended a
drama, not a philosophy, a self-justification, a demonstration of chromaticism, a consummation of romanticism, etc., etc.). Here I should like to follow
a point made by Una Ellis-Fermor in her admirable
and admirably lucid book *The Frontiers of Drama*:

Milton, in his prefatory note to *Samson Agonistes*, made
it clear that he regarded his play as a tragedy; but some
modern readers do not find it precisely the kind of play
that they have been accustomed to call tragedy, either
ancient or modern. It ends with the death of Samson,
and has a clear technical claim to inclusion in the category. But few of us, if thinking in terms of experience and
not of names, are content to call Samson's triumphant
death a tragic catastrophe. How could we, indeed, when
'nothing is here for tears'? We are accustomed to associate
with tragedy a balance between conflicting moods, be-

tween the sense of pain, grief, or terror on the one hand and, on the other, something that triumphs and illuminates. But in Milton's play we find instead a progression towards triumph and illumination which gradually subdues the sense of pain, grief, and loss and at the end transcends and utterly destroys it. Here is clearly something other than the balance of tragedy. Milton oversets the balance in the direction of positive interpretation; by justifying the ways of God to man he leaves no room for tragic ecstasy and substitutes ecstasy of another kind. He has written, that is, a play that belongs to the rare category of religious drama, a kind which, by the nature of some of its basic assumptions, cannot be tragic.

What is said here of *Samson Agonistes* applies very exactly, it seems to me, to *Tristan und Isolde*: the fundamental sense is of a progress towards a state of illumination which transcends yearning and pain. The fundamental rhythm of the piece is towards Tristan's conversion and the concluding *"Liebestod"* of Isolde—a triumphant ascent, not a tragic catastrophe. And *Tristan*, I believe, meets three other conditions that Miss Ellis-Fermor would wish to apply to religious drama. The nature of the experience is properly religious; the experience is the main matter of the drama; and the religious experience is actually, paradoxically, projected in a dramatic form.

That *Tristan und Isolde* is much more than a love story is only too evident. The extraordinary conception slowly and surely grips the audience: love is not merely an urgent force in life, but the compelling higher reality of our spiritual universe. The essential action of the opera is that the lovers are drawn more and more powerfully to perceive this reality and submit to it. In their vision of this reality, all the appurtenances of ordinary existence are sloughed off: subsidiary feelings, convention, personality, reason, and even life itself. If this is not to be called a religious experience, it is hard to know what meaning to attach to the term; and while it is certainly no Christian vision, it is one with some precedent in historical fact (or so we are told). Manifestly, too, this experience permeates and controls the drama with the greatest rigor. Mr. Francis Fergusson has reformulated the facts most recently, with a breadth of view and a dispassionate clarity unusual in Wagner criticism. The central "action," "to obey Passion as the one reality," subdues plot, setting, diction, imagery, dramatic rhythm, and, I am sure he would add, the music. This was the inexorable art that Maeterlinck and Debussy learned from Wagner. "Passion itself is taken as the paradoxical clue to human life transformed; to the true nocturnal scene of our existence; and to the 'absolute and despotic' form of the work itself."

Is Wagner's "absolute and despotic form" actually a *dramatic* form? This question is crucial, because the genuineness of Wagner's vision is not expressed by his intention, or by the pervasiveness or primacy of the vision in his piece, but by the success of the work of art in the particular form chosen. As everybody knows, fashionable opera-goers deplore *Tristan und Isolde* as the most undramatic thing in the world, just as many readers deplore *Samson Agonistes*. But dramatic criticism enters no such complaint. Mr. Fergusson, if anything, takes the dramatic efficacy of *Tristan* a little too much for granted, and does not bring out what I take to be the strongest point in the dramatic articulation. This is Wagner's presentation of the decisive progress in Tristan and Isolde. Miss Ellis-Fermor very truly observes that a relevant dramatic treatment of a religious experience is bound to involve progress into that experience. Religious drama, that is, centers about the act of conversion. So it is with *Tristan und Isolde*: the last act, which is the greatest in every way, is concerned specifically with the conversion of Tristan in a long scene known as the "Delirium," and with a reflection of this conversion in Isolde's "*Liebestod*." The preliminaries are long, sometimes undramatic and tedious, but every one of them falls into place with this incandescent climax in view. Needless to say, it is music that defines the conversion in *Tristan und Isolde*, and gives the sense of truth to the ultimate mystic vision.

2
_____

THE DRAMATIC structure of *Tristan und Isolde* shows hard lines of development superimposed upon elaborate symmetries. Each of the three acts is rather simply arranged to head towards one single active element of the myth as interpreted by Wagner: the drinking of the love-potion on the ship to Cornwall, the wounding of Tristan after the discovery of the lovers' tryst, and the death of Tristan in Isolde's arms. The limitation of action in each act is striking, ingenious, and very appropiate to Wagner's essentially psychological drama; and quite unlike the practice of Eugène Scribe, though some details of construction do betray Wagner's admiration for that notorious craftsman. Other symmetries may be pointed out. For example, each act opens impressively with some music actually heard on stage: the nostalgic song of the Sailor, the hunting-horns of Mark and Melot, and the Shepherd's piping in Kareol. These musical ideas are all symbolic, and permeate the beginnings of the acts in question—most profoundly in the case of the Shepherd's *"alte Weise"* of Act III. At the same time, the opera is planned to increase the concentration on Tristan, act by act. Act I is mainly about Isolde, with her long expository "Narration," but the final deed, the drinking of the love-potion, involves both lovers equally. They share the stage in Act II, but here the final deed is the wounding of Tristan. Act III is centrally concerned with him. Isolde does not enter until he is ready to die, and her *"Liebestod,"* an amplifying reflection of his more active conversion, completes the cycle by quietly returning the interest to her.

The three deeds that form the climaxes of the three acts are also highly symbolic in Wagner's scheme. In Act I, as is generally recognized, the drinking of the love-potion is a device to dramatize the love of Tristan and Isolde, or more exactly, their final confession of it. Wagner changed the myth with some care to indicate that this all-dominant love had smoldered long before the shipboard explosion. (Later, at the climax of the "Delirium" scene in Act III, Tristan makes things very clear: *"Den furchtbaren Trank! ich selbst, ich hab' ihn gebrau't!"*) Wagner changed the myth again in connection with the wounding of Tristan in Act II: it is not so much Melot who stabs Tristan, as Tristan who tries to kill himself on Melot's sword. Like Samson and Othello and Orpheus, Tristan has his time of weakness, and Act II leaves him in a crisis of despair; "day" is triumphant. Act I showed the lovers struggling to deny their love; the love-potion at the end symbolizes their inability or refusal to do so. Act II shows their attempt to realize their love in this world, the world of Melot and King Mark, of friendships, marriages, conventional loyalties, and sex. Tristan's wounding, by the thrust of Mark as well as by the thrust of Melot, symbolizes his abandonment of self under the shock of frustration and inner conflict. This is the price for his total involvement, paid with Tristan's characteristic passion.

However it is only at the start of Act III that the nature of the wound is properly revealed. The curtain rises on the bleak, sun-baked, ruined castle by the sea, Kareol; the wonderfully oppressive opening music on the strings gives way to the solo *cor anglais* of the Shepherd's strain, which hangs on the heavy air like lead. Tristan, brought home wounded by his faithful Kurvenal, has been languishing here in a coma. After

the disingenuous Shepherd has promised to signal the
arrival of Isolde's ship by means of a lustier tune,
Tristan wakes for the first time, his mind practically
a blank. To Kurvenal's joyful exclamations and ex-
planations he can only bring pathetic broken phrases,
which nevertheless show in the music a profundity that
Kurvenal does not grasp. His first speech of any length
is scarcely more coherent; the verse is almost formless,
and the music, with its unusual *absence* of passion, flow,
cadence, leitmotive, or musical idea of any sort, corresponds perfectly to Tristan's halting memory.

Wo ich erwacht,	Where I awoke
weilt' ich nicht;	there did I not stay;
doch wo ich weilte,	but where I stayed—
das kann ich dir nicht sagen.	yet that I cannot tell.
Die Sonne sah ich nicht,	The sun I did not see,
nicht sah ich Land noch Leute:	nor land, nor people;
doch was ich sah,	but what I saw—
das kann ich dir nicht sagen.	yet that I cannot tell.
Ich war—	I dwelt—
wo ich von je gewesen	where I have been from eternity,
wohin auf je ich gehe:	where I shall ever go:
im weiten Reich	the boundless realm
der Welten Nacht.	of worldwide Night.
Nur ein Wissen	One thought alone
dort uns eigen:	belongs us there:
göttlich ew'ges	blessed everlasting
Ur-Vergessen.	fathomless oblivion.

Tristan has wanted to escape; he has willed forgetful-
ness. The wound of Melot symbolizes what we would
call a complete nervous breakdown, with suicidal im-
pulses and amnesia, brought about by the collapse
of Tristan's values in Act II. It is perhaps only now that
our full interest and sympathy swing dramatically to
him.

As Mr. Fergusson remarks, it is tempting to substitute
a Freudian mythology here for the one offered by
Wagner. The long "Delirium" scene is a record of the

man pulling himself back together, dredging through his past life and feelings to reach a new synthesis—a synthesis, however, which psychoanalytic terminology remains powerless to illuminate. The process, which I have called Tristan's conversion, is the greatest dramatic feat in the opera, and, I would be inclined to say, in all of Wagner's works. Dramatic, even though no external agents are involved, and the more heroic exactly on that account. If the audience can only feel with Tristan, they will ask for no more explosive struggle, no greater agony, and no finer victory, than in his hour of darkness here. Certainly it could not have been matched in some set of violent thoughtless actions, such as Wagner might have salvaged from medieval saga material. And music, crucially, brings the audience to feel with Tristan.

His progress is organized into a large symmetrical double cycle—a typically Wagnerian pattern. After recalling his urge to oblivion, Tristan painfully wrenches back to memory one grief after another from the past. Leitmotives reflect them; Wagner's leitmotive technique never fell in with a dramatic situation more naturally and powerfully, or with such delicate psychological justness. At the start things are necessarily still vague for Tristan. Clarity grows only later. He remembers first his dreadful yearning, and in remembering of course feels it through again, and resents it bitterly, and with one part of his spirit wishes still for the oblivion ("night") that another part has rejected. His yearning seems the one reality to be found in life ("day"); he remembers no events yet, only this torturing complex of feeling—day, life, yearning, pain. As he summons up a great curse on them all, his surge of emotion is handled in a protracted musical *crescendo* of the kind that Wagner made peculiarly his own. After the curse on "day," Tristan sinks back exhausted, but also relieved and lightened. When Kurvenal tells him that Isolde has been summoned, he comes to life in another surging ecstasy of anticipation. But the ship is not yet there; Tristan is not yet ready. With a huge deceptive cadence characteristic of Wagner, and especially of this opera, the excitement yields pathetically to the sound of the Shepherd's piping, which we know to be a sign of a still empty sea. *"Noch ist kein Schiff zu seh'n."*

This then is the first cycle: *recollection—curse—relapse—anticipation.* It is now paralleled by another on the same plan, but in every way more profound than the first, which will indeed bring Tristan to Isolde. Up to now the introspection (*recollection*) has been in general terms; Tristan recaptures only the surface of his feelings. Such purgation (*curse*) as he accomplishes leaves him more or less as he was at the end of Act II: rejection of life, suicide, even abandonment of love. Yet this has been an essential and enormously arduous journey from willed amnesia to re-acceptance of the initial agony. This time Tristan can go on, and in the second cycle he will find his journey's meaning.

The Shepherd's piping, *die alte Weise,* had wakened Tristan for his first struggle; now it is heard again to begin the new cycle. This time Tristan's eyes are clear. He can penetrate into the events of his past and seek their significance, not only those that we already know from the opera, but also events from his childhood and even before, symbolized by the rich gloomy strain of the Shepherd, playing as he played when Tristan's mother and father died. By a fine inspiration, Wagner kept *die alte Weise* sounding all through this passage of introspection, combined with the other motives and woven into the musical texture. Thus Tristan sees everything now in the light of what we would classify as his traumatic past, or, as he says, the fate that has always governed his existence. This is a deeper motivation than "day"; the callow curse on day has yielded to an older memory, and a more thorough understanding. One by one the events related in Act I (all musically recalled by their motives) come back to Tristan, guiding his memory at last to the fatal love-potion. Suddenly there is a flood of revelation—that fearful drink: he himself was the one responsible, not day, not Isolde, but his fate, he himself. The music reaches its climax in a new motive, the most powerful and agonized of this whole intense score:

"I myself, it was I that brewed it!"—and the curse, the purgation, of his own guilt.

Just as this passage of *recollection—curse* is in every way deeper and more decisive than the earlier one—searching deeper into the soul, shifting responsibilities, seeing anew—so the subsequent *relapse* is more serious. Kurvenal thinks that Tristan is dead, and the orchestra plays a sweetly attenuated version of the famous "love-death" music which had opened the opera, and which soon is to accompany Tristan's actual dying. Tristan, however, now recovers, and the crowning episode that follows is without a precedent in the earlier cycle. The miracle, this time, has been accomplished: Tristan achieves a new integrity, a state of felicity, in which he can invoke Isolde with a purity apart from or above yearning, without undertones of day or anxiety or passion or curse. One's feeling of course is determined by the music; it is one of the great moments in the opera:

This represents an incredible intensity of consciousness for one who an hour before had abandoned being. The parallel step of *anticipation* for the ship bearing Isolde is more violent than before, and this time not to be frustrated. The Shepherd pipes his new tune, the miserable quality of which may perhaps be excused by the tremendous frenzied drive that masks it.* As Isolde enters and Tristan dies, the whole complex of themes of love and death sounds loudly in the orchestra—a complex stated strongly in the Prelude, and heard at many important junctures of the action. Paradoxically, the notorious shifting, atonal chromaticism acts here as a resolution to the excruciating prior surge. Tristan finds in death no longer oblivion, but triumph. The "Delirium" has been for him a novitiate, a great preparation.

The beatitude for which he prepared is left to Isolde. In Wagner's regular scheme, it is man who suffers and draws himself to the point of revelation, but woman whose sublime intuition complements life's struggle and expresses its meaning. This may be biologically questionable, but in this opera, at least, it is dramatically

* For this passage, Wagner coolly suggested that a special alphorn-type instrument be constructed. It would not help.

ingenious and just. Isolde's concluding *"Liebestod"* achieves the intense, ecstatic concentration on and identification with the ultimate reality of Passion, sharing Tristan's experience from a more inspired standpoint. Impossible for a woman just to expire in these circumstances, say critics who have swallowed the love-potion only with difficulty. But like the love-potion and the wound of Tristan, Isolde's death is another grandiose symbol: of the final mystic ascent, evaporating into a supreme nothingness, partaking of the divine, unworldly essence of Love.

3

WAGNER'S highly individual musical style, and only that style, made possible the dramatic achievement of *Tristan und Isolde*. In what does the Wagnerian reform consist? This is the most famous question in modern operatic criticism, and in approaching it, one has to take a solemn warning from the mass of generalization and aggressive plain statement that the question has promoted. I shall stress two points only: first a historical one, relating to a view of opera that has been implicit to this study, and then a specific one, concerning the scene of Tristan's "Delirium."

Musical form in opera, the essential articulating element of the drama, is always best understood as a reflection of, or as the original image of, musical form as it exists generally at the time in question. When opera was first created, Monteverdi gathered elements of operatic style from various musical genres of that vigorous, confused, transitional period. The orderly baroque plan of Metastasian aria and recitative finds expression also in the instrumental music of the time.

Mozart's operatic technique parallels his symphonic style. In a similar way, the Wagnerian operatic continuity adopts, defines, or consummates the characteristic formal ideal of romantic music.

I write "the ideal" deliberately, for today we have serious doubts as to its attainment; it was perhaps characteristic enough of romanticism to strive towards the unattainable. The ideal was of a grandiose organic unity according to the principles of the symphonic style. Beethoven took the first steps by gradually welding the movements of the symphony into a psychological whole lasting thirty or fifty minutes. I have related this symphonic unification to the unification of the operatic ensemble, the finale, and the composite aria. The sense of continuity in the last finale of *Fidelio*, with its several interlinked sections, is analogous to that of the sectional *Egmont* Overture; and ultimately to that of the Quartet in c♯ minor, whose seven movements flow into one another without a pause, sustaining the progress with an unparalleled certainty and beauty.

Wagner, who deserves credit for "discovering" this quartet, must have noted with great satisfaction that one theme in the last movement is very similar to the fugue subject of the first movement. Such thematic relationships are exceptional in Beethoven, but as his principles of musical organization were superseded or else simply misunderstood, composers sought more and more to achieve the large-scale, organic whole by means of long-range thematic connections of one kind or another. Berlioz's program symphony presents a series of movements held together (he hoped) by the use of an emphatic tune which suffers transformations as the work proceeds. Significantly, such tunes were given specific symbolic meanings. Soon themes were multiplied and shortened, the musical flow eased, and more intellectual techniques developed, in the symphonic poem of Liszt, the cyclic symphony of César Franck and others, and the frankly Wagnerian tone poem of Richard Strauss.

Opera had to share in this ideal. As it happened, opera spurred it on as Berlioz and Liszt never could. Wagner carried the organic ideal to a monstrous climax: a single, pulsing, theme-ridden ostensible continuity over four hours—over four evenings, even. Once opera in the nineteenth century had interested an *avant-garde* German composer like Wagner, it was bound to become strongly symphonic; for the motivic texture of the symphony (characteristically the texture of the first-movement development section) dominated musical thought in Wagner's time as melody did in the time of Handel, and declamation in the time of Monteverdi.

But beyond this point it is dangerous to make extreme statements about the Wagnerian musical continuity. Wagner was a big talker, but as an artist he was practical and opportunistic, a fact that his critics do not always keep firmly enough in mind. Some have enthusiastically claimed Wagner's operas as supreme, purely musical, organic unities. Alfred Lorenz so analyzed seven of them, with the aid of fantastic special pleading, and at a length dreadful to contemplate; his work is all the more infuriating as a *reductio ad absurdum* of certain valid insights. Sir Donald Tovey too, no fanatic, insisted that *Tristan und Isolde* is hugely organized on the same principles as a Beethoven symphony; but nowhere in his writings does he ever come to grips with this important concept. I would insist that "opera as symphonic poem" is no more viable dramatically than "opera as sung play." Opera must be regarded not as a purely musical form, but as a dramatic one in which music has an articulating function. The grief that Wagner causes many listeners is caused, or at least amplified, by a feeling that in being "sym-

phonic" Wagner sets up purely musical conditions
which then indeed he does not fill. But Mozart's operas
are not coherent in the same way as his symphonies,
though they reflect the same aesthetic preoccupations;
Wagner did not write symphonic poems, though his
operas tended in that direction. It has been said that
Tristan und Isolde could make its point without the
stage and without the singers. This is no more true of
Tristan than of *Don Giovanni*.

On the other hand, critics in the larger opposite
camp are equally wrong to claim that Wagner's continuity is altogether formless, amoebal, inarticulated.
When Nietzsche complains of unending melody, one
wonders (with all respects to our German friends)
whether his early love for Wagner was ever based on
any properly musical understanding at all. A hundred
years later there is little excuse for such deafness;
Wagner's mastery of musical shape in *Tristan und
Isolde* is a matter of fact, not opinion. One understands
Wagner no better with a weak musical ear than with
a head predisposed to theories of organic perfection.

As purely musical forms, Wagner's operas succeed
as well as any romantic symphonic poems of their
length might be expected to succeed; which is to say,
not too well. The program symphony and the symphonic poem never achieved the kind of unity to which
they seem to have aspired. Like Berlioz's symphonies,
Wagner's operas break down into passages of great
eloquence and power, loosely bound together. Long-
range connective effects, of detail and of larger intent,
are sometimes poetic and impressive, sometimes mechanical and esoteric; but Wagner never failed to use
the loose binding available in his technique as a forceful instrument of mood, and as with Debussy, this
binding in itself is of great dramatic value. As for the
coherence of the whole, that is determined by action as
well as music. *Tristan und Isolde*, like a Liszt sym-

phonic poem, includes musically dull passages such as neither Beethoven nor Brahms (nor Verdi in the late years, I might add) would willingly tolerate. The wonder is that these are so few, over the four hours. For the rest, there are passages that do, emphatically, succeed; not arias, as in Verdi, but passages of a symphonic, developmental nature. And more rigorously symphonic, of course, than such examples as may be found in *Otello* and *Falstaff*.

The point to be made about the "Delirium" scene in relation to the Wagnerian reform is this: not only is the scene one that emphatically succeeds, but as it is the climax of the opera, its success determines the success of the work as a whole. A good deal of Act I of *Tristan und Isolde* is rather on the blatant side; Act II includes, before and after the superb love duet, the monotonous conversation between the lovers and then the plaint of King Mark. But Act III is practically perfect, and the "Delirium" scene is one of the great long sustained passages in Wagner. It can be shown to relate to every other section of the opera, though with varying degrees of relevance. Considered simply in itself, the "Delirium" scene offers the most convincing evidence of the dramatic vitality of all of Wagner's dramaturgical techniques.

First and foremost, the idea of the leitmotive is particularly well realized here. With Debussy, as we have seen, a fastidious use of leitmotives contributes to the general atmospheric texture in a subsidiary way. With Wagner, leitmotive technique is central, far from reticent, and, from *Tristan und Isolde* on, highly involved.

The constructive and symbolic aspects of the leitmotive are worth distinguishing, though of course both aspects work together (even in Debussy). Short suggestive motives are the necessary material from which Wagner constructs his dense symphonic web. They are always present, always busy, recombined, reorchestrated, reharmonized, rephrased, developed. Now such symphonic writing, from Haydn to Schoenberg, has flirted with one main danger: in trying to make much out of slender material, music comes to a delicate point at which suddenly there is a feeling of effect without cause. Material can be pushed too far. Wagner was especially prone to this kind of bathos on account of the arrogant length to which he pursued the technique, and on account of certain undeniable blindnesses. In *Tristan und Isolde* an added danger came from the family likeness of all the music within the lovers' sphere; it was fatally easy to produce an overall impression of gum. On the other hand, much could be gained through the "organic" effect, to the extent that it could be carried off, and the composer could slip readily from one theme into the next, during a long developmental passage, without sounding arbitrary or forced.

The subtle introduction of the new theme of "Tristan's Guilt" (quoted on page 202) shows Wagner's manipulation of these conditions at its best. The motive is similar to all the others; when it finally appears, it carries a sense of consummation and inevitability, as well as the force of a revelation. Compare a famous earlier instance: the self-conscious, cryptic introduction of the new theme of "The Sword" (the C-major trumpet arpeggio) at the end of *Das Rheingold*. Another inspired stroke is the development of fragments of *die alte Weise* throughout the second, more serious cycle in Tristan's "Delirium." It is wonderfully suggestive, first of all, that so many pregnant motives grow out of what was originally a fairly coherent tune. With the greatest skill Wagner combined them contrapuntally with all the prior themes, which are thus modified or colored with unsuspected richness.

This thematic pervasiveness has a fine symbolic value too: under the spell of the Shepherd's ancestral strain, Tristan's renewed soul-searching takes on a deeper and more intense reality. Themes associated with every step of his spiritual journey return and order themselves in combination with the mournful tune of Tristan's past. The symbolic use of leitmotives, more generally recognized than the constructive use, is also more obviously precarious in its effect. The correspondence of musical symbol and its object easily becomes absurd, especially when the themes are as forthright as usual in Wagner; "The Sword" in *Das Rheingold* is an egregious example, if perhaps an attractively naïve one. As Erik Satie is said to have warned Debussy, the stage-trees do not shudder or grimace whenever a character walks on. But Wagner had revealed dramatic possibilities in the leitmotive technique that Debussy could not ignore. The virtue of the technique depends, as always, on the composer's sensitivity to the individual context.

Leitmotive symbolism in *Pelléas et Mélisande* is extremely elegant and restrained; in the *Ring*, often reckless; in Tristan's "Delirium," whole-hearted but imaginative and just, and dramatically central. As Tristan feverishly struggles to put his mind and memory in order, vague impressions out of the past struggle in his consciousness. To Tristan, each one of them is at the moment vital, terribly real, tangible, loud. Images combine and recombine musically—feelings associated with ideas, rather than clear concepts, such as the burghers in *Die Meistersinger* are represented as entertaining. To such feelings, as forceful and yet as indefinite as Tristan's raving words, the flux of always-related musical fragments is ideally suited.

Two other notorious Wagnerian techniques are especially well handled in the "Delirium" scene (and by "well" I mean, as always, dramatically well). The first is the long passage of plot résumé, during which some major character relates the course of previous action, with the liberal assistance of leitmotives. Most opera-goers suffer plot résumé for the purpose of initial exposition (Isolde's long "Narration" in Act I), barely tolerate it in the *Ring* (they may not have been there the previous evening), but object strongly when Wagner reviews in leisurely fashion action that they have actually just seen on the stage. This he does often enough—and what aware listener has not quailed at the beginning of Act III when that disingenuous Shepherd asks Kurvenal to explain Tristan's illness? But the principle behind such résumés is a genuinely dramatic one: to reinterpret past action in a new synthesis, determined by fresh experience. In Act II, for instance, the lovers review their early acquaintance with some dramatic force from quite a different standpoint than in Act I. Never has such a reinterpretation been more necessary than in the case of Tristan's conversion; the whole dramatic point of the opera depends on Tristan seeing his prior experience in a new mystic light. The newness of *die alte Weise* is of prime importance here.

The second matter is the firm and beautiful double construction of the scene. This was the feature that especially fascinated Lorenz; but Lorenz refused to see that the relevance of such structures depends sharply on the strength of their articulation. In the "Delirium" scene the musical parallelism is manifest thanks to the striking *alte Weise* placed at the start of each cycle. The dramatic structure is rigorously parallel too: in each cycle, quiet recollection growing in hysteria to a curse, then a relapse, then ecstatic anticipation. But the second cycle is in every way more profound than the first, and includes the crowning episode of beatitude, and reaches resolution. One can only admire that iron sense of form by which Wagner could sometimes span the great arcs of time that he dared to encompass.

The most emphatic formal pillar in *Tristan und Isolde* is the concluding "*Liebestod*" of Isolde; Tovey liked to make this point. The last eighty-odd bars of the score are rather closely repeated from the height of the love-duet in Act II, with new words, of course, and a new musical counterpoint of secondary interest for Isolde. But missing now is the rending deceptive cadence at the end of the love-duet, when Brangaene's scream greets the arrival of Mark and Melot to interrupt the lovers' passion; missing indeed is the whole sense of frenzy and yearning, the sexual excitement which has excited many critics. The mistaken effort to capture love in the terms of the "day" of this world is now transfigured, *verklärt*, into the consuming, serene mystic acceptance, the union in death. At last the continual surging, shifting, renewing, interrupting, and aspiring ceases, and the long-avoided cadence comes with unparalleled weight in B major. In fact Wagner's regular and exasperating cliché, the evasion of solid harmonic settling, finds its true symbolic place in *Tristan und Isolde*, the drama of the agony of yearning and its transformation. The final resolution is superb; the constructive force of the great recapitulation goes to define Wagner's ultimate meaning.

From the purely musical point of view, the effect of the "*Liebestod*" is unlike any effect obtainable by the use of leitmotives. It is more like the recapitulation of a Beethoven symphony movement, or (to get closer) like the reappearance of the first-movement theme in the final pages of the César Franck Symphony in d minor. It is more like the return of the music for the kiss at the end of *Otello*—a grand climactic repetition summing up the drama in a single gesture, rather than a momentary detail, however striking. Verdi had no sympathy for the patient funding of the leitmotive technique. But the "*Liebestod*" in itself constitutes no proof that *Tristan und Isolde* makes a stern, symphonic, Beethovenian, purely musical unity. This is no more true of *Tristan* than of *Otello* or of the César Franck (*pace* Tovey). Unlike Franck, Wagner was free of any such abstract formal commitment.

4
————

THE ANTI-WAGNERIANS, I know, will not be convinced; but dramatically speaking *Tristan und Isolde* is Wagner's best work, the clearest in form and idea, and the most complete in realization. This fact, no doubt, has recommended it to Mr. Fergusson and Mr. Bentley, and given it a general reputation as the most quintessentially Wagnerian of operas. Actually even imperfect Wagnerites know that in many ways *Tristan und Isolde* is technically inferior to the masterful later compositions. From the point of view of dramaturgy, the virtuoso exercise in well-madeness is *Die Meistersinger*, while *Parsifal*, on the other hand, realizes that purity of structure to which *Tristan* tends, admitting nothing so crude as the gratuitous disposing of Mark, Melot, Kurvenal, and Brangaene at the end of Act III. *Tristan* is the most thoroughly "symphonic" of Wagner's operas; but compared with the ripe texture of *Parsifal*, much of the music can appear insensitive, even gauche. It is not only the boisterous crew of Act I that makes one think of *The Flying Dutchman*.

But *Tristan*—four hours of unresolved chromaticism or no—has the terrible, grasping conviction of *The Flying Dutchman*, too. And final conviction is what the later operas somehow lack, for whatever reasons. The great thing about *Tristan und Isolde* is that Wagner forced himself to center his drama in the soul of his hero, and contrived to bring everything to a head in the "Delirium" scene and in its reflection, Isolde's "*Liebestod.*" These scenes equal anything in his later operas or in anyone else's for dramatic force; the music works best when it is most needed. Defining Wagner's unequivocal, intense mystic view, the conversion of Tristan and the symbolic death of Isolde draw everything in the drama to a consummation. Only the fury of Wagner's vision enabled him to justify his verbosity, defeat sentimentality, and subdue a tremendous wealth of detail to the central dramatic idea.

Of the religious experience and dramatic form, Miss Ellis-Fermor writes: ". . . the only type of conflict that this subject can offer for the use of drama is that of a heroic contest rising to exultation and passing on, in a few rare cases, into beatitude. This is the only point at which this content and this form can be reconciled, and it is at this point that, in all genuine religious drama, the reconciliation has been made. Are we now on the way to understand why the drama of religious experience is rare at all times and why the great plays of this kind can be counted almost upon the fingers of one hand?" *Tristan und Isolde* too, I suggest, "achieves what is apparently impossible, pushing forward the limits of drama into territory which, by the very nature of its mood, dimensions or form, seemed forbidden to it."

In the history of *dramma per musica*, the only other composer who had explored this territory with any real success was Johann Sebastian Bach. In certain of his sacred cantatas the Christian experience is presented in a bare, stiff form which has nonetheless the genuine outline of a dramatic form. A Bach cantata seems impossibly modest, to say nothing of conventional, next to Wagner's giant romantic effort, and is of course dramatic in a much more limited sense. There is no stage, no personality, only the abstracted quality of dramatic form. But like Wagner in *Tristan und Isolde*,

Bach deals centrally with religious conversion: the awareness and agony of sin, the acceptance of the Passion, and the final submersion in the universal, symbolized by the liturgical form of the chorale.

From Bach to Wagner is the great age of German music—the great age of German art, we may be inclined to say. Drama and the drama of ideas played an urgent role in the evolution of the German artistic effort. Characteristic was the attempt to present a psychological progress in the dramatic hero without the use of external agencies; a musical attempt indeed, and one that finds its echo in Florestan's extraordinary aria in *Fidelio*. For in Beethoven's lifetime music also became psychologically aware, and "dramatic," in the metaphor so well elaborated by Tovey. Conflicts, developments, and resolutions were incorporated into the musical continuity: into the single symphony movement, into the quartet as a whole, into operatic forms. It is not hard to see in Tristan's "Delirium" a fantastic development of the simple composite aria of Mozart and Beethoven, which was likewise a progressing soliloquy, rising from gloom to resolution to vision in Florestan's case. The tremendous machinery of Wagnerian reform and the techniques of the symphonic poem were never used more impressively than in the dramatic projection of Tristan's conversion.

Only at the end of Wagner's lifetime were the cantatas of Bach rediscovered, or to put it more precisely, published and admired for the first time outside the churches of Leipzig. The antiquarian efforts of the Bach Society, indeed, symbolize in a small way the transition to the characteristically modern attitude towards the musical tradition. We have a more vivid sense of it than Wagner did, one less governed by condescension and historicism. Music of the past is known and valued no less for being less chromatic, or less motivic, or less advanced in style than that of the present. Is Bach's presentation of the religious experience less real than that of Wagner in *Tristan und Isolde?* Questions of this sort were becoming troublesome at the end of the nineteenth century. Music's march into the Future seemed suddenly problematic.

Wagnerism exploded its way into the twentieth century, but with it went an equally violent reaction and a very general anxiety about artistic ends and means. Dramatic composers retrenched from the advanced positions of the late nineteenth century—from Debussy's ideal of opera as sung play, as well as from Wagner's ideal of opera as symphonic poem. Meanwhile, as Wagnerism recedes into the past as a burning musical issue, I should hope that historical perspective can help us view the creator of *Tristan und Isolde* himself in some reasonable proportion. He was neither the Prometheus nor the Polyphemus envisaged by his friends and enemies respectively, nor even the Proteus that he must seem to many critics. And his dramatic accomplishment is no myth. No doubt the man deserved the hatred of the early twentieth century; the question is, do we deserve the full onus of the anti-Wagnerian reaction? Bach too, after all, was thought intolerable for a time, by the generation immediately following his death.

RETRENCHMENT

*

8

Wozzeck *and* The Rake's Progress

THE retrenchment has been in dramaturgy; the major works have naturally not revealed any associated lapse in musical style or dramatic relevance. But in the matter of operatic dramaturgy, the twentieth century has seen economical new lines drawn behind the advanced positions of the nineteenth. This is true of most modern operas, whether valid works or pretentious ones, esoteric or popular, whatever their compositional schools.

As we have seen, late nineteenth-century opera carried the idea of continuity to extremes. One extreme was Wagner's, and the establishment of continuous opera was one of many reforms that the Wagnerians tried to interpret as the mission of the master. They could correctly point to the development itself as the one main fact in the history of operatic dramaturgy; but like all grand historical generalities, this one masks an enormous amount of complexity. The beginning, baroque opera, may have been straightforward enough, with its rigorous division of the drama into a speech level of recitative for plot exposition, intrigue, and dialogue, and a properly imaginative musical level for the essential dramatic articulation. The end product, however, opera with all the action incorporated into a single musical continuity, is very various, and its variety stems from the complexity of its evolution.

Wagner played a leading role, but even the Wagnerians acknowledged Gluck's pioneering; and actually the first steps were taken by unpretentious *opera buffa* composers, who enclosed still sharply limited dramatic actions within the tight musical form of the ensemble. Later the Italians gradually raised recitative to a pitch of musical coherence comparable to that of the arias or the other musical numbers. Those self-sufficient forms, meanwhile, were loosened and blended in to the rest. *Otello* and *Falstaff*, indeed, can be considered most clearly in terms of the stress between Verdi's desire for a more even, literary flow in opera and the lyric demands of the classical Italian tradition. A little later Debussy, with Wagner, Massenet, and Mussorgsky behind him, quietly demonstrated a new operatic aesthetic. He inserted a play whole into an opera, its literary values all fully preserved and even supported by a discreet, continuous musical web. Continuous opera would not have become the operatic "Art-Work of the Future" if Wagner alone had tended in its direction.

For fifty years—let us not speak of the future— opera of this kind held sway. They were the years dominated in the theater by Naturalism. Though the basic convention of all opera is far abstracted from actual life, continuous opera leans towards Naturalism in one important respect: it substitutes or tends to substitute a single convention for all phases of experience in the drama, instead of the sharp dualism of traditional opera. This allows composers to work more and more with ordinary lifelike dialogue; paradoxically, the shadowy symbolic play of Maurice Maeterlinck became the most naturalistic of operas. *Tosca, Der Rosenkavalier, Wozzeck,* and *The Saint of Bleecker Street* are all in their various ways more realistic than *Il Trovatore* or *The Magic Flute,* and all obviously reflect the Naturalism of the late nineteenth century.

Yet all of them retrench from the radical positions of the original reformers. Composers wished to adopt the naturalistic flow of opera as sung play without inhibiting the music as puritanically as in *Pelléas et Mélisande.* They wished to profit from the emphasis and emotional force of opera as symphonic poem without limiting the plot and conventionalizing the dialogue as in *Tristan und Isolde.* The dramaturgical purities of Debussy and Wagner were sacrificed gladly enough; indeed those composers themselves led the way to compromise, carefully fighting shy of attaining their own implied ideals. Finally —inevitably, perhaps, in our time—efforts have been made to retrench farther still, away from the quasi-naturalistic system of continuous opera itself.

From the standpoint of developments such as these, Alban Berg's *Wozzeck* of 1922 and Igor Stravinsky's *The Rake's Progress* of 1951 are interesting to see together. *Wozzeck* combines the dramaturgies of Wagner and Debussy with more originality and force than any other modern opera. It pursues both methods to unprecedented lengths; yet in its very un-dogmatism, in the very fact of combination, it reveals a shrewd retrenchment from their extremes. *The Rake's Progress,* on the other hand, is the most

convincing of operas that have retreated even farther, to eighteenth-century principles of construction. These principles were not dramatically exhausted in the early time, it appears, and much
that is fresh and still impressive can be derived from
them. *Wozzeck* and *The Rake's Progress* have been
claimed as the operatic masterpieces of two powerful
camps of contemporary music, the twelve-tone school
and the neoclassic school, and are generally discussed in partisan terms. But these operas do more
than illustrate dramaturgical trends or popularize certain twentieth-century musical styles. They justify
style and dramaturgy by creating unique dramatic
visions with the particular automatic urgency of contemporary art. Our interest, as always, is in the
drama, not in style or technique.

2

LIKE *Pelléas et Mélisande*, *Wozzeck* is a sung play.
The play is one of the most extraordinary in theatrical history: Georg Buechner's *Woyzeck*, which was
left in a fantastic jumble of notes at his early death
in 1837. Its proleptic theme is the savagery of society
towards the underprivileged. Woyzeck, a miserable
common soldier, is driven to half-insanity, murder,
and drowning by the taunts of his Captain, the
dietary experiments of his regimental Doctor, the
infidelities of his common-law wife, Marie, and the beating given him by her bull-like lover the Drum-Major.
Buechner's technique, as well as his theme and his
aura of sordid extremity, gave the play a special fascination for the expressionists who discovered it in the
1900's and staged it for the first time. Alban Berg

is said to have been deeply impressed by one of the early performances.

Woyzeck is made up out of a large number of very short, lifelike, cinematographic scenes. Berg selected from them and arranged them for his purpose with much skill, setting five scenes in each of his three acts, thus: Act I, scene i: Wozzeck, shaving the Captain, is beset by his crazy moralizing reproaches, but can make no articulate reply. Scene ii: In a weird, beautiful country sunset, Wozzeck sees a Masonic apocalypse. Scene iii: Marie notices the Drum-Major, engages in a cat-fight, sings to her child, and grows apprehensive at Wozzeck's strange behavior. Next day in the barracks (scene iv) Wozzeck is grotesquely goaded by the Doctor. Scene v: Marie and the Drum-Major go to bed. Act II, scene i: Marie with Wozzeck; signs of trouble. Scene ii: The Captain and the Doctor, now together, torment Wozzeck with lewd hints of Marie's backsliding. But when he confronts her (scene iii), she defies him, and at an inn (scene iv) passes him by to dance with the Drum-Major. Scene v: Wozzeck is beaten up in the barracks while his unconcerned comrades snore. Act III, scene i: Alone, Marie repents; but Wozzeck stabs her in scene ii. Scene iii: Quite mad now, he returns to the inn, raves, rushes out when blood is detected on his hands, and (scene iv) drowns while seeking the knife. The Captain and the Doctor walk by the pond; hearing a man flounder, they hurry away. At this point comes a climactic orchestral interlude with the curtain down, followed by a brief epilogue as scene v.

Berg scarcely changed the jabbing literary rhythm of the play. He no more attempted to fashion arias, duets, or choruses for musical convenience than Debussy did, though he did not disdain Marie's lullaby or her monologue in Act III, either. The quite exceptional speed, vividness, terror, and naturalism of the opera are due first of all to the fact that it uses no tailor-made libretto, but simply the stark original play. The practicability of such a method had been shown by Debussy.

Like *Pelléas et Mélisande*, *Wozzeck* depends on a highly individual kind of declamation. In a sung play, more than in any other operatic variety, declamation has to have a life of its own. Berg went farther even than Debussy in dissociating his speech from the orchestral background. Technically speaking, he used many vocal styles: sometimes plain speech, not sung at all, and at other times at least three different blends of *Sprechstimme*, half-spoken and half-sung, with musical pitches indicated, but to be followed only roughly. Generally the words are fully sung, but the listener distinguishes many shades here too: from fantastically chromatic and disjunct lines, close indeed to *Sprechstimme*, to an approximately Straussian, post-Wagnerian style of declamation. Even these sung sections refuse to adhere to their accompaniment, for the most part; the vocal lines are too eccentric and the accompaniment is too dissonant. By nature the voice is not too accurate in pitch, and the ear cannot instantly resolve imprecisions in a harmonic idiom as complex as that employed by Berg and Schoenberg. These deficiencies can be turned to good account. In *Wozzeck* Berg approaches the realism of a film soundtrack, in which speech and music are essentially disjoined. At the same time he courts its dramatic limitation, that the music acts as comment only and not integrally as part of the action. The orchestra pit is brought out into the audience instead of up onto the stage.

From a strictly dramaturgical point of view, the role of the orchestral music can also be said to be similar in *Wozzeck* and in *Pelléas et Mélisande*. In both operas, each scene is handled as a musical unit with its own particular mood, or at least its particular shade of the overall mood; and in both operas, the music gains most coherence during interludes between the scenes, in the dark theater. But Berg's musical technique itself makes the comparison with Debussy rather academic. Here most strongly his eclectic personality shows its Wagnerian side.

Together with Berg's later opera, the torso *Lulu*, *Wozzeck* consummates the German movement to organize opera as a grandiose symphonic unity. As I have suggested, this ideal is less explicit in Wagner's practice than in the rationalizations of post-Wagnerian critics. It is also explicit enough in the over-written operas of Richard Strauss, notably in *Salome* and *Elektra* of 1905 and 1909; during the years preceding their composition, Strauss had proved himself the most successful exponent of the symphonic poem. *Wozzeck* is a very Straussian work. Berg set out to bind each of his fifteen scenes into what are said to be fifteen different purely musical forms. Each act is said to make a larger unity: Act II, for instance, is a five-movement symphony, the movements corresponding to the five scenes. And of course, the opera as a whole is in musical terms "organic." At the end of the last scene ". . . the music seems still to be going forward. It does indeed go on! As a matter of fact the first measure of the opera could be directly attached to these concluding bars, whereby the circle would be closed."* There are more serious indexes to the musical coherence of *Wozzeck*, but I quote this one as a nice symbol, and one altogether characteristic of Berg's preoccupation and attitude, and his exaggerated care with the score.

Much propaganda has been devoted to the musical

* Willi Reich ostensibly records Berg's ideas in "A Guide to *Wozzeck*," reprinted in *The Musical Quarterly*, XXXVIII, January 1952. With the editorial reference to this guide as an "excellent analysis," I could not disagree more completely.

organization of *Wozzeck*, so much that it is well to emphasize that the ultimate judge is the ear, not the eye, and that the work is destined for the opera house, not for the analyst's study. Berg's more complicated musical constructions are simply not perceived in the theater, or rather, are perceived only to the extent of strong moods. Six of the fifteen scenes are built on *ostinato* forms (a speciality of the twelve-tone school, incidentally); these *are* perceived, and make their unesoteric dramatic effect by providing an overpowering sense of obsession to the action in question. Thus the murder scene, described as an "Invention on a Tone," revolves clearly around the note B; this note becomes more ominously insistent until, in the interlude after the scene, it is heard all alone in a famous gut-bursting crescendo, which resolves deceptively into the lowdown polka of the next scene—a deceptive distraction for Wozzeck. (But to link up this B with the gonged note that ends the previous act!) The next scene too is built on an *ostinato*: Wozzeck shows up at the inn raving, with Marie's blood on his hands, and a superb dramatic point is made by the constant repetition of a single rhythm. More mildly, much more mildly, this had been done in the gaming scene in *La Traviata*, Yniold's scene in *Pelléas et Mélisande*, and elsewhere. Without analytical abracadabra.

But that the piece is over-composed and has been over-analyzed does not distress the opera audience. What we hear makes its effect. Like *Pelléas et Mélisande*, *Wozzeck* creates an individual mood to bind each scene; unlike *Pelléas*, a shattering mood. The overall unity is of style and mood and action—as in *Pelléas*, as in *La Traviata*, but much more violently so. In certain scenes the music coheres with great force, producing a curious schizophrenic effect in relation to the firmly literary form established by the naturalistic dialogue. Debussy, who never let music take hold, carefully avoided any such disparity. I suspect that Berg deliberately sought it; Wozzeck seems to use every available means to refine a unique operatic vision of abnormality.

Abnormality is immediately evident; its exact nature, and the exact means by which it is projected, are more problematic. For some critics it is tempting to attribute the madness simply to the opera's Schoenbergian characteristics. Now to be sure, on the subartistic level those abrupt irregular rhythms and widely spaced vocal lines, the discontinuous orchestration and the high level of dissonance all evoke emotional responses more strained than (say) those suggested by Mozart's idiom. But the sub-artistic idiom is inevitably transcended, with Mozart as well as with Schoenberg. Music, art in general, is excellently resilient; with a little coaxing from the artist, any style will set up its own imaginative coherence, its own conventionalized rationale. Thus *Pierrot Lunaire*, however extreme in sentiment, establishes its own aesthetic normalcy. As a work of art, it is not mad at all, though its texture is from the conservative point of view more consistently perverse than that of *Wozzeck*. Perhaps consistency is the clue. Berg's opera is splendidly eclectic, undogmatic, inconsistent, and the powerful flux of style makes for his essential illusion.

The orchestral music, unlike that of *Pierrot Lunaire*, displays a subtle continuum from hearty twelve-tone formalism in some places to the stickiest post-Wagnerian tonal romanticism in others (notably the final climactic interlude, Marie's lullaby, and her later monologue in Act III). Whichever is momentarily accepted as normal qualifies the other to abnormality—and the shades are never entirely clear. The declamation establishes its own continuum from song to speech: from Marie's lullaby, where voice and orchestra are joined in the traditional way, to the final non-musical scream

of the Captain: *"Kommen Sie! kommen Sie schnell."*
Constant shifting within this continuum produces a
striking confusion between formalized declamation and
precise representation of the speech of persons in horrible extremity. Considered solely as recitative, *Wozzeck* would seem like Strauss made even more hyster-
ically unreal; considered solely as heightened speech,
it would seem like a grotesque caricature of old-style
elocutionary delivery. The interaction of these modes
adds a reality to the former and the credibility of
distance to the latter. It is their cunning confusion, I
believe, that builds into the illusion of hysteria, lying
just below the level of the naturalistic and often prosaic
dialogue.

Normality, in any case, never asserts itself in connection with the characters of the opera. This goes
against the play, which has its sane dullards (Marie,
Margret, Andres, the Drum-Major) along with its
generous share of eccentrics (Wozzeck, who is never
quite in his right mind, the Captain and the Doctor,
pervert and megalomaniac, the Idiot, and the marvelously drunk, preaching *Handwerksbursche*). In the
opera all inhabit a world of hysteria. The ones who
thrive best in it are the Captain and the Doctor; very
alarmingly, they are presented not as aberrations in
the world we know, but as ordinary denizens of a
distorted world. Wozzeck takes them for granted, without even protesting their persecutions, for captains
and doctors are apparently expected to behave as they
do.

The one thing that he does protest, Marie's infidelity, is actually the one normal element in the
play, coldly considering what Wozzeck is and what
Marie is—and we are certainly encouraged to see
Marie as coldly as Zola-esque methods allow. Shallow,
unintelligent, sentimental, she has been living unmar-

ried with Wozzeck for years, and makes a practice of sleeping with soldiers. Yet in the last act she abruptly dramatizes herself as Magdalen, and a maudlin scene it is too. What has she to regret in accepting the Drum-Major, who attracts her, as against Wozzeck, who cuts a poor figure indeed and (more important) arouses in her not the slightest affection? How seriously can we possibly take her morning-after repentance? Marie is a badly inconsistent character, unless she too, like the Captain and the Doctor, is regarded as a projection of what Wozzeck determines her to be.

Compare *Wozzeck* with Schoenberg's "monodrama" *Erwartung,* which was written in 1909 and deeply influenced Berg's opera in many ways. A woman, seeking her lover in a dark wood, comes upon or imagines she comes upon his dead body, and pours out around it her loves and fears and jealousies. Because this work establishes itself consistently within the subconscious, it evokes none of *Wozzeck's* peculiar terror or sense of aberration. Its macabre recital has no literal-minded meaning, and makes no musical reference to a normality without. *Wozzeck* on the other hand is rooted in actuality—the naturalistic plot and dialogue guarantee that; it takes place not in any dream world, but in the real world seen through abnormal eyes. The eyes are Wozzeck's, and the abnormality is evidently paranoia. Berg conceived the play with uncanny fidelity through the consciousness of his protagonist.* The dissection of a diseased mind gives the piece its supreme *frisson* for the twentieth century as surely as Buechner's blood-sniffing Idiot provided it for the early nineteenth.

At this point a question arises: is the paranoiac mind feasible dramatic material? *Frisson* is not tragedy. Much more than in the play, Wozzeck in the opera is

---

* The historical Woyzeck on whom Buechner based his play actually was a paranoiac, as Berg probably knew.

a dramatic nonentity, without personality or will (and with only the most tentative social consciousness, in spite of leitmotives). He is involved in no conscious conflict or action. He is simply obsessed altogether by his obsessions, and can only adjust to the world by going mad—which he does before the opera begins. Music articulates no progress while his agony is shown on the stage; what it does is document his derangement, that is, his dramatic irresponsibility. But *Wozzeck* does contain an extremely original kind of "musical action," one whose weakness is exactly that it lies outside the action on the stage, but whose strength in its own terms fortifies the opera even more than the naturalistic terror or the psychotic atmosphere. This musical action is of primary importance in considering the essential dramatic effect of the opera.

I refer to a large recurring musical rhythm from tension to relaxation. This is felt between many scenes and the orchestral interludes following them, but comes forward in all force only on the largest scale: between the opera as a whole and its final interlude, following Wozzeck's death and preceding the twenty-one-bar epilogue with the children. The first level on which *Wozzeck* is experienced is as a series of horrors mounting to a great release of tension in this last and longest interlude. And this primary experience must not be lost sight of in secondary subtleties.

The climactic orchestral interlude is the strongest and cleverest thing in *Wozzeck*, and its most genuinely Wagnerian feature. Berg saw the fault of Debussy's method even as he refined it. By not letting music take its head and seize an emotional crux in its own terms and do with it what it can, the sung play cuts off opera's chief source of power. Debussy was content with understatement; not so Alban Berg. Yet to have conventionalized to the extent of an aria or a Wagnerian aria-substitute would have broken the pace, and with it the immediacy and literalness of the presentation. So musical expansion, which the final force categorically demands, could take place only in the interludes between scenes. It is in the final interlude that one is first allowed leisure to feel what one has witnessed, here first that the enormity can be gauged in emotional terms. Wozzeck is dead, the curtain is down, and the music now connotes a sanity and a relief in warm contrast to the hysterical world of the stage, from which the audience has just been rescued. A forceful emotional place is provided without breaking the naturalistic illusion. Or more exactly, this illusion is broken by the curtain, a theatrical convention that Berg was careful not to override.

It is the dynamic of the symphonic poem, entirely Wagnerian in spirit. So is Berg's leitmotive parade. There is only one trouble, and for this incidentally no Wagnerian precedent exists. The great emphatic orchestral emotion is disconnected from the characters in the play; it is not *of* the action, but *about* the action.

Music qualifies the response of the audience instead of the response of the characters, who are now *todt Alles, Alles todt*, in King Mark's so applicable phrase. Boldly, and very unusually, Berg wrote an Aristotelian catharsis right into his drama. He himself was thoroughly in it; this is how he felt about the action, and this is how the audience is supposed to feel too. Everything, then, depends on the music of this interlude. If you surrender to its despotic demand, and if it rings true to you, it will define teleologically the tragedy of Wozzeck—which had not been articulated except in terms of this reaction to it. But once you have heard the interlude as a slow waltz in the lachrymose tradition of Gustav Mahler, you can no longer surrender, and everything is lost:

It brings to mind the last (and best) waltz in *Der Rosenkavalier*, the half-atonal one accompanying the winey tears of Octavian-Mariandel. Suddenly you see the deadly disparity between the tears and the dramatic action. On the basis of the play, blank Wozzeck has earned sympathy only to the extent of a baited animal. The emotion of the final interlude cannot properly adhere to him; it is, rather, self-indulgence after the shattering experience to which the audience has found itself subjected. The basic rhythm is from terror to self-pity, away from the action.

Puccini's practice comes to mind—but only very briefly, I must say. It is true that a piece like *Tosca* also ends with the composer's shrill demand for emotion essentially unearned by the action; but unlike *Wozzeck*, *Tosca* has presented no serious account of anything at any point previously. *Wozzeck* is also quite different from any of Puccini's operas in the effect of its actual conclusion. The epilogue following the interlude changes the mood strongly from the hysteria of the rest of the opera and the sentimentality of the interlude itself. Cold and entirely normal, it is the most naturalistic scene in the opera: children chanting a singing-game not in the disjunct chromatic style of Wozzeck's agony, but in the off-key tones of ordinary group unmusicality. They talk (*ganz gesprochen!*) to Marie's child: "You, your mother's dead!" Too little to understand or to talk himself, the child answers merely with two notes to giddy-up his rocking horse. The other children go out to review the corpse; then (a grisly touch neither in Buechner nor in his most imaginative editors) the child follows them out, equally curious. Throughout this very short, cinematographic epilogue the musical background is level and luminous, practically unrhythmicized by comparison with the rest of the piece, altogether impressionistic; sunlight. The music for the child's *"Hopp! hopp!"* recalls a passage in Debussy's *Gigues*; the final chord for the empty stage is pure Ravel—and what could be more clear-headed than Ravel? It is a final irony: the final *Schrecklichkeit* after the terror is past, understated as life is understated, set as unsentimentally as Berg knew how in the literal world of urchins.

It is a brutal juxtaposition, and for Berg must have been a heroic one: to place the children's icy reaction next to his and yours as boiled up in the immediately preceding interlude. By emphasizing an objective level of sanity, this concluding scene tends to give a new depth of reality to the psychosis of the earlier action, and an unexpected extent to the vision of degradation presented there. It comes too late, however. The scene seems disjoined from the essential business, and smacks fatally of a trick ending. Was Berg really interested in probing, or simply in twisting the knife? And for final relevance the action would have to be raised higher yet—higher than the level of consciousness of eight-year-old children.

What is genuine in this opera is the terror, not the

pity. The paranoiac dilemma was as real to Berg as to Wozzeck himself, and he was able to project it with a conviction and violence that make every other operatic shocker pale to the sphere of drawing-room comedy (I mean Strauss and Gian-Carlo Menotti). Nothing was too extreme that could add another shock to Buechner's grim play, another forceful detail to this arrogantly, fascinatingly overloaded score. When necessary Berg could out-brutalize Strauss, though he was rarely so blatant. He could evoke a mood as perfectly as Debussy, though he rarely needed Debussy's delicate sensuousness. What bravado to have written out the snoring in the barracks as a five-part male chorus—for all of nine bars of music! or to have coarsely mated Mahler and Stravinsky for the first Tavern Scene! Throughout, the dramaturgical surety is as amazing as its novelty; and the dramatic vision, whatever goes wrong, remains to wrench the subconscious: man oppressed and his hysterical, inarticulate struggle. *Wozzeck* is a central work in the contemporary theater on account of this vision, which cannot be wholly dimmed by the ultimate sentimentality.

3

THE ASPECT of contemporary music owes much to Alban Berg, and even more to Igor Stravinsky, who was born three years earlier. It is hard to think of two operas in more grating contrast than *Wozzeck* and *The Rake's Progress*. We tend to consider such artistic disparities as characteristic of our time; but the time of Buechner's *Wozzeck* was also that of *Prometheus Unbound*, of Berlioz and Stendhal, of young Mendelssohn and the old Goethe.

The Rake's Progress is a virtuoso exercise in twentieth-century neoclassicism. The libretto by W. H. Auden and Chester Kallman portrays no present-day neighbors, but fictional types in the comic spirit of Fielding. A handsome ne'er-do-well and his faithful country sweetheart take part in this moral "fable," a Bunyanesque progress wittily developed from the paintings by Hogarth. Fairy-tale elements blend in with the idealized eighteenth-century detail, color, and locale: the devil grants Tom a year and three wishes, and almost damns him at the end. There is even a clear link with classic myth. The dramaturgy retrenches to the Mozart line, employing *secco* recitative, arias, ensembles, and an almost ostentatious wealth of conventions culled from opera of the eighteenth and early nineteenth centuries. In particular, *Don Giovanni* is rather boldly evoked—comedy and tragedy, rakishness and retribution, Donna Anna/Anne Trulove, the graveyard and the moralizing *vaudeville* at the end. Through a veil, Stravinsky in his music seems sometimes to evoke Monteverdi, Pergolesi, Donizetti, Tchaikovsky, and others. He uses almost precisely Mozart's orchestra, but without trombones, and even resurrects the harpsichord for recitative.

Musical neoclassicism has its enemies, as many as the twelve-tone school of composition. But if *The Rake's Progress* has a final weakness, it is not a matter of neoclassicism, but of a flaw in the dramatic conception—the same fault as in *Wozzeck*: madness. Unlike Berg, Stravinsky shows madness as the climax of a long and thoroughly conscious progress on the part of his hero. Whether this is a more or less optimistic view of the condition of modern man, I shall not say; but I do have to say that from the dramatic point of view it is no more viable. The destination of the Rake's progress is not clear. The progress itself, like Wozzeck's agony, is magnificently presented, and is the lasting strength of the drama.

The libretto begins with a country tableau, a pair of lovers singing of "the festival of May":

ANNE: . . . The pious earth observes the solemn year.
TOM: Now is the season when the Cyprian Queen
With genial charm translates our mortal scene . . .

This is high talk for Hogarth's Tom Rakewell, and this opening duet has a strong ritual quality. Spring rites celebrate the annual return of Adonis from the underworld, and the lovers are preparing to re-enact the story of Venus and Adonis in a new interpretation. Adonis, a beautiful youth beloved of Aphrodite, rejects her love because he wishes to be free and devote himself to the pleasures of the chase. This life destroys him, but he is half-redeemed by the goddess and brought back to earth for half of every year. We are to see Tom reject Anne Trulove in order to follow his desire for freedom and pleasure in the brothels, fairs, and on the Stock Exchange of London. In "a year and a day" he is in the clutch of Hades, represented by his serving-man Nick Shadow, but is half-redeemed by Anne's love: not with a clear temporal division, as in the myth, but with a simultaneous one; he is both on earth and in hell at the same time—that is, insane. In Bedlam, Tom imagines himself Adonis in Hades, surrounded by Minos, Orpheus, and others, awaiting the return of Aphrodite. It is spring again, and she comes. But then she leaves for good; now we need the eighteenth-century story, and the twentieth-century moral.

Shadow is only half pagan shade. His Christian name is Nick, and the more important Christian fable is superimposed on the classic legend. Characteristically, Auden examines the soul of his Adonis, and enlists comedy, pathos, and lyricism to the task of turning our sympathies to him. The search for freedom and pleasure, it develops, is complex, equivocal, and very little fun. Tom can be resolute enough in the country, but when he comes with Nick to his first temptation, he draws back and has to be tricked into taking the plunge. He already half-repents, and continues to do so at every new step on his downward path, on which, indeed, he can only be propelled by the ingenuity of his domestic Satan. Tom is a weakling, but we must count it an act of bravery when, at the final reckoning, he throws away weakness and pride and trusts to Anne's love. In the graveyard, when the devil proposes a game of cards for Tom's soul, Tom bets on the apparently impossible Queen of Hearts, cheating Nick Shadow just as Shadow had cheated him in the first act. The Rake's progress, in other words, is first of all a proving, a preparation for Aphrodite, whom he finally wishes and deserves too late. The wordly search for pleasure and freedom is shown to be continuously vain.

This would seem to be clear and proper dramatic material; but the objection has been raised that Tom is not significantly a rake at all. The force of this objection is obscure. To be sure, Tom is not involved in so titillating a series of adventures as his prototype in the pictures, or even as Mozart's Don Giovanni. Tom is someone much more complicated, more a figure for our time. He may belong to the same family as Don Juan, together with Mr. Punch, Faust, Shaw's John Tanner, and Stravinsky's Soldier, but this family is fundamentally split on the matter of conscience. Punch and Don Juan have none; they do not change, and their dissoluteness and punishment are both handled unequivocally (*Don Giovanni* is admirably subtitled *Il dissoluto punito*). Faust and Rakewell do have consciences; the progresses through which they pass are intrinsically more interesting than their errors, and their sins and retribution are to varying degrees equivocal. Perhaps neither Faust nor Rakewell is possible today as a subject for comedy, unless the author disengage the sympathies, like Shaw. It is a question whether Don Juan is still a comic possibility, after Kierkegaard and Byron. But leaving aside the matter of comedy, Rakewell's case has all necessary urgency, timeliness, universality, and pathos, to say nothing of an honorable tradition.

A *priori* objection to Tom as a dramatic figure, then, is as absurd as Eduard Hanslick's mincing suggestion that the Othello story was too distasteful to be made into a decent opera. The only point is whether poet and composer can present him to us convincingly. In Auden's libretto the progress of the half-repentant Rake is direct, economical, well-shaped, and undeflected by secondary material. It is arranged around three wishes granted by Nick Shadow, who does not foresee that a fourth wish, for Anne, will save Tom at the end. In the country, Tom's callow desire is for money and the pleasures it will buy, but after his introduction to the brothel this palls, and Tom's understanding deepens. As he wishes more generally for happiness, Nick persuades him to marry a freak from St. Giles' Fair, Baba the Turk, *not* on the basis of gratification of the senses, but in order to exercise his noble gift of freedom; happiness comes only with freedom from the twin dictates of lust and conscience. Tom, never very clever, falls for this topical philosophy, but it proves altogether vain. Finally Shadow can incline him to wickedness only by appealing to his sentimental better nature—a low blow; the bread-making machine, Tom wishes and prays, may save his soul yet by spreading so much benefit in the world. For all this time he has been telling himself, with characteristic weakness or arrogance, that he is so far damned that he cannot return to Anne, even though she offers to forgive. Of course Tom is a little self-piteous; we laugh a little at that, too. "How handsomely he cries!" say the admiring Whores as Tom sings his most beautiful aria.

The record of Tom's progress is not deflected by the sub-plot concerning Baba the Turk, around which much of the humor turns. To have Tom assert his freedom by marrying is delightful and as cock-eyed as Shadow's philosophy. Moreover it has considerable value for the rest of the plot. If Anne was to do anything in the opera besides open and close it, she had tō appear in the middle, and about the only thing to have her do was chase after Tom in London (as in Hogarth—there to the point of tiresomeness). But then would not weak, good-hearted, repentant Tom go back to her, and foil Shadow ahead of time? That would destroy the plot; and mere whoring will not put off level-headed, determined girls like Anne. The only situation that can set her back (temporarily) is for her to find Tom married to someone else. As Anne is temporarily set back, Tom careers downward all the more clearly and dramatically.

Later Baba neatly befriends the wavering Anne, and actually gives her the final encouragement to seek Tom again, even though he had married another. Stravinsky rises to this occasion. Anne's epiphanic realization

> He loves me still! Then I alone
> In weeping doubt have been untrue . . .

is one of the most eloquent spots in the score. Potentially Anne is a fine character, much better than Hogarth's quite different girl, and we are sorry to see her evaporate at the end. Baba, however, is incisively and completely drawn, and her role is at every step co-ordinated to the main plot. The suspicions of exotic pleasures that Tom is presumably to taste with the circus freak are amusingly dispelled; it is only after the marriage and the scene with Anne that we learn (right at the curtain of Act II, scene ii) the nature of

Baba's great asset; heretofore we had only the dark information that "brave warriors who never flinched at the sound of musketry have swooned after a mere glance of her." In the following domestic scene Baba is revealed as a perfect caricature of commonplace femininity. It is hard to know what is more dreadful, her ceaseless chatter, her tantrum, or her saccharine little love song. But, as a parody of the eternal verities of Show Business, Baba has the inevitable heart of gold.

She also has the last laugh; and it is a matter of some importance that we always laugh at Tom. The three steps of his descent, corresponding to his Epicurean, existentialist, and Christian wishes, are each made to seem pointless in laughter. Mother Goose's Brothel is a carefully childish affair. The un-exotic Baba makes his life miserable. The "excellent machine" which deceives him is ludicrous. Obviously this use of humor is diametrically opposed to that in *Don Giovanni*, in which the fun is always turned against Don Giovanni's victims; we always laugh *with* him, even when he himself is fooled, for he always sees the joke (unlike Tom, who has no sense of humor). Attitudes towards these two protagonists are hardly determined by their actions or their degree of objective rakishness. Our different modes of sympathy are determined by the music, of course, and by the different directions of the comedy. We regard Tom always with some amusement, and with some compound of pity and impatience, whereas Don Giovanni earns our admiration.

The repentant Rake's progress is admirably projected in the libretto. If I have dealt with this libretto at unusual length, that is because it has been misunderstood, and because it is indeed unusually subtle for an opera book—though I should certainly not say unduly subtle. But as always, the dramatist is the composer, and the Rake's progress is essentially articulated by a progress in the music.

The dramaturgy is classical: basically a series of self-contained lyric numbers defining the developing stages of Tom's feeling and thus the stages of his growing awareness. His initial scorn for work and his trust in luck are sardonically greeted by a pair of bassoons, which grumble through his opening aria—a gay, Handelian piece, bold rhythmically, and simple-minded, with a proud high A as Tom calls on wishes to be horses: "This beggar shall ride!" But the wishes turn to nightmares. In the child-like brothel Tom is as if stunned; the audience should be stunned too by the sudden deepening of Tom's response as, helpless, he calls on Aphrodite for support in a *cavatina* of simple and direct sentiment. Remorse becomes more complex after the initiation. The long aria "Vary the tune" incorporates a painful, powerful account of Tom's disillusion worked over a chromatically rising bass progression, and returns pathetically to the clear-eyed opening tune. Tom's anguish is intensified in the very beautiful trio with Anne and Baba. In the graveyard he is too tense to feel or sing much; the realization in musical terms of his decisive act of faith is left until later, in Bedlam. Here the short duet with Anne is led by Tom, who seems certainly to regain his senses, and indeed to gain full awareness for the first time. The ending of this duet, breathlessly beating the air over the tonic pedal, is the most transcendental moment in the score:

> Rejoice, beloved: in these fields of Elysium
> Space cannot alter, nor Time our love abate;
> Here has no words for absence or estrangement
> Nor Now a notion of Almost or Too Late.

The pedal, the anapaestic rhythm, and the alternation of major and minor thirds (D and D♭) are typically

Text by W. H. Auden and Chester Kallman. Music by Igor Stravinsky. Copyright 1949, 1950, 1951 by Boosey & Hawkes, Inc. Reprinted by permission.

Stravinskian means of expression. Extra poignancy comes from the fact that this passage is fashioned out of the little ballad of Adonis sung by Tom when he was struck mad. After Anne leaves, Tom in his final accompanied recitative calls on Orpheus to lend him a swan-like music; the music vaguely recalls the music of Stravinsky's ballet *Orpheus*, with its uniquely reserved, penetrating grief. What is so striking about all these numbers is their clarity of feeling. Clarity, discreteness, is the great virtue of the traditional dramaturgical system of aria and recitative, and it is a virtue that Stravinsky is able to recapture.

To arrange a clear psychological progression in arias and ensembles seems an obvious enough resource, but it is one that was not fully appreciated in the time of the classic operatic tradition. I do not know that any opera employs it so extensively and centrally, so subtly, or so convincingly as *The Rake's Progress*. Of the baroque composers, perhaps Bach was the only one with the imagination to work in this way; in brief cantatas, at least, he left some impressive examples. Gluck certainly had the idea, but lacked the musical flexibility to fix developing stages of awareness. In *Don Giovanni*, Donna Elvira becomes the most interesting of the ladies on account of the progress in her lyric utterances—but only with the help of a thoroughly gratuitous piece, "*Mi tradì quell' alma ingrata*," which was forced into the last act for a singer in the Viennese performance. The early operas of Wagner and Verdi are enough in the classic manner to be counted, but neither composer was much of a psychologist yet. Stravinsky makes fresh use of a powerful dramatic possibility latent in the old convention.

Many other vitalizations of old conventions can be cited. Anne's scene at the end of Act I is a bold return to Donizetti's worst cliché, the aria with *cabaletta*. The singer begins with a lyric aria, then changes his mind because of a message or something heard off-stage, then sings a vehement *cabaletta* to ring down the curtain. A perfectly good device, when carefully used, as it rarely was; but we have seen how Verdi could turn it to dramatic account in Violetta's scene at the end of Act I in *La Traviata*—"*Ah fors' è lui*" leading to "*Sempre libera*." Stravinsky's aria is entirely serious, but his *cabaletta* is a parody of an old *da capo* aria, complete with absurd little modulation for the central section and then a thumping return. We love Anne all the more for being slightly ridiculous, like Mozart's Fiordiligi. And as with Violetta, some of Anne's music acts as a "hinge theme," later returning as a crucial dramatic reminiscence. Nick Shadow's one aria (also a *da capo* aria) wins Tom over to his esoteric philosophy with complete dramatic conviction, following the operatic maxim that every essential motivation has to be presented in musical terms. The musical style and form of the arias are strangely classical too, in spite of Stravinsky's characteristically modern methods. He has always refused to modulate forcefully in the manner developed by Mozart and Beethoven as the basis of the "dramatic" style in music, and the basis particularly of Wagnerian music. Stravinsky recreates the level quality of Handel and Bach, and their intensity and singleness of momentary emotion.

Stravinsky's use of the harpsichord is nicely symbolic of his entire effort and success. Nothing could be better than the brittle tone of this archaic instrument to shut off the imaginative level of the arias for the "business" of recitative. The old *maestri* would arpeggiate chords for greater clarity; Stravinsky writes a violently dissonant arpeggio every time that Shadow appears and grants a wish—but employs the technique less for aural clarity than for an intrinsic effect of scuttling menace. In the graveyard scene, suddenly, Nick Shadow's harpsichord comes to the fore and plays

all alone and coherently for minutes, during the excruciating game of cards for Tom's soul. The unholy
clatter, measured and terribly still, creates an incomparable impression of numb crisis—

> As wind in dry grass
> Or rats' feet over broken glass
> In our dry cellar
> Shape without form, shade without colour,
> Paralysed force, gesture without motion.

Entirely modern, the impression depends on the
more conventional use of the harpsichord earlier in
the opera. Arpeggios continue to characterize Shadow,
and two orchestral interruptions of the harpsichord
color have as devastating an effect as the trombones
in *Don Giovanni's* graveyard. The first (woodwinds)
is at Tom's despair: "O God, what hopes have I?"
The second (strings) is at his triumph: "Love, first
and last, assume eternal reign"; and the tune of Anne's
cabaletta returns, the dramatic reminiscence, guiding
him to the final trust and the defeat of Shadow.

After the painful intensity of the graveyard scene,
how exquisite the music becomes at the end, at spring's
return: the last duet between the lovers as Venus and
Adonis; Anne's gentle lullaby with the flutes; the tiny
dissonant *duettino* over a ground bass as Anne and
Trulove depart; Tom's dying recitative; the austere
monotone elegy of the Madmen's mourning chorus.
Sentiment is neither dessicated nor cloyed, and there
is a kind of consciousness and intelligence about it
that does indeed recall Mozart, in spite of the general
un-Mozartian pall. In sharp contrast to Alban Berg,
Stravinsky is outside his opera, viewing the progress
of the Rake with a grave detached sympathy which
is perhaps our most genuine response to crisis. Then,
in the epilogue, as lights flare on and the characters
step out in front of the curtain and take off their
wigs, and Baba takes off her beard, Stravinsky puts on

his Pulcinella-mask, which Picasso has drawn for us. Not even Pergolesi has captured the hard glitter of farce so well.

But while the music grows in eloquence, the dramatic meaning attenuates. Just as in *Don Giovanni*, it was necessary to try to re-establish the responses of comedy, dangerously weakened in the penultimate tableau; this was I think not quite feasible in either opera. It may pass for Hogarthian, this proverb recital —"The Devil finds work for idle hands." But it does not have Hogarth's lively cruelty; Auden made a decisive departure from the eighteenth-century view when he pitied the Rake and set about analyzing him. Once our sympathies are engaged, we want to know the destination of the Rake's progress, and what Tom feels about it, and what Anne feels about it, and what the dramatist feels about it. All of these must not be left in doubt.

Anne even comes to Tom in Bedlam, in order to fulfill dramatically his crucial act of faith in the graveyard. Indeed, if Tom's madness is regarded symbolically as obsession for Anne, his true reality, this too is resolved by his presumptive return to reason in the duet with her. But then Anne leaves; Tom awakes, and dies of a broken heart. ("My heart breaks. I feel the chill of death's approaching wing . . .") What is the significance of having Anne save him in the graveyard, only to betray him now? As her renunciation is not presented as saintly, it produces simply a dry, even cruel effect—and heretofore Anne has not been a dry person at all. Aphrodite did not leave Adonis to die in anguish. And in so specifically Faustian a tale, we want to know which way Tom goes when he dies—a matter treated squarely by Marlowe and Goethe and Thomas Mann, who, like Auden, brings his hero to insanity before death. In his madness, Tom's ravings cannot properly reflect his feelings about salvation,

Purgatory, Anne's departure, or the meaning of his
ordeal. Anne is extinguished. Neither of them touches
the theme of redemption or half-redemption on which
the opera promised to culminate. The chorus mourns
madly, making an undifferentiated aura of elegy, in itself moving, but inarticulate as to the consummation
implied by the earlier action.

"The Devil finds work for idle hands". . . I do not
think that moral fables are made out of people as
tragically alive as these. The ending epilogue seems
not to illuminate or to resolve, but to mask; the destination of the Rake's progress is quite unclear. It may
be a necessary characteristic of Auden's modern pil-
grim to find affirmation impossible. But unhappily this
is a state of mind that cannot be allowed to the dramatist, however anxious the age.

4

To HAZARD *Wozzeck* and *The Rake's Progress* as the
major operas of this century is probably to court less
argument than with any other pair that might be suggested. They are works of sensitivity and consummate
skill; each projects a relevant contemporary vision, even
though one of them is egregiously classical in technique, and even though both of them retrench from
the extreme positions of nineteenth-century operatic
dramaturgy. Like *Pelléas et Mélisande*, *Wozzeck* treats
an essentially undramatic idea with singleminded, terrifying conviction. Like *Don Giovanni*, *The Rake's
Progress* deals with man's mistaken journey penetrat-
ingly, but without finding a satisfactory dramatic consummation. These two works show most triumphantly
the continuing life to *dramma per musica* in our time
—a vitality all the more impressive on account of

their striking differences in mood, technique, and almost everything else. Compare the two lullabies, for instance. Both operas, I should think, must occupy an important place in any record of the serious contemporary theater.

And if this is not generally granted, the reason is that opera is generally considered only in its musical context rather than as drama at all. In fact, *Wozzeck* and *The Rake's Progress* are usually spoken of in terms of the conventional formulation of the state of contemporary music: the dichotomy between neoclassicism, which is mainly French in orientation, and the twelve-tone school, which is mainly German. This is a clumsy framework for criticism, and I have skirted it deliberately—wilfully, certain readers may think. *Wozzeck* and *The Rake* are extremely good works, but they are not at all parallel in respect to their positions in the history of the "schools." *The Rake's Progress*, certainly, is a climactic example of neoclassicism, from the hostile point of view a maddening caricature of it. *Wozzeck*, on the other hand, is a transitional piece and a highly eclectic one; only parts of it are written in the twelve-tone technique, and its essential large rhythm is Straussian. We may feel that in dramatic conception *The Rake* is finer and more meaningful than *Wozzeck*, even though it fails at the end. Such a judgement compares the two works, and to some extent the two composers, but hardly at all the virtues of the two schools. Straussian sentiments are no more intrinsic to the twelve-tone school than reminiscences of Tchaikovsky are to neoclassicism.

Both stylistic principles have been miserably abused, and both schools protect their fair share of the talentless. The great trouble with conventional discussions of contemporary music is that they center too much on style, and not enough on meaning. Style for what? The critical disparity is natural enough; meanings are hard to estimate while artists are in the process of formulating them, and hard to express under any circumstances. In the field of opera, perhaps, these difficulties are a little less intense than with purely instrumental music. We can see and say what an opera is trying to project. These masterpieces of Berg and Stravinsky are bigger than their schools, and it is parochial to regard them simply either-or as signposts to "the music of the Future."

9

Drama and the Alternative

> It would be possible to exhume
> hundreds of operas quite devoid of
> drama, but though they may be
> easily in the majority, they do not
> prove that Opera is undramatic.
> The best operas *are* dramatic; the
> failures are no evidence at all.
>
> —H. D. F. KITTO

DURING opera's relatively short history of three
hundred and fifty years, the ideal of *dramma
per musica* has animated many good composers and
many intellectuals. In the previous chapters I have
traced the evolution of this ideal, or better, its notable
successive embodiments, from the late Renaissance
humanism of Florence and Mantua to a very different
sort of neoclassicism in the 1950's. It should go without saying that the amount of genuine metal is small
by comparison with the slag-heaps that have kept opera
thriving. This is the case with any popular art. The
sixteenth century produced dozens of wretched imita-
tors of Petrarch for one Torquato Tasso; the eighteenth,
thousands of dreary trio-sonatas which we forget while
remembering those of Handel and Bach. And in the
twentieth, we need only think of the stacks of wasted
reels surrounding a single moving picture that seems

to deal imaginatively with the new art-form. Indeed, to read the history of opera in the early eighteenth or early nineteenth centuries is to be irresistibly reminded of the films today. The fantastic productivity and mortality; the stars and the ballyhoo; the meretriciousness, pretentiousness, and cynicism; the outrage of the critics and the enthusiasm of the paying public; the cult of the super-colossal—it all rings a familiar note. The casual critic may suppose that the conditions of opera, like those of the films, are simply antithetical to serious art. The more careful observer discerns at every point possibilities which some artists have chosen to wrestle with, always to some avail. Lesser men ignorantly or deliberately choose the lesser way.

The significant operatic canon is not large. Monteverdi, Purcell, Gluck, Mozart, Verdi, Wagner, Debussy, Berg, Stravinsky, and a few others have left a body of musical drama which is rich and various, but not large. The empirical eye of history notes the great bulk of operatic production that has been resolutely undramatic: seventy operas between 1795 and 1825 by a certain Simon Mayr, for instance, and so on and so on. But as Professor Kitto remarks, this is no evidence at all. The best operas *are* dramatic, and the successful works are plentiful and impressive enough to preserve the ideal, and preserve it triumphantly. History, if we give it time, will successively reject the mass of undramatic operas and maintain only those—only a fraction of those—which achieve some serious vision. Nothing seems so drab as the popular art of yesterday.

Perhaps I should say, the popular art of the day before yesterday; for the second-rate material of our immediate past is still very much in evidence. Our operatic repertory, in fact, is clogged with relics from the general period 1890 to 1914. This quarter-century, which brought much to a head and much to a conclusion, was the last period during which opera flourished as a lively contemporary thing, with a clear bond between the composer and the public. Society still found a place, though it was becoming narrow, for the last of the line of successful professional opera composers, men who fed and fed on the huge operatic traditions of the past, "men of the theater" writing rapidly for audiences which responded no less rapidly. Gluck, Mozart, and Verdi were such men who rose above the banalities of their condition—after years in the galleys, to use Verdi's own favorite metaphor. Among dozens who did not rise were Cesti and Campra, Caldara and Cimarosa, Simon Mayr, Flotow, Balfe, Mercadante, Massenet. The last of the line, I should suppose, were Richard Strauss and Giacomo Puccini. There is almost a sense of nostalgia, nowadays, in the way we store their work in the repertory, even to the point of making it a staple for some operatic theaters.

It is second-rate stuff. To be sure, Strauss and Puccini represent high types of the operatic professional: Puccini spent as much anxious care on each score as any composer, and Strauss had genuine literary connections and a reputation as a thinker, like Meyerbeer. They were hailed, rashly but pardonably at first, as the legitimate successors of Verdi and Wagner; but between Verdi and Puccini, between Wagner and Strauss, lies the decisive gulf between art and sensationalism. From the start Puccini and Strauss revealed a coarseness of sensitivity and a deep cynicism towards true dramatic values, characteristics that simply deepened as their techniques grew more and more impressive. Talent, craft, and pretentiousness are no substitute for spirit.

If I go on now to labor this point, it is not simply out of indiscriminate indignation against the second-rate. In art the poor is always with us, and ordinarily time treats it more effectively than indignation. At the moment, however, the aspect of operatic repertory differs in an important respect from what it has been traditionally. In the past, the repertory was mainly contemporary, formed by the constant honest sifting of the second-rate. That was to the good; the routine production of any age ought to be copiously presented, vigorously discussed, and decently buried. But today our opera houses do not fulfill this function; since the First World War they have come to occupy the positions of historical repositories. They serve the cause of Art, not the cause of Experiment. That is a tenable position too, and so long as it is clearly understood, no harm is done by mixing the serious works with a few curios from the past: a *Faust*, a *Martha*, even a *Louise*. Indeed we could use a few more of these, or at any rate a few different ones. What does seem to me harmful, though, is for the repertory to be practically dominated by material of this general category— inferior material without even the brashness of contemporaneity. Puccini looms larger in American musical life than any contemporary composer, and also larger than Mozart or Wagner as opera composers. The second-rate is granted fantastic authority.

Operatic taste is only what might have been predicted under these circumstances. On the one hand, Strauss and Puccini seem in the blinkered eye of history to stand as high as the great composers, on account of their freakish survival. This is stultifying enough, but actually less dangerous than the opposite tendency: artistic standards tend to be dragged down to the level of Strauss and Puccini. It is on this account, I believe, that so much confusion exists today as to the dramatic potential and achievement of opera. If Wagner is never expected to do more than Strauss, of course we can never appreciate his accomplishment— and the slighting of this accomplishment is more deplorable than the mere fact of Strauss's bloated pres-

tige. But the leveling of art and *Kitsch*, whether up-
ward or downward, is always damnable. An index of
how far things have gone with opera is afforded by
the common conjunction "Verdi and Puccini"; do we
speak so blandly of "Mozart and Clementi" or "Ibsen
and Galsworthy" or "Eisenstein and De Mille"? When
standards are formed indiscriminately on the second-
rate, genuine values are easily lost, and confusion up-
sets every judgement.

I am afraid that no effort to show the true metal of
opera would be complete without some dredging away
of the dross. It is imperative to keep emphasizing
that the difference is of crucial importance.

2
———

Tosca, that shabby little shocker, is no doubt admired
nowadays mostly in the gallery. In the parterre it is
agreed that *Turandot* is Puccini's finest work; no opera
at present, not even *Carmen*, has so inflated a reputation. But if *Turandot* is more suave than *Tosca* musically, dramatically it is a good deal more depraved,
and the adjective is carefully chosen. To be sure, as
Puccini died before quite finishing the score, his ultimate responsibility is in doubt. However he had already done most of the harm, and had approved the
libretto, and left a thirty-six-page draft which Franco
Alfano was able to follow in completing the piece.
Judging from the endings of other Puccini operas, I
cannot believe that the concluding scenes of *Turandot*
as he might have composed them would have been
much better, or even significantly different.

The story is an ancient one, which had served several
forgotten opera composers prior to Puccini. After long
journeys, Prince Calaf arrives in Peking and chances

upon his destitute old father with his sole support, the little slave-girl Liù, who has been secretly in love with Calaf for years. He listens to her meek avowal sympathetically, but falls in love with the icy Princess Turandot. He enters the usual contest, to guess three riddles, for the usual stakes, her hand or his head, and wins. When Turandot seeks to renege, Calaf offers her the chance to guess his name on the same terms; in order to find out, she tortures Liù, who kills herself without telling. Horrified, Calaf nevertheless kisses Turandot and tells her his name. But her fierce hatred for men evaporates, and as she crowns him next morning, she announces that his name is "Love." The Chinese rejoice that Turandot's bloody contests are at an end.

Nobody would deny that dramatic potential can be found in this tale. Puccini, however, did not find it; his music does nothing to rationalize the legend or illuminate the characters; it is consistently, throughout, of café-music banality. There is simply no insight into any emotions that might possibly be imagined in any of the situations, to say nothing of an imaginative binding conception. Thus the action shows Calaf's lust for Turandot increase as she grows more desperate; but his music is Puccini's eternal mawkish serenade, and his vitality is exhausted in *chinoiserie*. Liù's soft affection for Calaf, though prettily done, is altogether incommensurate with her gratuitous sacrifice. The three half-humorous councillors are gratuitous too, as is the Chinese chorus, for all its unusually large part; the Hymn to the Moon has as little to do with the action as the "*Miserere*" in *Il Trovatore*. Most damaging of all, Turandot's surrender has no motivation, except the obvious physical one, which Alfano dutifully wrote into the music, and which decorous opera directors ignore. Considering the size of his role, Timur (the father) is one of the weakest people in the whole operatic repertory as far as musical definition is concerned. He is of no real dramatic use, and we can hardly blame Calaf for forgetting all about him at the end.

The inescapable central message of the piece, then, is that the way to proceed with a frigid beauty is to get your hands on her. Then she will shout "Love"; in which sentiment you naturally share, even though previously she has shown her hand by murderous treachery towards you and by destroying the one half-appealing character in the play. The outlines of the story, and even these void characters, could have made a certain sense in the *verismo* setting of *Il Tabarro*. Then we might at least have been spared the claim that the drama illustrates "love." But in China, as Puccini's music portrays China, every gland has been torn from the tale. There is no organic reason for the bogus orientalism lacquered over every page of the score; the tremendous apparatus provides exoticism for its own sake, but also, more deeply, a chance for the artist to wriggle out of his irresponsibility. Puccini must have been afraid of this story. But in the mysterious, exciting, cruel, inscrutable world of Chinese myth anything can be excused, and shades of meaning can drift aimlessly from one pentatonic tune to the next, and from one sentimental phrase to its almost inevitable repetition. Rarely has myth been so emptily employed in this extravaganza. Genuine drama is entirely out of the question.

Aïda, and prior to that Meyerbeer's *L'Africaine*, had set a bad precedent in their careless application of local color. But the only well-known opera that goes as far as *Turandot* in this respect is *Boris Godunov*. The differences are striking, and fundamental to the problem of musical drama. Unlike *Turandot, Boris Godunov* is really about something: kingship, the relation between ruler and the ruled. The ruled are the people of Russia, a community which Mussorgsky knew and felt, and never dreamed of patronizing. It was no doubt the only community that he could honestly represent. His vision of a mystic, incoherent moving force in the Folk is realized by the pervasive Russian folk-character of the chorus and of the music for the minor characters, Pushkin's wonderful collection of "types." The Folk transcends personalities and Church, transcends individual actions and history. So the Tsar speaks in the accents of the Folk; Boris's conflict lies between his inevitable bond with Russia and his guilt, and his tragedy stems from his awareness of them both. Like the Tsar, the Church partakes of the spirit of the Folk. No opera, I think, has incorporated liturgical music—hymns and chants—into the drama so centrally and so convincingly. It is not a matter of technique, which was sketchy in Mussorgsky's case, but of a burning sincerity and purity of conception.

All this was far from Puccini's ken, though like so many other twentieth-century composers, he seems to have studied *Boris Godunov* with profit. The most extraordinary thing about this composer is his lack of penetration. He had, alas, a clear sense of the theater, a facility above the average, and a genuine talent for memorable little turns of melody within a narrow emotional span. In this respect Puccini is quite like George Gershwin, and a cut above most of his own contemporaries, such as Umberto Giordano, the composer of *Andrea Chénier*. But this lyric gift is quite unlike Verdi's. Puccini clings to his limited ideas and repeats them protectively; Verdi presses one into the next with an increasingly powerful sweep, an impressively broad control of sentiment, and a consummate sense of lyric form. Puccini applies his lyric melodies indiscriminately, as we have seen in the case of Calaf; Verdi, in *Otello*, bends lyricism always to the drama. Verdi had the soul for tragedy; only the pastoral, perhaps, was safely within Puccini's range, so long as the convention was not turned to any serious end. *La Bohème* stays so frankly on the surface that it will never lose its somewhat chlorotic charm. Puccini also had a good sense of fun; his indiscriminate lyricism cannot spoil *Gianni Schicchi*. Unfortunately conditions made it necessary for him to touch on torture, in *Tosca*; desertion, in *Madama Butterfly*; religion, in *Suor Angelica*; social consciousness, in *Il Tabarro*; and other matters for which he was altogether unequipped. There is almost a sense of despair in the meaninglessness of *Turandot*. Never did pretentiousness lead Puccini so far astray as in his most carefully wrought and most anxiously considered opera, the one that he did not live to complete.

Cecil Gray, the most reckless of reckless English critics, compared Richard Strauss with Puccini already in 1924, when it became apparent that the World War, unaccountably, had been insufficient to dislodge these masters of operatic pretension from the hardening repertory. It is certainly true that none of the egregious differences between these composers can obscure their firm common ground of insensitivity. Yet they seem to have come to it by different paths. Richard Strauss chose his subjects with considerable stylishness: Oscar Wilde, Hofmannsthal, modernized Sophocles, and Stefan Zweig, as opposed to Puccini's Sardou, Belasco, and Gozzi-by-way-of-Soho. At one period of his life, and it was his best period, Strauss belonged genuinely to the *avant garde*, especially in matters of harmony, while Puccini throughout his career skittishly borrowed and bowdlerized up-to-date techniques for his own conservative ends. Puccini cannot be said to have made any positive operatic innovation beyond the stage represented by the works of Massenet and Verdi's *Falstaff*. Strauss's realization of opera as symphonic poem was really something new, or at least something that had only been implied, and avoided, by Richard Wagner.

Strauss's operas are more complex and advanced and intellectual than Puccini's; at the same time they are just as hollow. The essential difference seems to be in consciousness, the difference in attitude between the unthinking opportunist and the decadent. There is a certain naïveté in Puccini's lack of taste and substance, but Strauss seems only too aware. His muse, as Cecil Gray put it, has lost her chastity—early, decisively, and repeatedly. No less insensitive than Puccini, Strauss adds an intellectual pretentiousness to Puccini's more innocent kinds.

In Gray's opinion *Salome* was Strauss's best work, and it does show his powers very clearly, as well as the absurdity to which they are turned. This opera, incidentally, sets a stage play verbatim, like *Wozzeck* and *Pelléas et Mélisande*, though of course Oscar Wilde's "poetic prose" is quite different from Maeterlinck's. Every gesture of every character is mirrored in the music; Strauss had a perfect genius for this sort of thing. But Salome, Jochanaan, Herod, and Herodias are as unreal as the less laboriously etched figures of *Turandot*, for only some kind of sympathy or interest on the part of the composer could make them live. This was not forthcoming, and so the sensational action is in the deepest sense irrelevant. Strauss probably intended the piece as an abstract display of sexual perversion, and as such it has been admired by some critics. But I find no reality on this plane either. Consistency, power, unity, ingenuity, yes; the overloading of detail is not as tedious as in other Strauss operas, and the whole is bound together with the greatest skill in a form comparable to that of the symphonic poem. The musical progress comes to its triumphant conclusion on the very last page, in a very famous, very loud passage which carries harmonic audacity farther than ever before. In musical technique, masterly; in sentiment, the most banal sound in the whole opera. John the Baptist's severed head might as well be made of marzipan. And it is for this sugary orgasm that all the fantastically involved aphrodisiac machinery has been required.

Baron Ochs at least lives the fullness of his lechery; we might wish that *Der Rosenkavalier* were really about him, for it is such a brilliant work, and he is the only one of the main characters who does not jerk at our heartstrings. But at the center stands the aging Marschallin, and close to her the youthful lovers. These characters are real enough; so is their unfailing shallowness of response. The opening tableau is already so ennervated in sentiment that the relationship between Octavian and the Marschallin seems as unappetizing as their affectionate nicknames. Her subsequent monologue is all the more so because she indulges her sentimentality so consciously—*"mit gar so klarem Sinn."* Sophie begins the second act promisingly; the first scene, a delightful conception: Strauss's nonsensical density of style is for once just right for the desperate confusion against which she sings determinedly of a humility so necessary but so impossible to achieve. But the scene of the presentation of the rose has all the solidity of a fifty-cent valentine, and when the young lovers come together at the end of the opera, all that Strauss can produce is a sort of feeble folk song. By any criterion, I think, it is the poorest thing in the opera. Was it for this minimal level of consciousness that we have had to suffer the Marschallin's self-pity and to sacrifice Ochs? for this, the silver rose and the white suit, the Three Noble Orphans and four finicky hours of leitmotives, modulations, and program-musical wit? The folk song is evidently a bow to a passage in *The Magic Flute*; Octavian and the

Marschallin recall *The Marriage of Figaro*. These were deadly comparisons to have courted, and bespeak an arrogance hard to credit in any true Mozartian.

The Viennese have managed thoroughly to debauch the waltz. Baron Ochs is the very personification of this inescapable dance. *"Die schoene Musi!"* In the operettas of Strauss's Viennese namesake, in a work like *Die Fledermaus*, the constant waltzing still has its pristine glitter and grace, setting perfectly the illusion of carnival, champagne, and feather-brained levity. But already with Brahms, and decisively with Gustav Mahler, the waltz began to assume the pretensions of sentiment that led Maurice Ravel to compose his savage, *verismo* parody. That was after the World War; but even after *Die Dreigroschenoper* had further satirized the waltz, a composer like Alban Berg was unable to shake off its traditional tawdry. Berg could never entirely shake off Mahler and Richard Strauss. *Salome's* Dance of the Seven Veils begins blatantly enough with music of the sort associated nowadays with Hollywood extravaganzas in a near-Eastern setting. When pseudo-orientalism yields climactically to a great swirling waltz running through all of Salome's leitmotives, the listener hardly knows whether to laugh or cry. Oscar Wilde, however artificial his sentiment, did at least have some sort of idea of the fascination of evil sexuality. Strauss—the characteristic touch—makes of it a *gemütlich* belly-dance.

The decline of Strauss as an opera composer after *Salome, Elektra*, and *Der Rosenkavalier* is well known. "Hailed on his appearance as the successor of Wagner —Richard the Second—only some ten years ago still, for most people the most commanding figure in modern music, he is today, apart from Germany and Austria, almost ignored by the leaders of progressive musical opinion"—Cecil Gray could say this even in 1924. The later operas are indeed almost ignored. But

even the three popular earlier ones are impossible today: how can we take *Salome* seriously as a study in
psychopathy after Alban Berg's *Wozzeck?* The difference is first of all the difference between Buechner
and Wilde, but *Elektra* serves to demonstrate, if demonstration is needed, that the taint in *Salome* lay
deeper than the libretto. No one who understood
The Marriage of Figaro could ever have taken *Der
Rosenkavalier* seriously, either, unless it was Strauss
and Hofmannsthal, and even that is not certain. For
these operas reveal finally a disconcerting quality of
cynicism. Puccini may have been innocent of any
dramatic ideas, but Strauss moved around among them
with deadly facility. Yet he was unable to match any
true feeling or any true idea with anything but a form
—and the form is always there, alarmingly precise,
alarmingly false. Somehow we sense that Strauss must
have understood this too. Anything he touched he
soiled as pervasively as the waltz soils the texture of
his music. Perhaps indeed *Salome*, which pretends to
no sympathies, is on that account the least objectionable of his three famous operas.

Many operas in the current repertory are obviously
less than perfect. Only a capricious critical bias, it may
be argued, would single out Strauss and Puccini for
attack. But some imperfections are worse than others,
and operatic criticism will never come to any account
unless it distinguishes emphatically, imperatively, between flaw and falsity in art. The operas of Strauss and
Puccini are false through and through; the trouble runs
much deeper than mere faults in conception or technique, such as we have seen in a number of good operas from Monteverdi's *Orfeo* on. *Orfeo* is a beautiful
work which unhappily fails to sustain its dramatic conception. *Salome* and *Der Rosenkavalier*, however, are
insincere in every gesture, meretricious and doubly
meretricious on account of their show of outer formal

integrity. *Orfeo* is a true work plainly gone wrong; *Salome* and *Der Rosenkavalier* are false works in which everything goes depressingly right. Defects of form, noncompletion, even ultimate failure, cannot altogether spoil works of art in which we divine the true metal. Dross, however consistent, belongs on quite another plane.

Drama requires not only the presentation of action, but an insight into its quality by means of response to action. Only the presentation of such quality justifies the dramatic endeavor; and in the best dramas, the response seems imaginative, true, illuminating, and fully matched to the action. This is never so in the operas of Strauss and Puccini. Monteverdi's *Orfeo* centers on a vision which is projected powerfully for four acts; then no element of action suggested itself —or, let us say, no element that was possible under the theatrical conventions of the day—to consummate and complete the drama. The same is true of Gluck's *Orfeo*. The same is true of *The Rake's Progress*. These are not perfect works, but for all their imperfections they are more meaningful than the technical successes of others.

Another, subtler kind of dramatic failure results when the guiding idea proves intractable to the necessities of dramatic form. Una Ellis-Fermor has argued ingeniously that there are several areas of human experience which are almost impossible to treat dramatically, and that nevertheless a few extraordinary dramas have overcome limitations of this sort. *Tristan und Isolde*, I have suggested, is such a one. *Pelléas et Mélisande* and *Wozzeck*, on the other hand, seem to me pieces which struggle on the whole unsuccessfully with essentially undramatic material—though the struggle creates a strong semblance of drama, and the genuineness of the composer's response is never in doubt. They are works of power and sensitivity, works of genius, even if we are bound to mind the misemployment of the dramatic form. These operas too belong centrally to the relevant canon.

Quite different is a piece in which the response, the quality of the action, is insensitive or simply sham all the way. The more shrewdly consistent the action and style, the more exasperating such a piece becomes. In the deepest sense the operas of Strauss and Puccini are undramatic, for their imaginative realm is a realm of emotional cant. They are unable to match any action, however promising, with anything but the empty form of drama. And the form is always there. Alarmingly precise, alarmingly false.

3

THAT works like *Turandot* and *Salome* will fade from the operatic scene, as decisively as have *L'Africaine* and *Lucrezia Borgia,* is scarcely to be doubted. At present they do a disservice by obscuring the true works of the operatic tradition, but of course the true works cannot actually be hurt. However, the persistence of the operas of Puccini and Strauss does more than affect taste; it seems to affect contemporary operatic composition. I have in mind the case of Gian-Carlo Menotti and the warm acceptance of his work. In himself an entirely trivial artist, Menotti is mainly interesting on account of his highly successful exploitation of the bad old ways. The whole genre, not only the musical style, belongs to another era. Menotti is a sensationalist in the old style, and in fact a weak one, diluting the faults of Strauss and Puccini with none of their fugitive virtues.

The Saint of Bleecker Street has been proclaimed his masterpiece, a cornerstone on which to base American opera. In this work the dramatic conflict is between a sickly Italian-American girl who suffers the stigmata and her loving but bitter and confused brother. In spite of all Michele's pleas and efforts, Annina finally takes the veil at a ceremony in the last scene—and dies; wearing the wedding-gown of a more terrestrial friend of hers, who has previously married a young man called Salvatore. At the wedding banquet, Michele had incensed the guests; he is something of a free-thinker, and lives with a whore, and resents the Italian community, which not unnaturally rejects him. But when the whore accuses him of incestuous wishes, he kills her. Michele has tried to prevent the faithful from visiting Annina at the time of her agonized visions, and also from carrying her in religious processions. His devotion is strong enough to make him return, though a fugitive, in order to forestall what he takes to be her fatal step (and so it turns out). But he fails, and is presumably apprehended as the curtain drops.

The material is lively enough; but what can it possibly come to when every attitude, every feeling, every response is on Menotti's own special level of banality? Menotti shows no kind of musical distinction comparable to that of Strauss or Puccini; only Puccini's eclecticism and Strauss's flair for the *épatant*. Puccini's lyricism, however limited, and Strauss's technical skill, however misdirected, are quite beyond him. *The Saint of Bleecker Street* is the crudest of all Menotti's operas in dramaturgy and symbolism, the feeblest in purely musical invention, and the most slovenly in dramatic effect. Briefly, the trouble is this: since Annina speaks always in the accents of a popular song, we necessarily take her religiosity at Michele's estimate: as a sentimental psychosis exploited by a corrupt Church. Exploited by Menotti too; he wants to take her seriously and yet indulge the skeptical view;

he wants all the sensationalism and demagoguery latent in both attitudes without the responsibility of either. Michele, for all his high talk, has no musical presence at all. The whore is called Desideria, and is to wear a red dress, and makes her smashing first entrance at the end of Act I to take down Michele from a symbolic crucifixion. Her music matches. Local color is smeared on with a putty-knife, but it is vivid and suitably sordid; indeed the one thing that seems real to the dramatist is the cheapness of Bleecker Street. Unfortunately this quality spreads only too convincingly to Annina the Saint, Don Marco the priest, and Michele the equivocal dissenter.

Television opera, let us charitably hope, deserves a better little cornerstone than Menotti's *Amahl and the Night Visitors*. American opera will build on something much more solid than *The Saint of Bleecker Street*. Michele's own disgust at his background is projected in the piece. The rest is sheer pretension.

4

To WRITE a prescription for contemporary opera would be a pretension on my part. A usurpation, too; for at the present time a number of good composers are coping with the operatic problem from various standpoints, while all composers, it seems, good and bad, are enthusiastically writing operas. The course of opera lies with composers, not critics, fortunately. The present study, furthermore, with its unpragmatic design, has been looking for no single path, no simple aesthetic or historical guidepost. Still, any consideration of the operatic tradition has to conclude with questions about the future, for the operatic tradition is continuing. Writing at a time fascinated by opera and saddled with Menotti, one feels that some sort of statement is called for over and above that of negative analysis.

What can one suggest? Only the truism with which we began: opera as drama. This ideal made opera possible in the first place, and has been reformulated by a line of enthusiasts, among whom Wagner was the most tireless, the most self-interested, and (thanks to his operas) the most convincing. An examination of the tradition shows how marvelously the ideal has been met by the few who were able to transcend the undramatic inertia of their contemporaries and turn stale conventions to serious account. The best operas *are* dramatic, and they stand with the best dramatic products of the modern age. None of the best opera composers has approached opera as a play with decorative musical additions—not even Debussy. None of them has approached it as a purely musical form vaguely adjusted to the stage—certainly not Wagner. Opera in their hands has shown itself to be an artform with its own integrity, with its own limiting and liberating conventions, and with its own unique areas of expression. As the dramatic form is articulated by music, great music is necessary, but only a great dramatic vision is sufficient.

For the composer, I should like to believe that the essential problem is to clarify the central dramatic idea, to refine the vision. This cannot be left to the librettist; the dramatist is the composer. If he lacks the sensibility and intellectual persistence to see the drama through, his opera will not succeed. Dramaturgy itself is the less urgent problem, though musicians naturally prefer to think in terms of technique—musical technique rather than expression, on the theory that one is consummated in the other. But with dramatic technique and drama, I do not think that this will quite do. The basic conception served by technique must be clear. In any case, the history of opera is full of ideas for operatic construction, so many of them that the modern composer cannot possibly make use of them all. And new forms will emerge; and certainly the present can still operate powerfully with forms of the past. In *Wozzeck* and *The Rake's Progress* the ideas are contemporary, and so are the musical styles that project the ideas. The dramaturgies actually retrench from the bold extremes which served other ideas at the end of the nineteenth century.

No particular dramaturgical plan can be prescribed for "the Art-Work of the Future." Confidence on this score would be possible only from the point of view of Wagnerian historicism. It is also dangerous to set down any limitation to or preference among the areas that are likely to be profitable for operatic treatment. Opera, we are told, should deal only in large, generalized emotions; luckily Mozart was not told. Who could have foreseen *The Marriage of Figaro,* or *Tristan und Isolde,* or *Falstaff?* Whatever convinces a good dramatic composer will serve; some areas of experience are more difficult than others, no doubt, but all are difficult. *Dramma per musica* should aim no lower than drama in verse or prose. However general and self-evident, this ideal is vital, as is quickly seen from the example of composers who have paid no attention to it. Retrenchment in imagination or sincerity, the retrenchments of Strauss and Puccini and Menotti —these are what one must really work to avoid.

The conditions of operatic composition are peculiar enough at present. Our opera houses are museums; half-amateur workshops impose their own odd limitations; performers and audiences are imponderable. The unproblematic position of the old opera composer, a position still held by Strauss and Puccini, can scarcely be regained today, unless Menotti succeeds in doing so, which I doubt. Popular art has other channels. One of them is musical comedy. Theoretically this might serve as a proving-ground for art, just as *opera buffa* did in the eighteenth century; but in over a hundred years operetta and musical comedy have come forth with not a single serious dramatist: only Auber and Offenbach, Suppé and Johann Strauss, Sullivan, Sigmund Romberg, Gershwin, and Kurt Weill. It seems to be no longer possible, as it was for Verdi, to evolve drama by fifty years of strenuous experiment in the theater. It is always possible to have the instant intuition of drama, like Mozart; but not probable. A good talent was not helped when Benjamin Britten's admirers proclaimed him years ago as the authentic Mozart of our age.

Our age is more likely to develop its concepts of drama by investigating the tradition, musical or non-musical. It is a historically and juridically minded age, both for the creative artist and for the audience, and we may as well make virtue out of necessity. Dramatic criticism of the operatic repertory may have its pragmatic value after all. In addition to making the theatergoer cognizant of musical values, it may also educate the composer a little about dramatic values as they have appeared in operas of the past. These values cannot be recaptured or repeated, of course. There is no simple path. In fact the study of history only deepens our impression of the fortuitous individuality of genius; the formulation of "trends" and "schools" in art helps us to dispose of the second-rate and codify techniques, but never explains the visions. The very presence of such visions, however, their variety, and their triumphant fulfillment in musical terms, ought to offer some kind of inspiration for idealism.

Index

JOSEPH KERMAN *was born in London on April 3, 1924,
the son of an American writer. He attended University
College School (London), New York University (A.B.,
1943), and Princeton University (Ph.D., 1951). Since
1948 he has regularly contributed articles on musical subjects to the* Hudson Review; *essays by him have also appeared in* The Musical Quarterly, *the* Partisan Review,
Opera News (*New York*), Opera (*London*), Perspectives
USA, *and other periodicals. In 1951 Mr. Kerman became
Assistant Professor of Music at the University of California
at Berkeley, and in 1956 became an Associate Professor.
In 1956 he received a Grant in Literature from the Na-
tional Institute of Arts and Letters. He is married and has
three children.* Opera as Drama *was published originally
by Alfred A Knopf, Inc., in 1956.*

*The text of this book was set in Electra; a Linotype face designed
by W. A. Dwiggins. This face cannot be classified as modern or
old-style. It is not based on any historical model, nor does it echo
any particular period or style. It avoids the extreme contrast between thick and thin elements that marks most modern faces, and
attempts to give a feeling of fluidity, power, and speed. Composed, printed, and bound by The Colonial Press Inc., Clinton,
Massachusetts. Cover design by Milton Glaser.*

VINTAGE FICTION, POETRY, AND PLAYS

V-131	Thackeray, W. M.	VANITY FAIR
V-713	Tolstoy, Leo	THE KREUTZER SONATA
V-154	Tracy, Honor	STRAIGHT AND NARROW PATH
V-202	Turgenev, Ivan	TORRENTS OF SPRING
V-711	Turgenev, Ivan	THE VINTAGE TURGENEV Volume I: SMOKE, FATHERS AND SONS, FIRST LOVE
V-712	Turgenev, Ivan	Volume II: ON THE EVE, RUDIN, A QUIET SPOT, DIARY OF A SUPERFLUOUS MAN
V-152	Waugh, Evelyn	THE LOVED ONE

VINTAGE BELLES-LETTRES

V-708	Aksakov, Sergey	YEARS OF CHILDHOOD
V-22	Barzun, Jacques	THE ENERGIES OF ART
V-191	Beer, Thomas	THE MAUVE DECADE
V-80	Beerbohm, Max	SEVEN MEN and Two Others
V-75	Camus, Albert	THE MYTH OF SISYPHUS and Other Essays
V-30	Camus, Albert	THE REBEL
V-216	Chamberlain, N. (ed.)	A VINTAGE FOOD SAMPLER
V-64	Evans, Bergen	THE NATURAL HISTORY OF NONSENSE
V-112	Gide, André	JOURNALS, Volume I: 1889-1924
V-113	Gide, André	JOURNALS, Volume II: 1924-1949
V-104	Huxley, Aldous	BEYOND THE MEXIQUE BAY
V-41	James, Henry	THE FUTURE OF THE NOVEL
V-235	Kaplan, Abraham	THE NEW WORLD OF PHILOSOPHY
V-167	La Rochefoucauld	MAXIMS
V-230	Leedom, William	THE VINTAGE WINE BOOK
V-193	Malraux, André	TEMPTATION OF THE WEST
V-55	Mann, Thomas	ESSAYS
V-232	Mencken, H. L.	TREATISE ON THE GODS
V-34	Montaigne, Michel de	AUTOBIOGRAPHY
V-197	Morgan, F. (ed.)	HUDSON REVIEW ANTHOLOGY
V-54	Nicolson, Harold	SOME PEOPLE
V-24	Ransom, John Crowe	POEMS AND ESSAYS
V-85	Stevens, Wallace	POEMS
V-53	Synge, J. M.	THE ARAN ISLANDS and Other Writings
V-194	Valéry, Paul	THE ART OF POETRY